Cross-Border Data Transfers Regulations in the Context of International Trade Law: A PRC Perspective

Yihan Dai

Cross-Border Data Transfers Regulations in the Context of International Trade Law: A PRC Perspective

Yihan Dai
East China University of Political Science
and Law
Shanghai, China

ISBN 978-981-16-4994-3   ISBN 978-981-16-4995-0 (eBook)
https://doi.org/10.1007/978-981-16-4995-0

© The Editor(s) (if applicable) and The Author(s), under exclusive license to Springer Nature Singapore Pte Ltd. 2022
This work is subject to copyright. All rights are solely and exclusively licensed by the Publisher, whether the whole or part of the material is concerned, specifically the rights of translation, reprinting, reuse of illustrations, recitation, broadcasting, reproduction on microfilms or in any other physical way, and transmission or information storage and retrieval, electronic adaptation, computer software, or by similar or dissimilar methodology now known or hereafter developed.
The use of general descriptive names, registered names, trademarks, service marks, etc. in this publication does not imply, even in the absence of a specific statement, that such names are exempt from the relevant protective laws and regulations and therefore free for general use.
The publisher, the authors and the editors are safe to assume that the advice and information in this book are believed to be true and accurate at the date of publication. Neither the publisher nor the authors or the editors give a warranty, expressed or implied, with respect to the material contained herein or for any errors or omissions that may have been made. The publisher remains neutral with regard to jurisdictional claims in published maps and institutional affiliations.

This Springer imprint is published by the registered company Springer Nature Singapore Pte Ltd.
The registered company address is: 152 Beach Road, #21-01/04 Gateway East, Singapore 189721, Singapore

About This Book

Currently, international trade cannot survive without cross-border data flows. The ongoing convergence of different industries and technologies, teeming with the emergence of new products and services, defies accurate classification between goods and services. Cross-border data transfers often encompass cross-sectional issues of privacy law, personal data protection law, trade law, to mention but a few. Therefore, these laws of several nations and regions must be considered together. In recent years, the People's Republic of China (PRC) has made good progress in enhancing its personal data protection through adopting related laws, regulations and guidelines, especially in the digital field. Like numerous other governments, such as those of Russia, Australia, South Korea, India, Brazil, Canada, Vietnam, Indonesia, Brunei or Iran, one of the PRC's endeavours is to regulate cross-border data transfers through direct and indirect data localization requirements. It is these restrictions on cross-border data transfers imposed domestically that have aroused great controversy because such restrictions might violate countries' treaty obligations and eventually impede international trade. Moreover, international trade may be further impeded by the fact that the existing world's international legal system is highly fragmented in nearly all areas, including data protection and cross-border data transfers. This fragmentation makes it very hard to harmonize the objectives of data protection laws with those of international trade liberalization in the near future.

As the most important laws governing these issues are usually adopted at the domestic level, it is important to prudently draft such data protection laws and regulations and to intelligently apply them so that countries can unlock the benefits of both technological innovation and global digital trade. For example, Artificial Intelligence (AI), big data and other new data-fuelled technologies benefit a lot from PRC's relaxed data privacy legislation and its system of Internet censorship. As data—particularly personal data—are now the most valuable assets of the digital age, data protection legislation is becoming one of the most important sources of competitive advantage of individual nations in the context of international trade and could have far-reaching implications for country's competitiveness in today's global digital economy. Overly stringent data privacy legislation might seriously weaken the development of digital economy, as well as international trade while too loose rules for the use of personal data might undermine privacy and data security. At the international level, it is necessary to find a common global language that clearly addresses some controversial issues that are closely related to the implementation of cross-border data flows. The conclusion of plurilateral trade agreements is a good starting point to build bridges between different systems of data protection and cross-border data flow regulations.

Keywords: PRC's Legislation on Cross-border Data Transfers, International Trade, Personal Data Protection, Foreign Trade Agreements, World Trade Organization (WTO), Industry Convergence, Technological Innovation, Regulatory Divergence, Competitive Advantage.

Contents

1	**Introduction**	1
2	**The PRC's Legislation on Cross-Border Data Transfers**	13
	2.1 Overview	13
	2.2 The PRC's Legal System and the Hierarchy of Norms	14
	2.3 Data or Information?	16
	2.3.1 The Definition of Personal Information in the PRC's Legal System	16
	2.3.2 The Difference Between "Personal Information" and "Personal Data"	19
	2.4 The PRC's Legislation on Cross-Border Data Transfers	23
	2.4.1 Laws and Regulations	23
	2.4.2 Non-Binding Guidelines	26
	2.4.3 Increasingly Tight Restrictions on Cross-Border Data Transfers	27
	2.5 Interim Remarks	34
3	**The Cross-Border Data Transfers in the Context of WTO Agreements—The PRC Perspective**	35
	3.1 Cross-Border Data Transfer Legislation in the Context of WTO Agreements	35
	3.1.1 General Remarks	35
	3.1.2 The PRC and the WTO	38
	3.1.3 The Tradability of Data	40
	3.1.4 Data as a Service	42
	3.1.5 Cross-Border Data Transfers: Service or Good?	44
	3.1.6 Cross-Border Data Transfers and the GATS	46
	3.2 The Information Silk Road	68
	3.3 A Comprehensive Outlook on Development	70
	3.4 Interim Remarks	76

4	**The Regulation of Cross-Border Data Transfers in the Context of Free Trade Agreements**		77
	4.1	Overview	77
	4.2	FTAs and Cross-border Data Transfers	81
		4.2.1 General Remarks	81
		4.2.2 E-Commerce Chapters	83
		4.2.3 Commitments Made on Service Sectors	95
		4.2.4 Economic and Technical Cooperation	96
		4.2.5 Other Chapters	98
	4.3	FTAs and RTAs in Which the PRC Is Involved	99
		4.3.1 E-Commerce Chapters	100
		4.3.2 Dispute Settlement	108
		4.3.3 Intellectual Property (IP) Chapters	108
	4.4	Regional Comprehensive Economic Partnership	110
	4.5	The Defects of Existing FTAs	111
	4.6	Interim Remarks	116
5	**Cross-Border Data Transfers Regulations in the Context of International Trade Law-Challenges and Perspective**		119
	5.1	The Necessity of Cross-Border Data Transfers	119
	5.2	Challenges Facing Legislatures	121
		5.2.1 Fragmentation of the Legal System	121
		5.2.2 Cross-Border Data Transfers and Emerging Concerns	129
	5.3	A Proposed Approach: Plurilateral Trade Agreements	133
	5.4	Interim Remarks	137
6	**Conclusion**		139
References			147

Abbreviation

2012 MIIT Provisions	Several Provisions on Regulating the Market Order of Internet Information Services
2013 MIIT Guidelines	Information Security Technology—Guideline for Personal Information Protection within Information System for Public and Commercial Services
2017 Guidelines for Cross-Border Transfer Security Assessment	Draft of Information Security Technology—Guidelines for Cross-Border Transfer Security Assessment
AI	Artificial Intelligence
APEC	Asia-Pacific Economic Cooperation
APPI	Act on the Protection of Personal Information
Art.	Article
ASEAN	Association of Southeast Asian Nations
BRI	Belt and Road Initiative
CAC	Cyberspace Administration of China
CEPA	Closer Economic and Partnership Arrangement
CEPA Hong Kong	Closer Economic and Partnership Arrangement with the government of the Special Administrative Region of Hong Kong
CEPA Macao	Closer Economic and Partnership Arrangement with the government of the Special Administrative Region of Macao
Chap.	Chapter
CII	Critical Information Infrastructure
CPC	United Nations Central Product Classification
CPG	Central People's Government
CPTPP	Comprehensive and Progressive Agreement for Trans-Pacific Partnership

DCD	Proposal for a Directive of the European Parliament and of the Council on Certain Aspects Concerning Contracts for the Supply of Digital Content
Draft of the Measures on Security Assessment	Draft of the Measures on Security Assessment of Cross-border Data Transfer of Personal Information and Important Data
DSB	Dispute Settlement Body
DSM	Digital Single Market
ECC	UN Convention on the Use of Electronic Communications in International Contracts
e-commerce	electronic commerce
EU	European Union
FTAs	Free trade agreements
Fig.	Figure
GATS	General Agreement on Trade in Services
GATT	General Agreement on Tariffs and Trade
GBDE	Global Big Data Exchange
GCC	Gulf Cooperation Council
GDPR	General Data Protection Regulation
GNS/W/120	Services Sectoral Classification List
HKSAR	Hong Kong Special Administrative Region of the PRC
Hong Kong-Macao CEPA	Hong Kong Special Administrative Region and Macao Special Administrative Region Closer Economic Partnership Arrangement
ICCPR	International Covenant on Civil and Political Rights
ICT	Information and communications technology
IP	Intellectual Property
ISPs	Internet Service Providers
KORUS FTA	FTA between the United States and South Korea
LDCs	Least-developed countries
MFN	Most Favoured Nation
MIIT	Ministry of Industry and Information Technology of the PRC
Model Law 1996	UNCITRAL Model Law on Electronic Commerce 1996
MPS	Ministry of Public Security
MSAR	Macao Special Administrative Region of the PRC
MTN/GNS/164	Scheduling of Initial Commitments in Trade in Services: Explanatory Note
NAFTA	North American Free Trade Agreement
NPC	National People's Congress

NT	National Treatment
OBOR	One Belt, One Road
OECD	Organization for Economic Co-operation and Development
PRC	People's Republic of China
RCEP	Regional Comprehensive Economic Partnership
RTAs	Regional trade agreements
SAFTA	Singapore-Australia FTA
SC-NPC	Standing Committee of the National People's Congress
TiSA	Trade in Services Agreement
TPP	Trans-Pacific Partnership
TRIPS	Agreement on Trade-Related Aspects of Intellectual Property Rights
TTIP	Transatlantic Trade and Investment Partnership
UDHR	Universal Declaration of Human Rights
UN	United Nations
UNCITRAL	United Nations Commission on International Trade Law
UNCTAD	United Nations Conference on Trade and Development
USMCA	United States–Mexico–Canada Agreement
WTO	World Trade Organization
WTO E-commerce Programme	WTO Work Programme on Electronic Commerce

Chapter 1
Introduction

...Law nowadays pervades all areas of life such that it can easily be termed a universal science. At the same time, all these areas of life are changing at unprecedented and truly breakneck speeds, as reflected in the pace of technological innovation and scientific progress.[1,2]

—Rostam J. Neuwirth

In this book, the focus of the discussion is on cross-border data transfers regulations in the context of international trade law, especially from the PRC's perspective. The legal confirmation of the right to privacy has undergone a long process in the PRC.[3] Currently, the right to privacy in the PRC is directly and indirectly protected by constitutional law, both private and public law as well as procedural law. Chinese authorities have gradually developed a comprehensive personal information protection system through introducing some of the landmark laws, such as Personal Information Protection Law(個人數據保護法) and Data Security Law(數據安全法) lately.[4]

---

[1] Introduction part is based on Yihan Dai, 'Data Protection Laws — One of the Most Important Sources of Competitive Advantage in the Context of International Trade' (2021) 4(1) Journal of Data Protection & Privacy 72.

[2] Rostam J. Neuwirth, *Law in the Time of Oxymora: A Synaesthesia of Language Logic and Law* (Routledge 2018) 4.

[3] The right to privacy known in western countries was not protected in the People's Republic of China (hereinafter: PRC) before the enforcement of the Tort Liability Law of the PRC which entered into force in 2010. The right to privacy has finally been confirmed by the General Provisions of the Civil Law of the PRC, Article 1 of which clearly stipulates that: 'a natural person enjoys the rights of…privacy…among others.' After that, the legal status and nature of privacy in civil law have been fully recognized in the PRC. See 'General Provisions of the Civil Law of the PRC.' (National People's Congress (hereinafter: NPC), 15 March 2017). http://www.npc.gov.cn/zgrdw/npc/xinwen/2017-03/15/content_2018907.htm, accessed 29 March 2021; see also Ashley Winton, Alex Zhang and others, 'Data Protection and Privacy in China' (White and Case LLP, February 2012). https://www.jdsupra.com/legalnews/data-protection-and-privacy-in-china-09725/, accessed 29 March 2021.

[4] On 10 June 2021, the Data Security Law of the PRC was officially passed during the 29th session of the Standing Committee of the 13th National People's Congress and came into force on 1 September 2021. On 20 August 2021, the Personal Information Protection Law of the PRC was officially

---

© The Author(s), under exclusive license to Springer Nature Singapore Pte Ltd. 2022
Y. Dai, *Cross-Border Data Transfers Regulations in the Context of International Trade Law: A PRC Perspective*, https://doi.org/10.1007/978-981-16-4995-0_1

Although the Chinese people, as well as the Chinese government's attitudes toward privacy as well as data protection, have shifted enormously in recent years, the right to privacy in the PRC is less respected in practice, as well as less protected in law compared to most western countries, which apparently leaves more room for the development of new technologies which are nourished by data. However, it is a debatable question whether the protection of data is actually conducive to the development of competitive technologies or not. Especially from the angle of a sustainable development of individual societies and the world as a whole, a balanced level of protection and freedom to transfer data is needed.

In recent years, the Chinese regulatory regime has evolved rapidly to address personal information protection issues and now comprises a large number of laws and regulations enacted at different legislative levels.[5] Although many laws and regulations of data protection are in place, it is notable that instead of providing subjects of personal information with the right to self-determination or power of control over their personal information, data protection legislation in the PRC is more intended to foster public trust, boost sales,[6] and safeguard the security of information.

In 2017, the Network Security Law of the PRC,[7] as well as various relevant implementing measures were challenged in the international arena as a violation of the PRC's treaty obligations, particularly under those arising from its membership in the WTO,[8] because "these measures would fall disproportionately on foreign service suppliers operating in the PRC, as these suppliers must routinely transfer data back to headquarters and other affiliates".[9] However, it is hard to conclude that the PRC

---

passed at the 30th meeting of the Standing Committee of the 13th National People's Congress by the Standing Committee of China's National People's Congress (hereinafter: SC-NPC) and will came into force on 1 November 2021.

[5] The Chinese regulatory regime addressing personal information protection issues now involves the Personal Information Protection Law, the Data Security Law, the Civil Code of the PRC, the General Provisions of the Civil Law of the PRC; the Criminal Law of the PRC; regulations such as the Network Security Law of the PRC, the E—Commerce Law of the PRC, the Consumer Protection Law of the PRC that were released by the SC—NPC; rules released by the Chinese Ministry of Industry and Information Technology(hereinafter: MIIT); rules released by various ministries and commissions; rules released by provincial governments; the PRC's international information protection obligations; a handful of accompanying measures and at least 10 draft standards.

[6] Paul De Hert and Vagelis Papakonstantinou, 'The Data Protection Regime in China, In—depth Analysis' (19 November 2015) 1(4) Brussels Privacy Hub Working Paper 1, 26. http://www.europarl.europa.eu/RegData/etudes/IDAN/2015/536472/IPOL_IDA(2015)536472_EN.pdf accessed 29 March 2021.

[7] 'Network Security Law of the PRC' (Chinese title: 中華人民共和國網絡安全法) (Cyber Administration of China (hereinafter: CAC) Homepage, 7 November 2016). http://www.cac.gov.cn/2016-11/07/c_1119867116.htm, accessed 30 March 2021.

[8] Trevor Schmitt, 'United States Flags China's VPN Ban as Possible WTO Violation' (Georgetown Law Technology Review, March 2018). https://georgetownlawtechreview.org/united-states-flags-chinas-vpn-ban-as-possible-wto-violation/GLTR-03-2018/, accessed 29 March 2021.

[9] 'Communication from the United States – Measures Adopted and under Development by China Relating to Its Cybersecurity Law' Art. 4 (WTO Council for Trade in Services, 2017). https://docs.wto.org/dol2fe/Pages/SS/directdoc.aspx?filename=q:/S/C/W374.pdf&Open=True, accessed 20 October 2021.

1 Introduction

is violating its commitments under its WTO obligations because the WTO does not explicitly forbid members to enact data localization laws.[10] The General Agreement on Trade in Services (GATS) rules on Computer and Related Services may substantially limit members' regulatory space in digital trade. However, the technical issue of the classification of services provides an excuse for a WTO member that does not follow its commitments. With respect to the trend of digital convergence and technological innovation, there exists considerable uncertainty in the application of WTO law to members' restrictions on cross-border data transfers.[11] The uncertainty covers, for instance, the preliminary question of categorizing the restricted data as goods or services, or within which of the four modes of services data fall,[12] as well as the interpretation of the schedules of commitments and the problem of explicitly determining to which sectors of service members have made a special commitment.[13] Current WTO laws have proven to be lag behind technological innovation and commercial development and not clear enough at regulating the barriers to cross-border data movement.[14]

---

[10] Allison S. Khaskelis and Anthony L. Gallia, 'Russian Federation: Russia's Data Localization Law, a Violation of WTO Regulations?' (Mondaq, 21 January 2016). http://www.mondaq.com/russianfederation/x/460342/data+protection/Russias+Data+Localization+Law+A+Violation+Of+WTO+Regulations, accessed 20 March 2021.

[11] Andrew D. Mitchell and Jarrod Hepburn, 'Don't Fence Me In: Reforming Trade and Investment Law to Better Facilitate Cross−Border Data Transfer' (2017) 19(1) Yale Journal of Law and Technology 182, 206; Cory Nigel, 'Cross−Border Data Flows: Where Are the Barriers, and What Do They Cost?' 16 (Information Technology and Innovation Foundation, May 2017). http://www2.itif.org/2017-cross-border-data-flows.pdf, accessed 16 March 2021; Aaditya Mattoo and Joshua P. Meltzer, 'International Data Flows and Privacy the Conflict and Its Resolution' Policy Research Working Paper 8431, 5 (World Bank Group, May 2018). http://documents.worldbank.org/curated/en/751621525705087132/pdf/WPS8431.pdf, accessed 12 March 2021; 'Working Party of the Trade Committee − Trade and Cross−border Data Flows' TAD/TC/WP(2018)19/FINAL, 27 (Organisation for Economic Co−operation and Development (hereinafter: OECD), 21 December 2018). http://www.oecd.org/officialdocuments/publicdisplaydocumentpdf/?cote=TAD/TC/WP(2018)19/FINAL&docLanguage=En, accessed 12 March 2021; Joshua P. Meltzer, 'The Internet, Cross−Border Data Flow and International Trade' (2014) 2(1) Asia and the Pacific Policy Studies 90, 97.

[12] Mitchell and Hepburn (n 11) 206.

[13] Mitchell and Hepburn (n 11) 196; Meltzer (n 11) 99; 'The General Agreement On Trade In Services (GATS): An Analysis' OCDE/GD (94) 123, 28 (OECD, 1994). http://www.oecd.org/officialdocuments/publicdisplaydocumentpdf/?doclanguage=en&cote=ocde/gd(94)123, accessed 16 March 2021; Fredrik Erixon, Brian Hindley and Hosuk Lee−Makiyama, 'Protectionism Online: Internet Censorship and International Trade Law'(2009) ECIPE Working Paper No. 12/2009, 10. https://ecipe.org/wp-content/uploads/2014/12/protectionism-online-internet-censorship-and-international-trade-law.pdf, accessed 24 March 2021.

[14] Susan Ariel Aaronson, 'CIGI Papers No. 197 − Data Is Different: Why the World Needs a New Approach to Governing Cross−border Data Flows' (Centre for International Governance Innovation, November 2018). https://www.cigionline.org/publications/data-different-why-world-needs-new-approach-governing-cross-border-data-flows/, accessed 18 March 2021; Stephen J. Ezell, Robert D. Atkinson and Michelle A. Wein, 'Localization Barriers to Trade − Threat to the Global Innovation Economy,' 69–70 (Information Technology and Innovation Foundation, September 2013). www2.itif.org/2013-localization-barriers-to-trade.pdf, accessed 18 March 2021.

The Doha negotiations remain stagnant and, as a result, the WTO faces difficulties in handling multifaceted and highly technical areas. Therefore, countries are increasingly turning to regional trade agreements (RTAs) for relief and the further development of the framework governing trade in data.[15] In recent years, numerous RTAs have attempted to establish a new legal landscape for cross-border data flows by somewhat compensating for the fragmented national rules on data and the availability of online information as well as overcoming the problems under the WTO law.[16] At present, 62 free-trade agreements (FTAs) with electronic commerce (e-commerce) provisions have entered into force since 2012.[17] Most of these 62 FTAs address, albeit to varying degrees, some of the issues left over by the WTO E-commerce Programme.[18] One of the principal problems, which cause concern among the treaty makers in the field of data, is the one of how to balance the relationship between the apparently divergent goals of fostering liberalization of and greater international cooperation in international trade by entering into RTAs on the one hand with those of much broader goals of domestic personal data protection legislation on the other.

The PRC—like many other jurisdictions—has begun to negotiate and conclude bilateral and regional free trade agreements to address e-commerce and other Internet

---

[15] There are 343 RTAs in force have been notified to the WTO until 4 April 2021. WTO RTA Database Homepage. http://rtais.wto.org/UI/PublicAllRTAList.aspx, accessed 4 April 2021.

[16] Joshua Meltzer, 'The Internet, Cross−border Data Flows and International Trade' (February 2013) 22 Issues in Technology Innovation, 17. https://www.brookings.edu/wp-content/uploads/2016/06/internet-data-and-trade-meltzer.pdf, accessed 4 March 2021.

[17] These FTAs include the PRC – Mauritius FTA, United Kingdom – Japan FTA, United Kingdom – Ecuador and Peru FTA, United Kingdom – CARIFORUM States FTA, United Kingdom – Central America FTA, United Kingdom– Chile FTA, United Kingdom–Côte d'Ivoire FTA, United Kingdom – Georgia FTA, United Kingdom – Korea, Republic of FTA, United Kingdom – Ukraine FTA, United Kingdom – Moldova, Republic of FTA, United Kingdom – Singapore FTA, United Kingdom − Viet Nam FTA, EU−United Kingdom FTA, United Kingdom–Colombia FTA, EU−Viet Nam FTA, Indonesia–Australia FTA, United States−Mexico−Canada Agreement (hereinafter: USMCA), Peru– Australia, EU−Singapore FTA, Hong Kong, China−Australia FTA, Hong Kong, China−Georgia FTA, EU−Japan FTA, the Comprehensive and Progressive Agreement for Trans−Pacific Partnership (hereinafter: CPTPP), PRC−Georgia FTA, Turkey−Singapore FTA, EU−Canada FTA, Canada−Ukraine FTA, EU−Ghana FTA, Eurasian Economic Union−Viet Nam FTA, Costa Rica−Colombia FTA, Korea, Republic of−Colombia FTA, Japan−Mongolia FTA, Pacific Alliance, PRC−Australia FTA, PRC−Korea, Republic of FTA, Korea, Republic of −Viet Nam FTA, Chile−Thailand FTA, Turkey−Malaysia FTA, Mexico−Panama FTA, Japan−Australia FTA, Canada− Korea, Republic of FTA, Korea, Republic of −Australia FTA, Canada−Honduras FTA, EU−Georgia FTA, EU−Moldova, Republic of FTA, EFTA−Central America (Costa Rica and Panama) FTA, EU−Ukraine FTA, Singapore−Chinese Taipei FTA, New Zealand−Chinese Taipei FTA, Gulf Cooperation Council (GCC)−Singapore FTA, EU−Central America FTA, Costa Rica−Singapore FTA, Canada−Panama FTA, EU−Colombia and Peru FTA, Malaysia−Australia FTA, United States−Panama FTA, Canada−Jordan FTA, Mexico−Central America FTA, United States−Colombia FTA, EU−Eastern and Southern Africa States FTA and Korea, Republic of − United States FTA. See WTO RTA Database Homepage. http://rtais.wto.org/UI/PublicSearchByCrResult.aspx, accessed 4 April 2021.

[18] 'Work Programme on Electronic Commerce', WTO Doc. WT/L/274 (WTO General Council, 30 September 1998). https://view.officeapps.live.com/op/view.aspx?src=https%3A%2F%2Fdocsonline.wto.org%2Fdol2fe%2FPages%2FFormerScriptedSearch%2Fdirectdoc.aspx%3DDFDocuments%2Ft%2FWT%2FL%2F274.DOC, accessed 27 March 2021.

issues. For example, specific provisions on e-commerce have been integrated into the Regional Comprehensive Economic Partnership (RCEP) agreement, the PRC-Mauritius FTA, the PRC-Korea, Republic of FTA, the PRC-Australia FTA, the PRC-Georgia FTA, the PRC-Chile Upgrade FTA negotiations, the Closer Economic and Partnership Arrangement with the government of the Special Administrative Region of Hong Kong (CEPA Hong Kong) and the government of the Special Administrative Region of Macao (CEPA Macao).[19]

However, except for the RCEP agreement,[20] the CEPA Hong Kong[21] and the CEPA Macao,[22] the PRC has neither included language regarding the free flow of information nor formulated and implemented a concrete and distinct strategy for digital trade in its FTAs.[23] Hong Kong Special Administrative Region of the PRC (HKSAR) and Macao Special Administrative Region of the PRC (MSAR) are two special administrative regions of China. The Central People's Government (CPG) shall be responsible for the defense and the foreign affairs relating to the HKSAR and MSAR.[24] The CPG authorizes the HKSAR and MSAR to conduct relevant external affairs on their own.[25] Requiring personal data to be stored in the PRC is a default data localization rule that is very broad in scope and possibly inconsistent with international trends.[26] The examination of status and the trend of PRC's domestic legislation related to cross-border data transfers as well as the position towards globalization

---

[19] These FTAs all can be found in CHINA FTA NETWORK Homepage which is approved by the Ministry of Commerce of the PRC and supported by the China International Electronic Commerce Center. See CHINA FTA NETWORK Homepage. http://fta.mofcom.gov.cn/topic/enmauritius.shtml, accessed 1 April 2021. See also WTO Regional Trade Agreements Database. http://rtais.wto.org/UI/PublicMaintainRTAHome.aspx, accessed 1 April 2021.

[20] See 'Regional Comprehensive Economic Partnership (RCEP) Agreement', Art. 12.15 (Ministry of Foreign Affairs of Japan, 8 February 2021). https://www.mofa.go.jp/policy/economy/page1e_kanri_000001_00007.html, accessed 1 April 2021.

[21] 'Mainland and Hong Kong Closer Economic Partnership Arrangement–Agreement on Economic and Technical Cooperation', Art. 14(7). See 'Agreement on Economic and Technical Cooperation' (Trade and Industry Department of HK Homepage). https://www.tid.gov.hk/english/cepa/legaltext/cepa15.html, accessed 15 March 2021.

[22] The CEPA Macao–Agreement on Economic and Technical Cooperation, Art. 13(7). 'Agreement on Economic and Technical Cooperation' (Economic Bureau of Macao). https://www.economia.gov.mo/en_US/web/public/pg_cepa_cepa_aetc?_refresh=true, accessed 15 March 2021.

[23] After reviewing all the FTAs that the PRC involved, I came to this conclusion.

[24] Basic Law of the Hong Kong Special Administrative Region of the PRC (hereinafter: HKSAR), Art. 13 and 14, see 'The Basic Law of the Hong Kong Special Administrative Region of the PRC' (HKSAR Government). https://www.legco.gov.hk/general/english/procedur/companion/chapter_15/mcp-part3-ch15-n1-e.pdf, accessed 7 March 2021; Basic Law of the Macao Special Administrative Region of the PRC, Art. 13 and 14, see 'The Basic Law of the Macao Special Administrative Region of the PRC' (MSAR Government). https://bo.io.gov.mo/bo/i/1999/leibasica/index.asp, accessed 7 March 2021.

[25] See Basic Law of the HKSAR, Art. 13; Basic Law of the MSAR, Art. 13.

[26] Carl E. Schonander, 'Chinese Proposed Cross–border Data Flow Rules Contradict an Emerging International Default Norm for Cross–Border Data Flows' (Linkedin, 19 April 2017). https://www.linkedin.com/pulse/chinese-proposed-cross-border-data-flow-rules-default-carl-schonander, accessed 31 March 2021.

and economic integration is showing a paradox: on the one hand, the government is eager to position itself as a pioneer and supporter of globalization and liberalization of global trade, while on the other hand, the government is cautious and discrete regarding the free movement of data across borders because of national security, privacy, public moral, and other concerns. The paradox is exhibited through the contradiction between two strategies being implemented simultaneously: one side involves the de facto cross-border data restriction policies in the Network Security Law and other domestic regulations, and the other side is actively entering into international FTAs as well as calling for greater international cooperation in cross-border e-commerce by advancing the concept of a digital silk road (or the Information Silk Road).[27]

Cross-border data transfer restrictions may have "an impact that ripples quickly and resolutely outward into other countries".[28] Therefore, laws of several nations and regions must be considered together because they are interrelated in protecting the privacy of personal data sent over the Internet.[29] However, existing data protection systems are highly fragmented and regulated in different ways at the global, regional and national level.[30]

First, the right to the protection of personal data is explicitly considered a fundamental human right by European Union (EU) law such as the General Data Protection

---

[27] 'China Unveils Action Plan on BRI' (Xin Hua, 28 March 2015). http://english.gov.cn/news/top_news/2015/03/28/content_281475079055789.htm, accessed 3 March 2021.

[28] Manuel E. Maisog, 'Making the Case against Data Localization in China' (IAPP, 20 April 2015). https://iapp.org/news/a/making-the-case-against-data-localization-in-china/, accessed 5 March 2021.

[29] Bu−Pasha Shakila, 'Cross−Border Issues under EU Data Protection Law with Regards to Personal Data Protection' (2017) 26(3) Information and Communications Technology Law 213, 214; John P Carlin, James M Koukios, David A Newman and Suhna N Pierce, 'Data Privacy and Transfers in Cross−border Investigations' (Global Investigations Review, 9 August 2017). https://globalinvestigationsreview.com/insight/the-investigations-review-of-the-americas-2018/1145431/data-privacy-and-transfers-in-cross-border-investigations, accessed 26 March 2021.

[30] 'Data Protection Regulations and International Data Flows: Implications for Trade and Development' UNCTAD/WEB/DTL/STICT/2016/1/iPub, xi (United Nations Publication, 2016). http://unctad.org/en/PublicationsLibrary/dtlstict2016d1_en.pdf, accessed 29 March 2021.

Regulation (GDPR),[31] the Charter of Fundamental Rights of the EU,[32] the Comprehensive and Progressive Agreement for Trans-Pacific Partnership (CPTPP),[33] to mention but a few. While in other jurisdiction, for example, the PRC and the Asia–Pacific Economic Cooperation (APEC) forum, the right to the protection of personal data is not explicitly considered a fundamental human right. Second, the extent of the data protection provided by legislation varies worldwide. According to the United Nations Conference on Trade and Development (UNCTAD), 128 out of 194 countries have enacted laws to protect data and privacy. Sixty-six percent of the United Nations (UN) countries have enacted data protection legislation while 10 percent of UN countries have had draft legislation of data protection.[34] Third, existing data protection systems vary greatly at the national level. Comprehensive data protection and privacy laws have been adopted by over 130 countries and independent jurisdictions or territories worldwide to protect the personal data held by private and public bodies.[35] Some other countries, do not have a comprehensive data protection law but have sector-specific laws or policies in place. Fourth, the strength of jurisdictions' measures regarding data localization differ and can be divided into strong, partial, mild, and sector-specific.[36] Fifth, the approaches to cross-border data transfers diverge in different legal frameworks. Some jurisdictions adopt approaches based on the "adequacy" of the data protection in foreign jurisdictions.[37] Some jurisdictions

---

[31] Article 1(2) and 1 (3) of the General Data Protection Regulation (hereinafter: GDPR) stipulate that 'this Regulation protects fundamental rights and freedoms of natural persons and in particular their right to the protection of personal data. (3) The free movement of personal data within the Union shall be neither restricted nor prohibited for reasons connected with the protection of natural persons with regard to the processing of personal data'. See 'Regulation (EU) 2016/679 of the European Parliament and of the Council of 27 April 2016 on the protection of natural persons with regard to the processing of personal data and on the free movement of such data, and repealing Directive 95/46/EC (General Data Protection Regulation) (Text with EEA relevance)'(EUR−Lex). https://eur-lex.europa.eu/legal-content/EN/TXT/?uri=CELEX%3A32016R0679, accessed 5 March 2021.

[32] Article 8 of the Charter of Fundamental Rights of the European Union stipulates that: 'everyone has the right to the protection of personal data concerning him or her', see 'Charter of Fundamental Rights of the European Union' 2012/C 326/02 (Official Journal of the European Union). https://eur-lex.europa.eu/legal-content/EN/TXT/?uri=CELEX:12012P/TXT, accessed 21 March 2021.

[33] 'Comprehensive and Progressive Agreement for Trans−Pacific Partnership Text' (New Zealand Foreign Affair and Trade). https://www.mfat.govt.nz/en/trade/free-trade-agreements/free-trade-agreements-in-force/comprehensive-and-progressive-agreement-for-trans-pacific-partnership-cptpp/comprehensive-and-progressive-agreement-for-trans-pacific-partnership-text-and-resources/, accessed 16 March 2021.

[34] 'Data Protection and Privacy Legislation Worldwide' (United Nations Conference on Trade and Development (hereinafter: UNCTAD), 2 April 2020). https://unctad.org/en/Pages/DTL/STI_and_ICTs/ICT4D-Legislation/eCom-Data-Protection-Laws.aspx, accessed 4 April 2021.

[35] David Banisar, 'National Comprehensive Data Protection/Privacy Laws and Bills 2020' (15 December 2020). https://ssrn.com/abstract=1951416, accessed 5 April 2021.

[36] Igor Runets, 'Meeting the Challenge of Data Localization Laws' (Linkedin, 27 September 2016). https://www.linkedin.com/pulse/meeting-challenge-data-localization-laws-igor-runets/, accessed 4 January 2021.

[37] Christopher Kuner, 'Regulation of Transborder Data Flows under Data Protection and Privacy Law: Past, Present and Future', OECD Digital Economy Papers No. 187, 20 (OECD

adopt approaches based on the person's consent, like the EU.[38] Other jurisdictions, such as Australia, adopt approaches based on the accountability principle.[39] Finally, several regulations such as the GDPR are legally binding, while others such as the Organization for Economic Co-operation and Development (OECD) Privacy Guidelines[40] and the APEC Privacy Framework[41] are not legally binding. There exist also initiatives, such as international human rights treaties and instruments adopted by UN bodies, that have been enacted at the global level, while others, such as the APEC Privacy Framework, that have been enacted at the regional level. A uniform and comprehensive law governing data protection issues is absent at the international level, and this situation can realistically not be expected to change in the short term. Data-related issues (data security, data protection, data transfer, data usage etc.) are still mostly regulated at the domestic level even though numerous new technologies are contributing to a de-territorialization of factual problems.[42] In this regard, Rostam J. Neuwirth has noted as follows:

> As far as the economic theory of international trade is concerned, absolute and comparative advantage gradually evolved to what can be termed a "competitive" or "creative advantage". In brief, this means that given natural conditions favouring the production of certain economic offerings, such as climate, have gradually become replaced by man-or policy made conditions.[43]

As data—particularly personal data are now the most valuable assets in the digital age, data protection legislation is becoming one of the most important sources of

---

publishing 2011). https://www.oecd-ilibrary.org/docserver/5kg0s2fk315f-en.pdf?expires=1604549314&id=id&accname=guest&checksum=62C9388AB859B25CE75D219D1AC46D74, accessed 4 January 2021.

[38] For example, Article 7(1) of the GDPR stipulates that: 'where processing is based on consent, the controller shall be able to demonstrate that the data subject has consented to processing of his or her personal data'.

[39] For example, Article 8.1 of the Australian Privacy Principles stipulates that: 'Before an APP entity discloses personal information about an individual to a person (the overseas recipient): who is not in Australia or an external Territory; and who is not the entity or the individual; the entity must take such steps as are reasonable in the circumstances to ensure that the overseas recipient does not breach the Australian Privacy Principles (other than Australian Privacy Principle 1) in relation to the information.'. See 'Chapter 8: Australian Privacy Principle 8 — Cross−border disclosure of personal information (Version 1.2)' (July 2019). https://www.oaic.gov.au/__data/assets/pdf_file/0006/1230/app-guidelines-chapter-8-v1.2.pdf, accessed 21 March 2021.

[40] 'OECD Guidelines governing the Protection of Privacy and Transborder Flows of Personal Data (OECD, 2013). oecd.org/sti/ieconomy/2013−oecd−privacy−guidelines.pdf, accessed 29 March 2021.

[41] 'APEC Privacy Framework' (APEC, 2005). https://www.apec.org/groups/committee-on-trade-and-investment/~/media/files/groups/ecsg/cbpr/cbpr-policiesrulesguidelines.ashx, accessed 4 March 2021.

[42] Janne E. Nijman and André Nollkaemper, 'Deterritorialization in International Law: Moving Away from the Divide between National and International Law' in Janne E. Nijman and André Nollkaemper, *New Perspectives on the Divide Between National and International Law* (1st edn, Oxford University Press 2007) 84–109.

[43] Rostam J. Neuwirth, '"Novel Food for Thought" on Law and Policymaking in the Global Creative Economy' (2014) 37(1) European Journal of Law and Economics 13, 21.

competitive advantage for individual nations in the context of international trade. The regulation of personal data shall, therefore, be at the heart of policy-making nowadays to ensure the goal of a "sustainable" development and competitive development of trade, science and technology, as well as society.

One the one hand, it has been argued that the world's most valuable resource is no longer oil, but data.[44] The pace and scope of technological innovation such as the development of AI, autonomous driving cars, and the Internet of Things all require vast amounts of data. In the digital world, data are tradeable, no matter as goods, services or contents. The Internet is considered a 21st-century trade route.[45] The borderless nature of the Internet has dramatically reduced the high entry costs to export markets, which paves the way for businesses of all sizes to reach international markets.[46] As the Internet is playing an increasingly important role in international trade, blocking access to data is tantamount to blocking access to trade.[47] Global e-commerce totaled US$ 27.7 trillion in 2016, up from US$ 19.3 trillion in 2012.[48] Increasing cross-border data flows nowadays create more economic value than traditional flows of traded goods.[49] Imports and exports of PRC's cross-border e-commerce totaled US$ 261.5 billion in 2020.[50] The modern battlefield in the regime of international trade is over the flows of information,[51] and moves from legislation to

---

[44] Ramona Pringle, '"Data Is the New Oil": Your Personal Information Is Now the World's Most Valuable Commodity' (CBC News, 25 August 2017). http://www.cbc.ca/news/technology/data-is-the-new-oil-1.4259677?cmp=rs, accessed 23 March 2021; 'The World's Most Valuable Resource Is No Longer Oil, But Data' (Economist). https://www.economist.com/leaders/2017/05/06/the-worlds-most-valuable-resource-is-no-longer-oil-but-data, accessed 12 September 2020.

[45] 'Enabling Trade in the Era of Information Technologies: Breaking down Barriers to the Free Flow of Information', 8 (Google, 2011). https://www.google.com/googleblogs/pdfs/trade_free_flow_of_information.pdf, accessed 23 March 2021; Meltzer (n 11) 1.

[46] 'Enabling Trade in the Era of Information Technologies: Breaking down Barriers to the Free Flow of Information' (n 45) 4; Nelson Cabrera, 'How the Internet Affects International Trade' (Lilly and Associates, 30 May 2010). http://www.shiplilly.com/blog/how-the-internet-affects-international-trade/, accessed 24 April 2021; Joshua Paul Meltzer, 'Supporting the Internet as a Platform for International Trade' (Brookings, 12 March 2015). https://www.brookings.edu/research/supporting-the-internet-as-a-platform-for-international-trade/, accessed 24 April 2021.

[47] 'Enabling Trade in the Era of Information Technologies: Breaking down Barriers to the Free Flow of Information' (n 45) 8.

[48] 'WTO Trade Report 2018: The Future of World Trade: How Digital Technologies Are Transforming Global Commerce', 5 (WTO Secretariat, 3 October 2018). https://www.wto.org/english/res_e/publications_e/world_trade_report18_e_under_embargo.pdf, accessed 1 March 2021.

[49] James Manyika and others, 'Digital globalization: The New Era of Global Flows' (Mckinsey Global Institute, February 2016), 2. https://www.mckinsey.com/business-functions/digital-mckinsey/our-insights/digital-globalization-the-new-era-of-global-flows, accessed 19 December 2020.

[50] 'Cross−border E−Commerce Contributes to China's Foreign Trade in 2020, With 31.1% Annual Growth Amid Pandemic' (Global Times, 14 Jan 2021). https://www.globaltimes.cn/page/202101/1212876.shtml, accessed 13 March 2021.

[51] Usman Ahmed and Anupam Chander, 'Information Goes Global: Protecting Privacy, Security, and the New Economy in a World of Cross−border Data Flows', E15Initiative, Geneva: International Centre for Trade and Sustainable Development (ICTSD) and World Economic Forum

technical standards.[52] On the other hand, cross-border digital trade builds on the foundation of users' trust.[53] The privacy of individuals should be well protected to elicit the confidence of users. Privacy is under serious threats at present. Google's parent company, Alphabet, runs the world's most popular search engine (Google), smartphone operating system (Android), web browser (Chrome), video site (YouTube) and email service (Gmail),[54] giving the company unprecedented details about its users. Everyone's daily activities—what one eats, reads or buys; where one works, shops, or passes by; whom one chat with, hang out with—are collected by different apps, and used or sold primarily for marketing.[55] More and more data about individuals will be generated and will persist under the control of others.[56] How to balance the relationship between privacy protection and data usage in the context of international trade is an important issue that WTO members' governments are facing in the legislative process, whether domestically or internationally.

Technological innovation changes the language and way of thinking, although in a slow pace. Finding a common language that clearly differentiates among some controversial concepts that are closely related to the implementation of cross-border data flows, though difficult to achieve in practice, is essential.[57] These concepts include but are not limited to those of "personal data and personal information", "data privacy and data security", "data controller and data processor", or "services and goods".

To highlight the deficiencies of the present international legal framework in place causing a problematic relationship between privacy protection, data usage, and the

---

(2015), 1. http://e15initiative.org/wp-content/uploads/2015/09/E15-Digital-Chander-and-Ahmed-Final.pdf, accessed 24 May 2021.

[52] The PRC is striving to develop new standards for 5G. For example, Huawei has been proactively involved in the formulation of 5G standards. Elsa Kania, 'China's Play for Global 5G Dominance – Standards and the "Digital Silk Road"' (ASPI, 27 June 2018). https://www.aspistrategist.org.au/chinas-play-for-global-5g-dominance-standards-and-the-digital-silk-road/, accessed 7 March 2021.

[53] 'Building Trust and Confidence for a Successful Digital Economic Era' (UNCTAD, 14 March 2017). http://unctad.org/en/pages/newsdetails.aspx?OriginalVersionID=1450, accessed 20 March 2021; see also 'Report on what's the Big Deal with Data?' 18 (Software Alliance, 21 October 2016). https://data.bsa.org/wp-content/uploads/2015/12/bsadatastudy_en.pdf, accessed 24 October 2020.

[54] Drew Harwell, 'Facebook Is Now in the Data Privacy Spotlight. Could Google Be next?' (Washington Post, 11 April 2018). https://www.washingtonpost.com/news/the-switch/wp/2018/04/11/facebook-is-now-in-the-data-privacy-spotlight-could-google-be-next/?noredirect=on&utm_term=.2d318050f81d, accessed 23 September 2020; William L. Hosch and Mark Hall, 'Google Inc.' (Encyclopedia Britannica). https://www.britannica.com/topic/Google-Inc, accessed 23 September 2020.

[55] Omri Ben−Shahar, 'Privacy Is the New Money, Thanks To Big Data' (Forbes, 1 April 2016). https://www.forbes.com/sites/omribenshahar/2016/04/01/privacy-is-the-new-money-thanks-to-big-data/?sh=fd2a4fa3fa2e, accessed 24 October 2020.

[56] John Podesta and others, 'Big Data: Seizing Opportunities, Preserving Values Interim' (Executive Office of the President, May 2014), 9. https://obamawhitehouse.archives.gov/sites/default/files/docs/big_data_privacy_report_5.1.14_final_print.pdf, accessed 24 March 2021.

[57] Rostam J. Neuwirth, 'Essentially Oxymoronic Concepts' (2013) 2(2) Global Journal of Comparative Law 147, 149.

progressive liberalization of international trade, the laws of the PRC related to cross-border data transfers are compared and contrasted/discussed with the relevant WTO treaty provisions, and various RTAs and FTAs entered into after 2012.

More precisely, the PRC legislation on cross-border data transfers is analysed in Chap. 2 in order to show that rules and measures restricting cross-border data transfers in the PRC are increasingly restrictive and have the potential to make the PRC a target of WTO disputes. Chapter 3 addresses the convergence of industries and technologies notably caused by digitization; the issue of conflicts between goods and services; the General Agreement on Tariffs and Trade (GATT) and GATS as well as the difficulty of classifying service sectors under WTO members' commitments. Chapter 4 examines the FTAs that entered into force after 2012 and surveys the FTAs and RTAs in which the PRC is involved that regulate digital trade beyond the venue of the WTO and analyses their rules of relevance for cross-border data flows and international trade. It asks whether and how these FTAs have deliberately reacted to the increasing importance of data flows as well as to the trouble of governing them in the context of global governance. The so-called "spaghetti-bowl" effect of FTAs may significantly undermine the value and impact of multilateralism. Cross-border data transfer restrictions are therefore largely a global issue. The highly fragmented current system for data protection and transfer is discussed in Chap. 5. This chapter proposes an appropriate legislative approach to strike a balance between the free flow of data across borders and public policy objectives in the context of international trade liberalization. At the end, Chap. 6 summarizes the discussion in this book.

Chapter 2
The PRC's Legislation on Cross-Border Data Transfers

> Law may be diametrically opposed to the objective of technology, as the former aims to maintain, preserve, and avoid sudden changes in order to guarantee the rule of law in terms of legal predictability and certainty, whereas the latter constantly pushes for change, and for improvement through innovation.[1]
>
> —Rostam J. Neuwirth

2.1 Overview

International trade in today's economy, whether regarding physical goods or virtual services, is supported by cross-border data movement. The direct or indirect data localization requirements are adopted into domestic law at a large-scale by many countries and regions.[2] Policy and regulatory environments affect the development and deployment of digital technologies that facilitate trade.[3] Some restrictions on cross-border data transfers are truly and undeniably for the purpose of safeguarding public policy objectives, but digital protectionism may also be a motivator.[4]

---

[1] Rostam J. Neuwirth, 'The UNESCO Convention and Future Technologies: "A Journey to the Centre of Cultural Law and Policymaking"' (31 October, 2016) in Lilian Richieri Hanania and Anne–Thida Norodom, *Diversity of Cultural Expressions in the Digital Era*, 87 (Buenos Aires: TESEO 2016). https://www.teseopress.com/diversityofculturalexpressionsinthedigitalera/chapter/the-unesco-convention-and-future-technologies-a-journey-to-the-centre-of-cultural-law-and-policymaking/, accessed 23 March 2021.

[2] Andrada Coos, 'Data Protection Legislation Around the World in 2021' (Endpoint Protection, 8 January 2021). https://www.endpointprotector.com/blog/data-protection-legislation-around-the-world/, accessed 23 March 2021.

[3] 'Trade in the Digital Economy—A Primer on Global Data Flows for Policymakers', 2 (International Chamber of Commerce Homepage, 19 July 2016). https://iccwbo.org/publication/trade-in-the-digital-economy, accessed 19 March 2021.

[4] Shahmel Azmeh and Christopher Foster, 'The TPP and the Digital Trade Agenda: Digital Industrial Policy and Silicon Valley's Influence on New Trade Agreements', 11 (2016). https://www.southcentre.int/wp-content/uploads/2017/09/Ev_170925_SC-Workshop-on-E-Commerce-and-Domestic-Regulation_Presentation-The-TPP-and-the-Digital-Trade-Agenda-Shamel-Azmeh_EN.pdf, accessed 23 March 2021; Henry Gao, 'Google's China Problem: A Case Study on Trade,

© The Author(s), under exclusive license to Springer Nature Singapore Pte Ltd. 2022
Y. Dai, *Cross-Border Data Transfers Regulations in the Context of International Trade Law: A PRC Perspective*, https://doi.org/10.1007/978-981-16-4995-0_2

2.2 The PRC's Legal System and the Hierarchy of Norms

Understanding the PRC's legal system and legislation hierarchy is essential to analysing legislation on personal information and cross-border data transfers against the appropriate background. According to the Constitution of the PRC and the Legislation Law of the PRC,[5] the National People's Congress (NPC) and its permanent body—the Standing Committee of the National People's Congress (SC-NPC)—both have state legislative power.[6] The NPC is at the top of the political power structure of the PRC; only it can enact basic laws and amend the Constitution.[7] The SC-NPC is the second-highest legislative organ in the PRC that has extensive legislative power. The SC-NPC develops and amends laws other than those developed by the NPC and partially supplements and amends laws developed by the NPC when the NPC is not in session.[8] The power to interpret the law is also vested in the SC-NPC if the specific meaning of the law needs to be further clarified or if the changing environment makes it necessary to define the basis of the law after its enactment.[9] In addition, the State Council of the PRC, under the authorization of the NPC and the SC-NPC, has the power to enact administrative regulations in accordance with the Constitution and national law.[10]

After obtaining preliminary approval from the State Council, the relevant agencies of the State Council, such as the People's Bank of China and the State Audit Administration, can enact administrative regulations as well.[11] According to the Legislation Law of the PRC:

> In light of the specific situations and actual needs of the jurisdiction, the People's Congress of a province, autonomous region, municipality directly under the central government and the

---

Technology and Human Rights Under the GATS' (24 December 2011) 6 Asian Journal of WTO & International Health Law and Policy 347, 347; Chander Anupam and P. Le Uyen, 'Data Nationalism' (2015) 64(3) Emory Law Journal 677, 681; Mike Herrick, 'With GDPR in the Background, Digital Protectionism is on the Rise and It has Been Building for a While' (Adweek, 10 April 2018). https://www.adweek.com/performance-marketing/with-gdpr-in-the-background-digital-protectionism-is-on-the-rise/, accessed 12 February 2021.

[5] The Legislation Law of the PRC (Chinese title: 中華人民共和國立法法) was adopted at the third Session of the Ninth NPC on 15 March 2000, promulgated on 15 March 2000, and amended on 15 March 2015. 'Legislation Law of the PRC' (NPC Homepage, 18 March 2015). http://www.npc.gov.cn/zgrdw/npc/dbdhhy/12_3/2015-03/18/content_1930713.htm accessed 9 March 2021. The Constitution of the PRC (Chinese title:中華人民共和國憲法) was adopted at the Fifth Session of the Fifth NPC and promulgated for implementation by the Announcement of the NPC on 4 December 1982, with further revisions in 1988, 1993, 1999, 2004 and 2018. 'Constitution of the PRC (2018 Version)' (State Council, 22 March 2018). http://www.gov.cn/guoqing/2018-03/22/content_5276318.htm, accessed 29 March 2021.

[6] Constitution of the PRC, Art. 62(3), 67(2) (3); see also the Legislation Law of the PRC, Art. 7.

[7] Constitution of the PRC, Art. 62(1) (3); see also the Legislation Law of the PRC, Art. 7.

[8] Legislation Law of the PRC, Art. 7; see also the Constitution of the PRC, Art. 67(2) (3).

[9] Legislation Law of the PRC, Art. 45; see also the Constitution of the PRC, Art. 67(1) (4).

[10] Legislation Law of the PRC, Art. 89(1); see also the Constitution of the PRC, Art. 45.

[11] Legislation Law of the PRC, Art. 80.

2.2 The PRC's Legal System and the Hierarchy of Norms

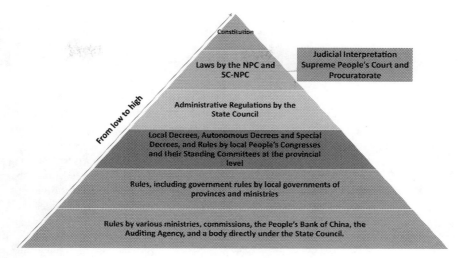

Fig. 2.1 .

Standing Committee thereof may enact local decrees provided that they shall not contravene any provision of the Constitution, national law and administrative regulations.[12]

The hierarchy of PRC domestic laws and regulations can be summarized as follows (Fig. 2.1).

(According to Art. 88, 89, 90, 91 and 92 of the Legislation Law of the PRC)

The Supreme People's Court and the Supreme People's Procuratorate have been vested with the power to develop interpretations on the specific application of law in trial or procuratorial work.[13] These judicial interpretations, which can be cited directly during the trial, have a legal effect but cannot contradict the constitution and law. In addition, international treaties ratified by the PRC are directly applicable and prevail if they conflict with domestic law.[14]

---

[12] Ibid, Art. 72.

[13] Ibid, Art. 104. The legislature of the PRC hasn't clarified the level of authority of judicial interpretations. Judicial interpretations are outside the formal hierarchy of legal norms. Nowadays, leading standpoint of academic filed is that the judicial interpretations of specific provisions of law have the same legal effect as the enacted law itself. See Chen Wang (王成), 'Research on the Legal Effect of Judicial Interpretations' (Chinese title: 最高法院司法解釋效力研究) (2016) 1 Peking University Law Journal (Chinese title:中外法學) 263, 279.

[14] 'If any international treaty concluded or acceded to by the People's Republic of China contains provisions differing from those in the civil laws of the PRC, the provisions of the international treaty shall apply, unless the provisions are ones on which the PRC has announced reservations.' See General Principles of the Civil Law of the PRC, Art. 142.

2.3 Data or Information?

2.3.1 The Definition of Personal Information in the PRC's Legal System

There is no uniform definition of personal information in the PRC legal system. Most data-related law and regulations in the PRC adopt their own customized definition of personal information.

The Decision of the SC-NPC on Strengthening Information Protection on Networks (Chinese title: 全國人民代表大會常務委員會關於加強网络信息保護的決定) (SC-NPC Decision) protects electronic information by which individual citizens can be identified and that involves the privacy of citizens.[15] It provides the scope of protection of electronic information rather than a definition of personal information.

The Provisions on Protection of the Personal Information of Telecommunications and Internet Users (2013 MIIT Provisions) define a user's personal information as a user's name, date of birth, identity card number, address, telephone number, account number, passwords and other information through which the identity of the user can be distinguished independently or in combination with other information as well as the time of use and location of the user using the service and other information collected by telecommunications service operators and Internet information service providers in the process of providing services.[16] It is the first time that personal information has been defined independently, and it is also the first time that the core legal characteristic of personal information, i.e. "identifiability", has been specified in Chinese law.

The Notice of the Supreme People's Court, the Supreme People's Procuratorate and the Ministry of Public Security on Legally Punishing Criminal Activities Infringing upon the Personal Information of Citizens 2013[17] stipulates that the

---

[15] The Decision of the SC—NPC on Strengthening Information Protection on Networks (Chinese title: 全國人民代表大會常務委員會關於加強网络信息保護的決定) (hereinafter: SC—NPC Decision) was passed on 28 December 2012 at the 30th Committee Meeting of the 11th SC—NPC. Art. 1. See 'Decision of the Standing Committee of the National People's Congress on Strengthening Information Protection on Networks' (Central People's Government of the PRC Homepage, 28 December 2019). http://www.gov.cn/jrzg/2012-12/28/content_2301231.htm, accessed 8 March 2021.

[16] The Provisions on Protection of the Personal Information of Telecommunications and Internet Users (Chinese title: 電信和互聯網用戶個人信息保護規定) are deliberated and adopted at the 2nd executive meeting of the Ministry of Industry and Information Technology of the PRC on 28 June 2013, and come into force on 1 September 2013. 'Provisions on Protecting the Personal Information of Telecommunications and Internet Users', Art. 4 (Global Law). http://policy.mofcom.gov.cn/claw/clawContent.shtml?id=4835, accessed 17 November 2018.

[17] The Notice of the Supreme People's Court, the Supreme People's Procuratorate and the Ministry of Public Security on Legally Punishing Criminal Activities Infringing upon the Personal Information of Citizens 2013 (Chinese title: 最高人民法院、最高人民檢察院、公安部關於依法懲處侵害公民個人信息犯罪活動的通知2013) was published by the SPC, the Supreme People's

2.3 Data or Information?

personal information of citizens includes the name, age, valid certificate number, marital status, employer, educational background, resume, family address, phone number and other information or data that can identify a citizen or involve the personal privacy of a citizen,[18] and divides personal information into two broad categories: (1) information that can identify a citizen; and (2) information that involves the privacy of a citizen. This definition is broad and distinguishes personal information from personal privacy.[19]

The Information Security Technology—Guideline for Personal Information Protection within Information System for Public and Commercial Services (2013 MIIT Guidelines) divide personal information into "general personal information" and "sensitive personal information"—similar to the distinction in the EU data privacy regime[20] and for the first time clearly define what might be considered "personal information" as well as "sensitive personal information". In the 2013 MIIT Guidelines, personal information is referred to as:

> Information or an information aggregate which is capable of effectively and feasibly identifying a particular user, separately or in combination with other information, such as name, date of birth, identification certificate number, address, telephone number, account number and password.[21]

Additionally, so-called "sensitive personal information" is described by the 2013 MIIT Guidelines as follows:

> Personal information that, once it is leaked or altered, may bring about harmful influence to the subject of the indicated personal information. The concrete content sensitive personal information in different sectors is to be determined on the basis of the wishes of the subject of the personal information who receives the service and the particular characteristics of different sectors. Personal information listed as sensitive may include identity

---

Procuratorate and the Ministry of Public Security on 23 April 2013. See 'Notice of the Supreme People's Court, the Supreme People's Procuratorate and the Ministry of Public Security on Legally Punishing Criminal Activities Infringing upon the Personal Information of Citizens 2013' (Supreme People's Procuratorate and the Ministry of Public Security Homepage, 9 May 2017). http://www.spp.gov.cn/xwfbh/wsfbt/201705/t20170509_190088.shtml, accessed 8 March 2019.

[18] Notice of the Supreme People's Court, the Supreme People's Procuratorate and the Ministry of Public Security on Legally Punishing Criminal Activities Infringing upon the Personal Information of Citizens 2013, Art. 2.

[19] Ibid.

[20] In November 2012, the MIIT issued the first national standard on personal data protection—the Information Security Technology—Guideline for Personal Information Protection within Information System for Public and Commercial Services (Chinese title: 信息安全技術公共及商用服務信息系統個人信息保護指南) (hereinafter: 2013 MIIT Guidelines). See 'Information Security Technology—Guideline for Personal Information Protection within Information System for Public and Commercial Services' GB/Z 28828–2012 (National Public Service Platform for Standard Information). https://max.book118.com/html/2019/0409/8073014027002016.shtm, accessed 17 March 2021. Article 3.2 of the 2013 MIIT Guideline stipulates that: 'Personal information Computer data that is handled in computer systems, that are related to a specific natural person, and that can be used independently or in combination with other information to distinguish that specific natural person. Personal information may be divided into sensitive personal information and common personal information'.

[21] 2013 MIIT Guidelines, Art. 4.

card numbers, mobile telephone numbers, ethnicity, political viewpoints, religious beliefs, genes, fingerprints, etc.[22]

If personal information is anonymized or de-identified, and particular users cannot be identified, the 2013 MIIT Guidelines do not apply.[23]

The Provisions of the Supreme People's Court on Several Issues Concerning the Application of Law in the Trial of Cases involving Civil Disputes over Infringements upon Personal Rights and Interests through Information Networks (2014)[24] do not define personal information but list the information that relates to a natural person's individual privacy and stipulate in the following way:

> Where a network user or NSP discloses through network a natural person's individual privacy such as genetic information, medical records, health inspection materials, criminal records, home address, and private activities, or any other personal information, which causes damage to any other person, and the infringed party requests the assumption of tort liability by the network user or NSP, the people's court shall support such a request, unless under any of the following circumstances.[25]

Privacy and personal information are not distinguished in the article.

A relatively comprehensive concept of personal information is formed in the Network Security Law of the PRC in the following way:

> Personal information means all kinds of information recorded in an electronic or other forms, which can be used, independently or in combination with other information, to identify a natural person's personal identity, including but not limited to the natural person's name, date of birth, identity certificate number, biology-identified personal information, address and telephone number.[26]

This definition used summarizing and enumerating methods to provide a relatively comprehensive concept of personal information. Although the Network Security Law applies to the "construction, operation, maintenance and use of the network as well as the supervision and administration of cybersecurity within the territory of the PRC,"[27] the definition of personal information is technology neutral. It does not matter how the personal information is stored—in electronic or other forms, such as on paper or in a CCTV system.[28]

The Supreme People's Court and the Supreme People's Procuratorate of Several Issues Concerning the Application of Law in the Handling of Criminal Cases of

---

[22] Ibid, Art. 3.7.

[23] Ibid.

[24] 'Provisions of the Supreme People's Court on Several Issues Concerning the Application of Law in the Trial of Cases involving Civil Disputes over Infringements upon Personal Rights and Interests through Information Networks' (Chinese title: 最高人民法院關於審理利用信息網絡侵害人身權益民事糾紛案件適用法律若干問題的規定2014) (SPC Homepage, 21 October 2014). http://www.court.gov.cn/zixun-xiangqing-6777.html, accessed 8 March 2019.

[25] Ibid, Art. 12.

[26] Network Security Law of the PRC, Art. 76.

[27] Ibid, Art. 2.

[28] Ibid, Art. 76.

2.3 Data or Information?

Infringement on Citizens' Personal Information defines citizens' personal information in Article 253(a) of the Criminal Law as follows:

> All kinds of information recorded in electronic form or any other form, which can be used, independently or in combination with other information, to identify a specific natural person's personal identity or reflect a specific natural person's activities, including the natural person's name, identity certificate number, communication and contact information, address, account password, property status, and whereabouts, among others.[29]

This article expands the scope of citizens' personal information from information that can be used to identify a natural person's personal identity to information that can be used to identify a natural person's personal identity or to reflect a specific natural person's activities.

A consistent cognition of the definition of personal information has not been formed. The definition of personal information is departmentally oriented and fragmented across different Chinese laws and regulations, which creates a great challenge in determining the scope of personal information in judicial practice. The chaos of the concept has brought much confusion to the practice of enforcement owing to the lack of uniform norms. Judges have discretionary power over the definition of personal information. In judicial practice, there is considerable dispute over whether certain information could be considered personal information and thus be subject to legal protection.[30]

2.3.2 The Difference Between "Personal Information" and "Personal Data"

Personal information and personal data are two often-used phrases in the Internet age. Regarding the legal terminology, the PRC adopts the term "personal information" as the same choice was made in Japan,[31] Russia,[32] and in South Korea.[33] By

---

[29] Interpretation of the Supreme People's Court and the Supreme People's Procuratorate of Several Issues Concerning the Application of Law in the Handling of Criminal Cases of Infringement on Citizens' Personal Information, Art. 1.

[30] For example, *Zhu Ye v Baidu 2015 Case (Chinese title: 北京百度網訊科技有限公司與朱燁隱私權糾紛)*.

[31] 'The purpose of this Act is to protect the rights and interests of individuals while taking consideration of the usefulness of personal information.' See 'Act on the Protection of Personal Information of Japan', Art.1 (Act No. 57 of the 2003). http://www.cas.go.jp/jp/seisaku/hourei/data/APPI.pdf, accessed 30 December 2020.

[32] 'Data Protection Laws of the World, Russia, Data Protection Laws of the World Full Handbook' (DLA PIPER). https://www.dlapiperdataprotection.com/system/modules/za.co.heliosdesign.dla.lotw.data_protection/functions/handbook.pdf?country=all, accessed 12 November 2020.

[33] 'Data Protection Laws of the World, South Korea, Data Protection Laws of the World Full Handbook' (DLA PIPER). https://www.dlapiperdataprotection.com/system/modules/za.co.heliosdesign.dla.lotw.data_protection/functions/handbook.pdf?country=all, accessed 12 November 2020.

contrast, most EU countries adopt the term "personal data". As a combined approach, Canada,[34] and the Chinese Taipei use both terms.[35]

The Network Security Law of the PRC differentiates information from data by defining network data as "all kinds of electronic data collected, stored, transmitted, processed and generated through the network".[36] Personal information as information that can be used, independently or in combination with other data, to identify a natural person's identity, such as the person's name, address, telephone number, birthday, ID number and biometric data.[37]

According to the Oxford Dictionary, one meaning of data that closely relates to the discussion in this thesis is as follows:

> 1 Facts and statistics collected together for reference or analysis. 1.1 The quantities, characters, or symbols on which operations are performed by a computer, which may be stored and transmitted in the form of electrical signals and recorded on magnetic, optical, or mechanical recording media.[38]

At the same time, information in computing is defined by the Oxford Dictionary as data that are processed, stored, or transmitted by a computer.[39]

Data and information are interconnected but are not the same. Data usually refers to "raw data", i.e. the basic form of data that have not been analysed or processed in any manner. It is popular to say that "data is the oil of the 21st century", which means that data have value, as does oil, but only after being broken down and analysed.[40] After the data are processed, stored, or transmitted by a computer, they become information. Data can stand alone, while information depends completely on the

---

[34] 'Guidelines for Processing Personal Data Across Borders' (Office of the Privacy Commissioner of Canada). https://www.priv.gc.ca/en/privacy-topics/airports-and-borders/gl_dab_090127/, accessed 30 December 2020.

[35] 'Data Protection Laws of the World, Taiwan, Data Protection Laws of the World Full Handbook' (DLA PIPER). https://www.dlapiperdataprotection.com/system/modules/za.co.heliosdesign.dla.lotw.data_protection/functions/handbook.pdf?country=all, accessed 12 November 2020.

[36] Network Security Law of the PRC, Art. 76(4).

[37] Ibid, Art. 76(5).

[38] 'Definition of Data in English' (English Oxford Living Dictionaries). https://en.oxforddictionaries.com/definition/data, accessed 16 May 2021.

[39] 'Definition of Information in English' (English Oxford Living Dictionaries). https://en.oxforddictionaries.com/definition/information, accessed 16 May 2021.

[40] Clive Humby, UK Mathemetician, and architect of Tesco's Clubcard, 2006, widely credited as the first to coin the phrase: 'Data is the new oil. It's valuable, but if unrefined it cannot really be used. It has to be changed into gas, plastic, chemicals, etc. to create a valuable entity that drives profitable activity; so must data be broken down, analyzed for it to have value.' See Michael Haupt, 'Data Is the New Oil – a Ludicrous Proposition Natural Resources, the Question of Ownership and the Reality of Big Data' (Medium). https://medium.com/twenty-one-hundred/data-is-the-new-oil-a-ludicrous-proposition-1d91bba4f294, accessed 16 May 2021.

2.3 Data or Information?

Fig. 2.2 .

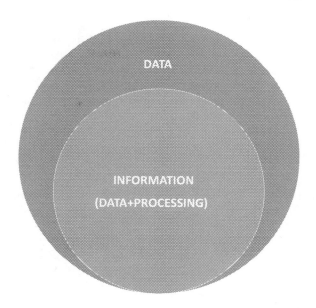

data.[41] Standalone data are useless, while information is meaningful and valuable.[42] Information is the message that is being expressed and conveyed, while data are simple facts. Data are considered the language of the computer. They are the output of the computer. However, information is the way in which we process or translate language or data. It is the human interpretation of data. Data are an objective record of things. Information refers to the content that has useful value and form after the data have been processed. The scope of personal data is broader than that of personal information. The relationship between these two can be summarized as follows in Fig. 2.2.

Based on this, it can be inferred that network data in the Network Security Law of the PRC refers not to raw data but to network information. The personal information in the Network Security Law of the PRC refers not to the content that forms after the data have been processed but to identification data. These two definitions are confusing and should be changed to be consistent with the meaning that is widely known and accepted. Although the Network Security Law of the PRC differentiates these two concepts, personal information in the judicial practice of the PRC actually refers to personal data.

---

[41] Tarun Kumar, '10 Main Differences between Data and Information' (Loginworks, 13 July 2018). https://www.loginworks.com/blogs/10-main-differences-between-data-and-information/, accessed 16 May 2021.

[42] Ibid; S. Surbhi, 'Difference between Data and Information' (Key Differences, 15 September 2016). https://keydifferences.com/difference-between-data-and-information.html, accessed 16 May 2021.

Regarding personal information protection on the Internet, the case *Zhu Ye v Baidu 2015* is a highly representative case.[43] In this case, Internet user Ms. Zhu Ye claimed that her privacy rights were violated because she could not stop seeing advertisements on weight loss, abortion and breast implants when she browsed webpages after using Baidu's search engine to search related information. The Intermediate People's Court of Nanjing City, Jiangsu Province, made the decision that Baidu's use of cookies to personalize advertisements does not infringe on consumers' rights to privacy.[44] The question arising from this case is what kind of information could be considered personal information and thus obtain protection under Chinese law. The court held the opinion that users' information, such as the Internet activity and Internet preferences collected by the Baidu cookies, could not be viewed as personal information under Chinese law because such information was in a separate form and could not be used to identify the user. The prerequisite for personal information being protected under the PRC legal system is that the information, independently or in combination with other information, must enable the identification of a specific individual.[45] Therefore, only identifiable personal information can be protected by law in the PRC. Although different names are adopted, the range of personal data or information protected by law is similar among different countries and regions mentioned above, focusing on the "identifiable" data or information.[46]

Both personal data and personal information, independently or in combination with other data and information, enable the identification of a specific individual. Both personal data and personal information can be related to privacy. For more comprehensive protection, it is better to adopt the term "personal data" rather than "personal information" in the data protection legislative process. Since personal information in the PRC legal system actually refers to personal data,[47] these two terms are used interchangeably in the following discussion.

---

[43] Sherry Gong and Nolan Shaw, 'Chinese Appellate Court Provides Guidance for Lawful Use of Cookies' (Hogan Lovells, 3 August 2015). http://www.hldataprotection.com/2015/08/articles/international-eu-privacy/chinese-appellate-court-provides-guidance-for-lawful-use-of-cookies/, accessed 16 May 2021.

[44] Ibid.

[45] 2013 MIIT Guidelines, Art. 4.

[46] GDPR Rec.26. Art. 4(1); OECD Guidelines, Art. 1.

[47] For more detail, please refer to Sect. 2.3.2 The Difference Between "Personal Information" and "Personal Data".

2.4 The PRC's Legislation on Cross-Border Data Transfers

2.4.1 Laws and Regulations

When the Network Security Law of the PRC came into force on 1 June 2017, the PRC information protection legislation entered a new stage.[48] This law contains a whole chapter that regulates personal information protection issues and proffers specific requirements regarding the collection, use, and protection of personal information, albeit from the perspective of emphasizing network information security rather than protecting personal privacy rights.

The Network Security Law embraces the new concept of the "critical information infrastructure" (CII), which refers to that:

> Public communication and information services, power, traffic, water, finance, public service, electronic governance and other critical information infrastructure that if destroyed, losing function or leaking data might seriously endanger national security, national economy and the people's livelihood, or the public interest.[49]

The PRC, in its Network Security Law, for the first time, expressly requires that the personal information and important data of Chinese citizens that are collected, generated and produced by operators of CII be stored in servers located in mainland China.[50] Such information and data can be transferred to overseas parties only if they are "indeed necessary" and "pass the security assessment".[51] The security assessment shall be conducted by the competent agencies unless otherwise specified by laws and regulations.[52] The Network Security Law of the PRC defines CII broadly as infrastructure that will result in serious damage to state security, the national economy and people's livelihood and public interest if it is destroyed, loses function or encounters data leakage.[53] Specific reference is made to key fields such as public communications and information services, energy, transport, water conservancy, finance, public services, and e-government affairs.[54] This definition is sufficiently broad to cover numerous sectors and industries. Since many domestic and multinational companies may fall within the scope of the CII, these companies will likely be subject to restrictions and impediments from the new data storage and transmission requirements of the Network Security Law.

CII operators are subject to more stringent compliance requirements. High-level security measures are justifiably expected from large Internet companies such as

---

[48] Jason Meng and Fan Wei, 'China Strengthens Its Data Protection Legislation' (International Association of Privacy Professionals, 2016). https://iapp.org/news/a/china-strengthens-its-data-protection-legislation/, accessed 10 March 2021.

[49] Network Security Law, Art. 31.

[50] Ibid, Art. 37.

[51] Ibid.

[52] Ibid.

[53] Ibid, Art. 31.

[54] Ibid.

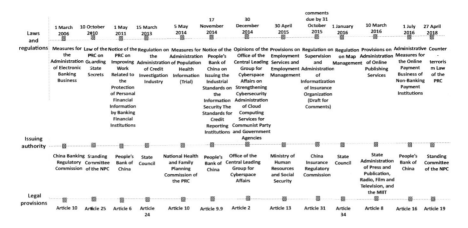

Fig. 2.3

Alibaba, Baidu, and Tencent. The Network Security Law explicitly requires the network operators to provide technical support and assistance to the government for activities related to safeguarding state security and investigating crimes.[55] However, this obligation may become clear only through further interpretation and application. The uncertainty of some definitions and concepts also hinders the implementation of the Network Security Law. The law must clarify the definition and scope of some key concepts (e.g., sensitive data) and the required procedures and processes (e.g., the process of undertaking a security assessment for cross-border CII information transfer). Furthermore, whether enterprises and nonprofit organizations that play roles as network operators should be treated equally or differently is unclear. Like many other laws in the PRC, the Network Security Law leaves much room for interpretation and requires more detailed implementation rules to work together with the high-level principles.

Besides the Network Security Law, the PRC has adopted broad, cross-border, domestic data restriction policies. In the PRC, rules and policies regarding restrictions on cross-border data transfers are scattered around several regulations. The figure above shows the PRC's existing data localization and cross-border data transfer requirements in a time sequence (Fig. 2.3).

From above, it is observed that restrictions on cross-border data transfers in the PRC have been enacted on a sector-by-sector basis. The strictest transfer restriction applies to sensitive data such as personal banking and financial information, personal credit reference information, personal health information and, most importantly, information related to state secrets, national security and national sovereignty—such as information with terrorist or extremist content. The PRC's new Counterterrorism Law requires telecommunications business operators and Internet Service Providers (ISPs) to cooperate more extensively with the public security authorities or

---

[55] Ibid, Art. 28.

2.4 The PRC's Legislation on Cross-Border Data Transfers

the relevant government departments.[56] Like the Network Security Law, the details and interpretation of the Counterterrorism Law remain unclear and call for further explanation.[57]

On 20 August 2021, the NPC of the PRC passed the Personal Information Protection Law.[58] The Personal Information Protection Law gets a lot of attention as it is going to be the first comprehensive and dedicated personal information protection law in the PRC. It comprises 8 chapters and 74 articles, covering a variety of matters relating to personal data protection, as well as cross-border data transfers.[59] Under the Personal Information Protection Law, in addition to CII operators, personal information handlers that process personal information reaching certain threshold amounts are required to store the personal information within mainland China.[60] Where they need to provide it abroad, they shall pass a security assessment organized by the Cyberspace Administration of China (CAC).[61] The Personal Information Protection Law basically introduces four mechanisms that could be relied upon before a data exporter provides personal information outside the borders of the PRC for business or other such requirements: (i) passing a security assessment organized by professional certification bodies as designated by the CAC according to Article 40 of this Law; (ii) obtaining relevant personal information protection certification from specialized body as designated by the CAC; (iii) concluding an agreement with its foreign data recipients to ensure foreign data recipients process personal information in accordance with the personal information protection standards provided in this Law; or (iv) other conditions as may be provided by laws, administrative regulations or other conditions as may be prescribed by the CAC, where treaties or international agreements that the People's Republic of China has concluded or acceded to contain provisions such as conditions on providing personal data outside the borders of the People's Republic of China, it is permitted to act according to those provisions. Personal information handlers shall adopt necessary measures to ensure that foreign receiving parties' personal information handling activities reach the standard of personal information protection provided in this Law.[62]

Similar to the Data Security Law[63] the Personal Information Protection Law also stipulates that relevant competent department's approval should be obtained before

---

[56] Counterterrorism Law of the PRC (2018 Amendment), Art. 19. See 'Counterterrorism Law of the PRC' (Chinese name: 中華人民共和國反恐怖主義法) (NPC Homepage, 12 June 2018). http://www.npc.gov.cn/zgrdw/npc/xinwen/2018-06/12/content_2055871.htm, accessed 1 March 2021.

[57] Alan Charles Raul, 'Global Overview' in Alan Charles Raul *Privacy, Data Protection and Cybersecurity Law Review* (4th edn, Law Business Research Ltd 2017) 3.

[58] 'Personal Information Protection Law of the PRC'(Chinese title: 中華人民共和國個人信息保護法) (NPC, 20 August, 2021). http://www.npc.gov.cn/npc/c30834/202108/a8c4e3672c74491a80b53a172bb753fe.shtml, accessed 1 September 2021.

[59] Ibid.

[60] Ibid, Art. 40.

[61] Ibid.

[62] Ibid, Art. 38.

[63] 'Data Security Legislation' (NPC). http://www.npc.gov.cn/npc/sjaqfca/sjaqfca.shtml, accessed 1 March 2021.

providing personal information for international judicial assistance or administrative law enforcement assistance outside mainland China.[64]

Regulations on Data localization and cross-border transfer are key considerations for international companies operating in the PRC.[65] The Personal Information Protection Law appears to introduce several positive mechanisms allowing for the cross-border transfer of personal information. However, details on the procedure and implementation of the proposed mechanisms remain unclear, further clarifications are needed to enable companies operating in the PRC to understand and comply with the new law.[66]

In addition to the laws and regulations mentioned above, restrictions on cross-border transfer are also suggested under two non-binding industry guidelines.

2.4.2 Non-Binding Guidelines

First, personal information stored on an entity's information system in the PRC is subject to the requirements of the 2013 MIIT Guidelines.[67] The 2013 MIIT Guidelines require that the express consent of individuals be obtained before their personal information is transmitted overseas unless the information export has been authorized under the applicable PRC laws and regulations or by the competent PRC authority.[68] The overseas recipients must also meet the requirements set out in the 2013 MIIT Guidelines; for example, they must implement protective measures against the loss, leakage, and destruction of and tampering with the personal information.[69] Therefore, the recipient may be required to enter into a written data transfer agreement with the transmitter to clarify the recipient's responsibilities.[70] Although the 2013 MIIT Guidelines are non-binding and no fixed sanction exists for failure to comply, the Chinese authorities actively encourage entities to implement them on a voluntary basis.[71]

---

[64] Ibid, Art. 41.

[65] Clarice Yue and others, 'China Data Protection Update and Deep Dive (1): Data sharing and cross−border data transfer rules under the Draft Personal Information Protection Law' (October 2020, Bird & Bird). https://www.twobirds.com/en/news/articles/2020/china/china-data-protection-update-and-deep-dive-1, accessed 17 March 2021.

[66] Ibid.

[67] See 'Information Security Technology—Guideline for Personal Information Protection within Information System for Public and Commercial Services' GB/Z 28828–2012 (National Public Service Platform for Standard Information). https://max.book118.com/html/2019/0409/8073014027002016.shtm, accessed 17 March 2021.

[68] Ibid.

[69] Ibid, Art. 5.4.

[70] Ibid, Art. 5.4.2.

[71] Ibid, Art. 1.

2.4 The PRC's Legislation on Cross-Border Data Transfers

In addition, the Standards for Assessment of Personal Information Protection of Internet Enterprises (Internet Enterprises Standards)[72] are the first series of standards in the field of the Internet that have been proposed by independent third parties, namely, the China Law Association on Science and Technology and the Peking University Internet Law Centre (Chinese title: 北京大學科技法研究中心). The Internet Enterprises Standards adopt general rules for transferring personal information to any third party rather than just personal information that is transferred overseas. The express consent of the users is the precondition for transfer except in four special situations.[73]

Cross-border information transfer is severely restricted under these two standards. Without the consent of the subjects, personal information cannot be transferred unless certain special situations exist. However, both of these standards lack legal remedies and liability provisions and are not legally binding.

2.4.3 Increasingly Tight Restrictions on Cross-Border Data Transfers

Although there are several Chinese laws and regulations governing the collection, use, and storage of personal data, no comprehensive law existed that governed data transfers across Chinese borders before the enforcement of the Network Security Law. A series of regulations have been developed from the enforcement of the Network Security Law.[74] The two most important are: (1) the Draft of the Measures on Security Assessment of Cross-border Data Transfer of Personal Information and

---

[72] The Standards for Assessment of Personal Information Protection of Internet Enterprises (hereinafter: Internet Enterprises Standards) (Chinese title: 互聯網企業個人信息保護測評標準) was published and effective on 25 March 2014. See 'Evaluation Standard for Internet Enterprises' Protection of Personal Information' (Legal and Judicial Information Center for China–ASEAN Countries, 15 March 2014). http://www.cac.gov.cn/2017-04/11/c_1120785691.htm, accessed 8 March 2021.

[73] Four special situations include: (a) Special provisions of laws and regulations with regard to maintaining public security and critical necessity, etc. (b) For purposes of academic research or social and public interests. (c) Compulsory actions were taken by an administrative department under the law; (d) Decisions, rulings or judgments rendered by a judiciary under the law. The Internet Enterprises Standards applies to all the data transfer (not only cross–border data transfers). See Internet Enterprises Standards, Art. 5.2.

[74] On 13 June 2019, the Cyberspace Administration of China (hereinafter: CAC) has, in conjunction with the relevant departments, drafted the Measures for the Security Assessment for Cross–border Transfer of Personal Information (Exposure Draft), and requests public comments thereon.However, this Measures solely focuses on the Transfer of "personal information," without any mention of data localization requirements. See 'Notice by the Cyberspace Administration of China of Requesting Public Comments on the Measures for the Security Assessment for Cross–border Transfer of Personal Information (Exposure Draft)' (Chinese title: 國家互聯網信息辦公室關於《個人信息出境安全評估辦法 (徵求意見稿)》公開徵求意見的通知) (CAC Homepage, 13 June 2019). http://www.cac.gov.cn/2019-06/13/c_1124613618.htm, accessed 8 March 2021.

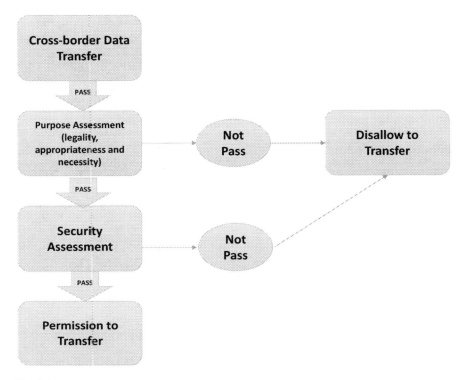

Fig. 2.4

Important Data (Draft of the Measures on Security Assessment),[75] and (2) the Draft of Information Security Technology—Guidelines for Cross-Border Transfer Security Assessment (2017 Guidelines for Cross-Border Transfer Security Assessment), which was first published in May 2017 (First Draft) and subsequently amended in August 2017 (Second Draft).[76] The legal hierarchy and effect of these measures as can be seen in Fig. 2.4.

---

[75] 'Draft of the Measures on Security Assessment of Cross−border Data Transfer of Personal Information and Important Data' (hereinafter: Draft of the Measures on Security Assessment) (Chinese title: 個人信息和重要數據出境安全評估辦法 (徵求意見稿)) was published by the CAC on 11 April 2017 to solicit public opinion. (CAC Homepage, 11 April 2017). http://www.cac.gov.cn/2017-04/11/c_1120785691.htm, accessed 8 March 2021.

[76] 'Draft of Information Security Technology—Guidelines for Cross−Border Transfer Security Assessment' (hereinafter: 2017 Guidelines for Cross−Border Transfer Security Assessment) (Chinese title: 信息安全技術 數據出境安全評估指南 (草案)) was published by the General Administration of Quality Supervision, Inspection and Quarantine of the PRC (Chinese title: 國家質量監督檢驗檢疫總局) and the National Information Security Standardization Technical Committee (Chinese title: 國家信息安全標準化技術委員會) (National Information Security Standardization Technical Committee Homepage, 27 May 2017). https://www.tc260.org.cn/ueditor/jsp/upload/20170527/37491495878030102.pdf, accessed 8 March 2021.

2.4 The PRC's Legislation on Cross-Border Data Transfers

To provide further explanation of problems not mentioned in the Network Security Law, specifically how the Chinese government intends to conduct the security assessment and the criteria for such an assessment, the Draft of the Measures on Security Assessment was published to solicit public opinion.[77]

First, the Draft of the Measures on Security Assessment expands the scope of the data localization and security review requirements of the PRC, namely, from "critical information infrastructure"[78] to all "network operators", which are defined as any owners or administrators of a computerized information network system, as well as network service providers.[79] As a general principle, if personal data and important data have been collected or generated within the territory of the PRC, network operators are required to store them within the territory of the PRC.[80] It is noteworthy that the cross-border transfer of personal data and important data that are collected or generated by individuals or organizations other than network operators are also subject to security assessment, as outlined above.[81]

Second, the Draft of the Measures on Security Assessment states that before any personal data are transferred to overseas countries, the relevant subjects must be notified of the purpose, scope, content, and receipt of the transfer as well as the country or area where the recipient is located.[82] In addition, the subjects' consent must be obtained before the transfer.[83] No exceptions to the requirement for consent are provided in the Draft of the Measures on Security Assessment. In contrast, such exceptions exist under Article 42 of the Network Security Law, under which the consent of personal information subjects is not required if the personal information is unidentifiable.

The Draft of the Measures on Security Assessment does not clarify whether network operators include only domestic network operators in the PRC or also foreign-invested network operators. According to the 2017 Guidelines for Cross-Border Transfer Security Assessment (Second Draft), network operators that are not registered in the PRC would still be considered to be conducting domestic operations if they conduct business, or provide products or services within the territory of the PRC.[84] Even if the data collected by a network operator are not retained outside the PRC, there could still be a cross-border transfer of the data if overseas entities, institutions or individuals are able to access the data remotely (public information

---

[77] 'Notice of the Cyberspace Administration of China on Assessment of Cross-border Data Transfer of Personal Information and Important Data' (Chinese title: 國家互聯網信息辦公室關於《個人信息和重要數據出境安全評估辦法 (徵求意見稿)》公開徵求意見的通知) (Office of the Central Leading Group for Cyberspace Affairs, 11 April 2017). http://www.cac.gov.cn/2017-04/11/c_1120785691.htm, accessed 28 October 2020.

[78] Network Security Law of the PRC, Art. 37.

[79] Draft of the Measures on Security Assessment, Art. 17.

[80] Ibid, Art. 2.

[81] Ibid, Art. 16.

[82] Ibid, Art. 4.

[83] Ibid, Art. 11(1).

[84] 2017 Guidelines for Cross-Border Transfer Security Assessment (Second Draft), Art. 3.2.

and web access are excluded from this regulation).[85] In addition, even if all personal information and/or important data collected by subsidiaries are stored within the PRC, the data transfer to an offshore parent company could still be a cross-border transfer.[86] The same rules apply to the transfer of data collected or generated in the course of operations within the PRC to affiliated group companies outside the PRC. The broad definition of cross-border transfer will generate an important legal issue for most foreign-invested companies located in the PRC that provide Internet services via offshore entities or collect personal information via servers established outside the PRC.

The 2017 Guidelines for Cross-border Transfer Security Assessment (Second Draft) which are consistent with the Draft of the Measures on Security Assessment, also extend cross-border transfer requirements to "network operators"—a much broader term than the "operators of critical information infrastructure" in the Network Security Law.[87] The 2017 Guidelines for Cross-Border Transfer Security Assessment (Second Draft) require network operators to conduct an annual security self-assessment and to initiate the self-assessment in certain circumstances.[88] It is worth noting that those who request cross-border data transfers in cloud services are responsible for the self-assessment.[89] For example, the customers of a cloud service are responsible for the self-assessment if they transfer data across borders. If the transfer is initiated by the cloud providers instead of customers, the cloud providers are responsible for the self-assessment. The 2017 Guidelines for Cross-Border Transfer Security Assessment (Second Draft) instruct both network operators and regulators to evaluate (i) whether the transfers are lawful, legitimate, and necessary and (ii) the risks associated with the transfers.[90]

Under the Draft of the Measures on Security Assessment, personal data refers to any information recorded by electronic or other means that can identify an individual, either independently or combined with other information, including but not limited to an individual's name, date of birth, ID number, personal biometric data, address and telephone number.[91] This definition remains in step with the definition provided in the Network Security Law. Although this definition seems relatively all-encompassing, it does not include information that can identify the user of the service, independently or in combination with other information (such as the time of use and location of the user), which has been embraced by the the Several Provisions on Regulating the Market Order of Internet Information Services (2012 MIIT Provisions).[92] The Draft

---

[85] Ibid, Art. 3.7 note 1(b).
[86] Ibid, Art. 3.7 note 1(c).
[87] Ibid, Art. 3.2.
[88] Ibid, Art. 3.9.
[89] Ibid, Art. 4.2.2.
[90] Ibid, Art. 4.1.
[91] Draft of the Measures on Security Assessment, Art. 17.
[92] The Several Provisions on Regulating the Market Order of Internet Information Services (Chinese title: 規範互聯網信息服務市場秩序若干規定) (hereinafter: 2012 MIIT Provisions) was adopted at the 22nd executive meeting of the MIIT of the PRC on 7 December 2011 and come into force

of the Measures on Security Assessment states that the scope of important data will be specified in the relevant standards and guidance[93] but does not enumerate the names and details of the relevant standards and guidance. The 2017 Guidelines for Cross-Border Transfer Security Assessment (Second Draft) fill the gap by providing a specific scope[94] and adding an exception clause for important data. If data are legally disclosed through the government information disclosure channel, they shall no longer be considered important data.[95]

The network operator who conducts the security assessment is responsible for the results of the assessment.[96] However, the legal term "security assessment" is unclear, and the authorities therefore potentially have the discretionary power to restrict any transfer of personal information overseas in the name of national security or the public interest.[97] In addition, the Draft of the Measures on Security Assessment requires that a security assessment organized by the authorities be completed within 60 working days[98] but does not provide further details of the requirements or procedures for how to conduct a security assessment. The 2017 Guidelines for Cross-Border Transfer Security Assessment (Second Draft) fill the gap and provide detailed information regarding the assessment procedures as can be seen in Fig. 2.5.

(According to Article 4.1 of the 2017 Guidelines for Cross-Border Transfer Security Assessment (Second Draft))

A combined reading of the 2017 Guidelines for Cross-Border Transfer Security Assessment (Second Draft) and the Draft of the Measures on Security Assessment and the Network Security Law indicates that even if all personal information collected by subsidiaries is stored within the PRC, a data transfer to an offshore parent company could also be subject to the relevant business supervisory authorities for a security assessment organized by the authorities,[99] especially if the data involve the personal information of more than 5,00,000 users or exceed one Terabyte and the information includes nuclear facilities; chemico-biology; national defence and the military; population health data; or data relevant to large-scale engineering activities, the ocean environment or sensitive geographic information.[100]

---

on 15 March 2012. 'Several Provisions on Regulating the Market Order of Internet Information Services' (CAC Homepage). http://www.cac.gov.cn/2011-12/30/c_1111550424.htm, accessed 17 November 2020, Art. 4.

[93] Draft of the Measures on Security Assessment, Art. 17.

[94] 2017 Guidelines for Cross−Border Transfer Security Assessment (Second Draft), Art. 3.5 note (2).

[95] Ibid, Art. 3.5 note (1).

[96] Draft of the Measures on Security Assessment, Art. 7.

[97] Thomas M. Shoesmith, Julian Zou, and Liang Tao, 'China's New Rules on Cross−Border Data Transfer' (Pillsbury, 19 June 2017). https://www.jdsupra.com/legalnews/china-s-new-rules-on-cross-border-data-50685/, accessed 12 November 2020.

[98] Draft of the Measures on Security Assessment, Art. 10.

[99] Draft of the Measures on Security Assessment, Art. 17; 2017 Guidelines for Cross−Border Transfer Security Assessment (Second Draft), Art. 3.7 note 1(c).

[100] Draft of the Measures on Security Assessment, Art. 9.

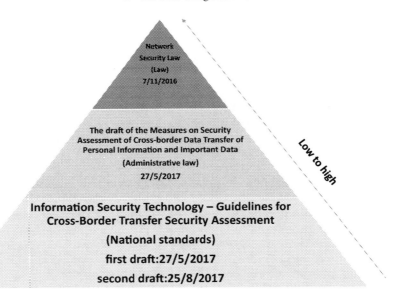

Fig. 2.5

Although the Draft of the Measures on Security Assessment and the 2017 Guidelines for Cross-Border Transfer Security Assessment (Second Draft) are both not legally binding, compared to the Network Security Law, the 2017 Guidelines for Cross-Border Transfer Security Assessment (Second Draft) and the Draft of the Measures on Security Assessment adopt much stricter standards for cross-border data transfers. These standards will affect not only foreign Internet entities but also other foreign entities, such as educational institutions, healthcare organizations, wearable equipment manufacturers, and insurance companies, that usually collect personal information and transfer that information to offshore parent companies for assessment and market promotion.[101]

In addition, on 13 June 2019, the CAC released Notice of Requesting Public Comments on the Measures for the Security Assessment for Cross-border Transfer of Personal Information (Exposure Draft).[102] Regulations and guidelines provided in the Measures for the Security Assessment for Cross-border Transfer of Personal Information (Exposure Draft) are for the purpose of guaranteeing the security of personal information in the process of cross-border data flow, and pertain to network

---

[101] Shoesmith and others (n 97).

[102] See 'Notice by the Cyberspace Administration of China of Requesting Public Comments on the Measures for the Security Assessment for Cross—border Transfer of Personal Information (Exposure Draft)' (Chinese title: 國家互聯網信息辦公室關於《個人信息出境安全評估辦法 (徵求意見稿)》公開徵求意見的通知) (CAC, 13 June). http://www.cac.gov.cn/2019-06/13/c_1124613618.htm, accessed 12 November 2020.

2.4 The PRC's Legislation on Cross-Border Data Transfers

operators that transfer the personal information across borders.[103] The 2017 Guidelines for Cross-Border Transfer Security Assessment apply to both "important data" and "personal information". However, the Measures for the Security Assessment for Cross-border Transfer of Personal Information (Exposure Draft) solely focus on the cross-border transfer of "personal information." The removal of the term "important data" implies that "important data" and "personal information" are treated as separate categories and subject to different requirements in the PRC.[104] The Measures for the Security Assessment for Cross-border Transfer of Personal Information (Exposure Draft) introduce a range of activities that organizations should undertake prior to any cross-border transfer of personal information, including but not limited to: conduct a security impact assessment which has been approved by the CAC[105]; enter into data transfer agreements with all offshore data recipients and ensure sufficient contractual safeguards,[106] to mention but a few. The Measures for the Security Assessment for Cross-border Transfer of Personal Information (Exposure Draft) do not mention any data localization requirements. However, it does not mean that network operators are exempt from data localization.[107]

Moreover, the E-Commerce Law expands the application of the Network Security Law by taking the Network Security Law, as well as other regulations related to violations of data protection obligations, as references.[108] The first draft of the E-Commerce Law comprises concrete rules for collecting and using consumer information. However, the formal law deletes these provisions and requires e-commerce operators to comply with the Network Security Law.

The combined reading of the Network Security Law and the E-Commerce Law shows that foreign companies that engage in e-commerce business in the PRC, such as Apple, Amazon.com and other e-commerce companies, will have to abide by the Network Security Law's requirements to store personal data on servers within the PRC.

The Network Security Law applies to any companies selling goods or providing services to Chinese consumers in covered domestic operations.[109] Companies beyond

---

[103] Ibid.

[104] 'China Issues Draft Regulation on Cross−Border Transfer of Personal Information' (Hunton Andrews Kurth LLP, 19 June 2019). https://www.huntonprivacyblog.com/2019/06/19/china-issues-draft-regulation-on-cross-border-transfer-of-personal-information/, accessed 12 March 2021.

[105] Measures for the Security Assessment for Cross−border Transfer of Personal Information (Exposure Draft), Art. 3. http://www.cac.gov.cn/2019-06/13/c_1124613618.htm, accessed 12 November 2020.

[106] Ibid, Art. 4 and 13.

[107] Daniel Albrecht, 'Measures on Security Assessment of Cross−Border Transfer of Personal Information (2019 Draft)' (Your IP Insider, 27 February 2020). http://www.youripinsider.eu/measures-security-assessment-cross-border-transfer-personal-information-2019-draft/, accessed 12 March 2021.

[108] E−Commerce Law of the PRC, Art. 79. See 'E−Commerce Law of the PRC' (Chinese title: 中華人民共和國電子商務法) (NPC Homepage, 31 August 2018). http://www.npc.gov.cn/zgrdw/npc/lfzt/rlyw/2018-08/31/content_2060827.htm, accessed 9 September 2020.

[109] Network Security Law of the PRC, Art. 2.

the PRC may be liable for the security screening of any data collected from users in the PRC. If foreign companies engaging in e-commerce business in the PRC will export data to their headquarters or affiliated companies outside the PRC, they will have to be assessed for security concern. The assessment will be a self-assessment unless it reaches a certain threshold, in which case it will be sent to the regulators for assessment. The requirement that personal data be stored within the PRC presents challenges for foreign e-commerce companies that set up local transaction processing and cloud storage centers and use cloud services to store data. It will be costly and ineffectual for them to improve their business efficiency and data security.

The E-Commerce Law also refers to the obligations of the state by requiring it to maintain the security of e-commerce transactions, to protect the information of e-commerce users, to encourage the development and application of e-commerce data, to protect the orderly and free flow of e-commerce data by law, to take measures to promote the establishment of a public data sharing mechanism, and to encourage e-commerce businesses to use public data by law.[110] However, these clauses are soft and unconsolidated and are more similar to slogans than to binding rules.

2.5 Interim Remarks

The regulatory landscape for cross-border data transfers in the PRC has changed completely since the enforcement of the Network Security Law. The PRC has become another important jurisdiction that restricts data transfers across borders. If the final version of the Draft of the Measures on Security Assessment is enacted in its current form, it will become very difficult for foreign companies that are based in the PRC to be exempted from the security assessment regime and will impose an additional burden on companies conducting transnational business in the PRC. Moreover, the PRC will establish security assessments on both incoming and outgoing data, thus giving more power to government agencies, especially those relevant to the country's military and security agencies, to request data and confidential information from domestic and foreign companies, particularly those in the IT sector.

Although the 2017 Guidelines for Cross-Border Transfer Security Assessment (Second Draft) are not legally binding, once they are finally adopted, they will play the role of supplements to the Draft of the Measures on Security Assessment and be important parts of a comprehensive legal regime governing PRC cross-border data transfers, which will in turn determine whether the cross-border data transfers conducted by a company can continue, will have to be adjusted or will be prohibited.

---

[110] E-Commerce Law of the PRC, Art. 69.

Chapter 3
The Cross-Border Data Transfers in the Context of WTO Agreements—The PRC Perspective

> War is ninety percent information.[1]
> —Napoleon Bonaparte, French Military and Political Leader

3.1 Cross-Border Data Transfer Legislation in the Context of WTO Agreements

3.1.1 General Remarks

Cross-border data restriction policies can be broad or narrow in scope.[2] The cross-border data restriction policies introduced by the PRC are considered broad.[3] In 2016, the Chinese government's restriction on political information that is circulated online was considered a barrier to trade by the United States Trade Representative in its National Trade Estimate Report.[4] The Report stipulates as follows:

> Over the past decade, Chinese filtering of cross-border Internet traffic has posed a significant burden to foreign suppliers. Outright blocking of websites appears to have worsened over the past year, with 8 of the top 25 most trafficked global sites now blocked in China. Much of the blocking appears arbitrary…[5]

---

[1] "Napoleon: War Is Ninety Percent Information: So, All War Is Cyber War" (CTOvision.com). https://ctovision.com/quotes/war-is-ninety-percent-information-so-all-war-is-cyber-war/, accessed 1 October 2020.

[2] John Selby, 'Data Localization Laws: Trade Barriers or Legitimate Responses to Cybersecurity Risks, or Both?' (13 July 2017) 25 International Journal of Law and Information Technology 213, 215.

[3] Ibid.

[4] USTR, 'The 2016 National Trade Estimate Report' (USTR, 2016). https://ustr.gov/sites/default/files/2016-NTE-Report-FINAL.pdf, accessed 23 February 2021.

[5] Ibid.

In 2017, the Network Security Law of the PRC and various relevant implementing measures were accused of damaging global trade in services by the United States in a document submitted for debate at the WTO Services Council.[6] In the document, the United States claimed that the PRC's measures towards data protection:

> would impose special scrutiny, particular procedures, or bans on the cross-border transfer of expansive and loosely-defined categories of data. The result would be to discourage cross-border data transfers and to promote domestic processing and storage. The impact of the measures would fall disproportionately on foreign service suppliers operating in China, as these suppliers must routinely transfer data back to headquarters and other affiliates. Companies located outside of China supplying services on a cross-border basis would be severely affected, as they must depend on access to data from their customers in China.[7]

On 22 January 2017, the Ministry of Industry and Information Technology (MIIT) of the PRC published a Notice on Cleaning Up and Regulating the Internet Access Service Market,[8] which seems to impose new restrictions on virtual private networks (VPNs) and leased lines.[9] The United States argued that PRC's proposed restrictions would impose significant new constraints on market access opportunities for cross-border service suppliers,[10] violating the terms of the WTO GATS, particularly with regard to the treatment of cross-border data processing services.[11] This is the first time the PRC has sought to pass a trade resolution to address serious human rights issues facing Internet users of the PRC.[12] There is no doubt that this kind of regulation preventing the cross-border transfer of data from foreign countries in and out of the PRC has some leverage over international trade. PRC's rules and measures restricting cross-border data transfers have the potential to make the PRC a target of WTO disputes.[13]

---

[6] 'Communication from the United States—Measures Adopted and under Development by China Relating to Its Cybersecurity Law' Art. 4 (WTO Council for Trade in Services, 2017). https://docs.wto.org/dol2fe/Pages/SS/directdoc.aspx?filename=q:/S/C/W374.pdf&Open=True, accessed 20 March 2021, see also Tom Miles, 'U.S. Asks China not to Enforce Cyber Security Law' (Reuters, 26 September 2017). https://www.reuters.com/article/us-usa-china-cyber-trade/u-s-asks-china-not-to-enforce-cyber-security-law-idUSKCN1C11D1, accessed 12 December 2020.

[7] 'Communication from the United States—Measures Adopted and under Development by China Relating to Its Cybersecurity Law' (n 6).

[8] 'Notice of Ministry of Industry and Information Technology on Clearing and Regulating Internet Network Access Service Market' (Chinese title: 工業和信息化部關於清理規範互聯網網络接入服務市場的通知) (State Council Information Office of China, 22 January 2017). http://www.scio.gov.cn/xwfbh/xwbfbh/wqfbh/35861/36970/xgzc36976/Document/1559330/1559330.htm, accessed 6 March 2020.

[9] 'Communication from the United States—Measures Adopted and under Development by China Relating to Its Cybersecurity Law' (n 6) Art. 4 and 5.

[10] Ibid., Art. 5 and 6.

[11] Ibid., Art. 5; See also Miles (n 6).

[12] Panday Jyoti, 'The Post–TPP Future of Digital Trade in Asia' (Electronic Frontier Foundation, 2 March 2018). https://www.eff.org/deeplinks/2018/02/rcep-negotiations-face-obstacles-member-nations-unwilling-commit, accessed 6 March 2021.

[13] Cory Nigel, 'Cross-Border Data Flows: Where Are the Barriers, and What Do They Cost?' 16 (Information Technology and Innovation Foundation, May 2017). http://www2.itif.org/2017-cross-border-data-flows.pdf, accessed 16 March 2021.

3.1 Cross-Border Data Transfer Legislation in the Context of WTO Agreements

The purposes of the PRC's restriction on cross-border data transfers are diverse: first, the restriction aims to ensure that all online information that is circulated within the PRC, no matter where it comes from, is consistent with public morals,[14] particularly with reference to sustaining core socialist values (Chinese title: 社會主義核心價值觀).[15] Second, commercial purposes are claimed to be another motivation for the restriction. Removing foreign competitors from the PRC grants local enterprises the opportunity to gain market share because people have no choice but to use what is left.[16] For instance, the Chinese search engine Baidu benefits greatly from the blocking of Google in the PRC. In 2002, Google held 24% of the Chinese market, while Baidu only held 3%. However, at the end of 2008, Google's share was reduced to just 19% of the Chinese search market, while Baidu accounted for 65%.[17]

The transfer of data across national borders drives today's global economy.[18] The Internet grants companies the ability to access billions of potential customers beyond their borders. Even small enterprises and companies are capable of competing based on the quality of their offerings, free from geographic limitations.[19] The proper function of international trade currently needs reliable and continuous access to data, wherever they are located.[20] International trade activities especially international service trade activities require cross-border data transfers from service providers to customers and others located around the world.

Countries' attitudes towards cross-border data transfers can be divided into two main types: those in favour of restrictions on cross-border data flows, particularly data localization legislation, and those opposed to it. The supporters of data localization policies, such as the PRC and Russia, argue that the goals of the restrictions on

---

[14] Cindy Chiu, Chris Ip, and Ari Silverman, 'Understanding social media in China' (McKinsey Insights, 1 April 2012). https://www.mckinsey.com/business-functions/marketing-and-sales/our-insights/understanding-social-media-in-china, accessed 12 December 2020.

[15] The Core Socialist Values, including freedom, equality, patriotism, dedication, prosperity, democracy, civility, harmony, justice, rule of law, integrity and friendship are promoted at the 18th National Congress of the Communist Party of China in 2012. Kiki Zhao, 'China's "Core Socialist Values", the Song—and—Dance Version' (New York Times, 1 September 2017). https://www.nytimes.com/2016/09/02/world/asia/china-dance-socialist-values.html, accessed 22 October 2021.

[16] Michael A. Santoro and Wendy Goldberg, 'Fair Trade Suffers When China Censors the Internet. It's Not Just a Human Rights Issue' (Huffpost, 2011). https://www.huffpost.com/entry/chinese-internet-censorsh_b_156212, accessed 17 December 2020.

[17] Ibid.

[18] 'Business Without Borders: The Importance of Cross—Border Data Transfers to Global Prosperity' (United States Chamber of Commerce and Hunton and Williams LLP), 1. https://www.huntonprivacyblog.com/wp-content/uploads/sites/28/2014/05/021384_BusinessWOBorders_final.pdf, accessed 1 March 2021.

[19] Ibid.

[20] David Dreier and Joshua Paul Meltzer, 'Growing the Global Internet Economy by Ensuring the Free Flow of Data across Borders' (Brookings, 23 May 2013). https://www.brookings.edu/blog/up-front/2013/05/23/growing-the-global-internet-economy-by-ensuring-the-free-flow-of-data-across-borders/, accessed 19 May 2020.

cross-border data transfers that they pursue are legal and reasonable.[21] Opponents, such as the United States, label such policies trade barriers.[22] Cross-border data flow restrictions can be temporary or permanent, partial or complete. On the one hand, a national government's right to regulate the service industry is broadly considered "necessary to protect consumers from harmful or unqualified providers".[23] On the other hand, a country's attempt to impose restrictions on cross-border data flows should be prudent and should not violate its treaty obligations. There are some arguments about whether the PRC legislation regarding cross-border data transfers could be challenged in the international arena as a violation of the PRC's treaty obligations, particularly under those arising from its membership in the WTO.[24]

3.1.2 The PRC and the WTO

The WTO is the most important global and multilateral organization dealing with the rules of trade between nations.[25] It aims to "ensure that trade flows as smoothly, predictably and freely as possible".[26] The GATT,[27] the GATS,[28] and the Agreement on Trade-Related Aspects of Intellectual Property Rights (TRIPS)[29] form the three crucial pillars of WTO law (plus Dispute Settlement Body (DSB)). The GATT acts as the WTO's "principal rule book for trade in goods".[30] The TRIPS is powerful in combination with DSB on IP rights. The TRIPS sets minimum standards for

---

[21] William Alan Reinsch, 'A Data Localization Free−for−All?' (Center for Strategy and International Studies, 9 Match 2018). https://www.csis.org/blogs/future-digital-trade-policy-and-role-us-and-uk/data-localization-free-all, accessed 22 March 2021.

[22] In 2017, in the National Trade Estimate (an annual report on significant barriers to American exports), data localization is considered category of digital trade barrier. See 'Key Barrier to Digital Trade' (Office of U.S. Trade Representative Homepage, March 2017). https://ustr.gov/about-us/policy-offices/press-office/fact-sheets/2017/march/key-barriers-digital-trade, accessed 27 December 2020.

[23] Rachel F. Fefer, 'U.S. Trade in Services: Trends and Policy Issues Analyst in International Trade and Finance' (Congressional Research Service, 30 June 2017) 10. https://fas.org/sgp/crs/misc/R43 291.pdf, accessed 12 December 2020.

[24] Trevor Schmitt, 'United States Flags China's VPN Ban as Possible WTO Violation' (Georgetown Law Technology Review, March 2018). https://georgetownlawtechreview.org/united-states-flags-chinas-vpn-ban-as-possible-wto-violation/GLTR-03-2018/, accessed 29 March 2021.

[25] 'The WTO in Brief' (WTO website). https://www.wto.org/english/thewto_e/whatis_e/inbrief_e/inbr00_e.htm, accessed 6 January 2021.

[26] Ibid.

[27] Multilateral Agreements on Trade in Goods, 15 April 1994, Marrakesh Agreement Establishing the WTO, Annex 1A, 1867 U.N.T.S. 187.

[28] GATS, 15 April 1994, Marrakesh Agreement Establishing the WTO, Annex 1B, 1869 U.N.T.S. 183.

[29] TRIPS, 15 April 1994, Marrakesh Agreement Establishing the WTO, Annex 1C, 1869 U.N.T.S. 299.

[30] 'The WTO in Brief' (n 25).

3.1 Cross-Border Data Transfer Legislation in the Context of WTO Agreements

IP protection provided by each WTO member.[31] Principles of trade in service are managed by the GATS. WTO members have also made individual commitments under the GATS regarding which service sectors they are willing to open to foreign competition and the extent to which these markets are open.[32]

A dispute settlement mechanism is critical to the operation of the WTO,[33] WTO members must accept dispute settlements because they are part of a package that includes the WTO agreements and the first three annexes.[34] The WTO requires that all members respect the rules in the interests of a safer and more reliable multilateral trading system. Therefore, WTO members have agreed that when they judge that other members have failed to meet their treaty obligations or have broken international trade rules, they will refer the dispute to the WTO dispute settlement mechanism rather than adopting unilateral measures. The WTO law to some extent can be considered "hard" law in the sense that it is binding on its members like all public international law. WTO law includes "deep intervention in domestic regulatory regimes and can impose certain sanctions for breach of obligations".[35]

The PRC has not entered any bilateral treaties or multilateral treaties that explicitly prohibit it from restricting cross-border data transfers. Agreements under the WTO are the most important agreements related to this issue. The PRC officially became a member of the WTO on 11 December 2001.[36] The PRC's remarkable economic growth has made it an attractive trading partner.[37] Information must continue to flow in and out of the PRC so that international enterprises can ensure that their staff in the PRC are able to access data that are necessary to carry out their job functions.[38] On the one hand, on a global scale, and particularly with China as one of the leading economies,[39] laws regulating data protection and transfer are indispensable because without such laws, many multinational companies trading with the PRC are exposed to various risks stemming from lack of transparency and

---

[31] 'Overview: The TRIPS Agreement' (WTO website). https://www.wto.org/english/tratop_e/trips_e/intel2_e.htm, accessed 6 January 2021.

[32] 'The General Agreement on Trade in Services (GATS): Objectives, Coverage and Disciplines' (WTO website). https://www.wto.org/english/tratop_e/serv_e/gatsqa_e.htm, accessed 6 April 2021.

[33] William J. Davey, 'Implementation in WTO Dispute Settlement: An Introduction to the Problems and Possible Solutions' (March 2005) RIETI Discussion Paper Series 05-E-013, 1. https://www.rieti.go.jp/jp/publications/dp/05e013.pdf, accessed 22 March 2021.

[34] Xavier Philippe, 'The Dispute Resolution Mechanism of the WTO Five Years after Its Implementation', Law. Democracy and Development 69, 75. www.saflii.org/za/journals/LDD/1999/5.pdf, accessed 22 March 2021.

[35] Gregory C. Shaffer and Mark A. Pollack, 'Hard vs. Soft Law: Alternatives, Complements, and Antagonists in International Governance' (2010) 94 Minnesota Law Review 706, 715 and 760.

[36] 'China and the WTO' (WTO). https://www.wto.org/english/thewto_e/countries_e/china_e.htm, accessed 13 December 2020.

[37] Aimee Boram Yang, 'International Issues: China in Global Trade: Proposed Data Protection Law and Encryption Standard Dispute' (2008) 4(3) Journal of law and policy for the information society 893, 897.

[38] Ibid.

[39] Ibid.

data manipulation.[40] On the other hand, there is an inherent conflict between the logic of the PRC's data localization efforts and the policy objectives that the Chinese government is pursuing by joining FTAs as well as the WTO and promoting the "Belt and Road Initiative" (BRI). Cross-border data transfer restrictions imposed by national laws have increasingly raised concern that this kind of restriction might violate countries' WTO obligations and impede international trade.

3.1.3 The Tradability of Data

Data—in the quantities in which they are available today—are increasingly seen as an entirely new commodity. It is productive to consider whether data are tradable and, if so, whether trading them generates value and benefits for humans. Tradable refers to "something that can be bought and sold".[41] Whether data are tradable depends on whether they can be bought and sold.

The initial question "Are data a tradable commodity?" could be split into two molecular questions: "Are data a commodity?" and "Are data tradable?" The Cambridge Dictionary defines commodity as: "1. a substance or product that can be traded, bought or sold. 2. A valuable quality".[42] The Merriam-Webster dictionary describes commodity as follows:

> an economic good; something useful or valued; a good or service whose wide availability typically leads to smaller profit margins and diminishes the importance of factors (such as brand name) other than price; one that is subject to ready exchange or exploitation within a market.[43]

The Longman Dictionary of Contemporary English describes commodity as: "1. a product that is bought and sold; 2. (formal) a useful quality or thing".[44] The Oxford Living Dictionaries of English defines commodity as "1. A raw material or primary agricultural product that can be bought or sold, such as copper or coffee; 2. A useful or valuable thing such as water or time".[45] From the above definitions, it is obvious that a commodity is distinguished from other products of labour by being useful and having value.

---

[40] Ibid.

[41] 'Meaning of "Tradable" in the English Dictionary' (Cambridge University Press). https://dictionary.cambridge.org/dictionary/english/tradeable, accessed 24 March 2021.

[42] 'Meaning of "Commodity" in the English Dictionary' (Cambridge University Press). https://dictionary.cambridge.org/dictionary/english/commodity?q=Commodity, accessed 24 March 2021.

[43] 'Definition of Commodity' (Merriam–Webster). https://www.merriam-webster.com/dictionary/commodity, accessed 24 March 2021.

[44] 'Commodity' (Longman Dictionary of Contemporary English). https://www.ldoceonline.com/dictionary/commodity, accessed 24 March 2021.

[45] 'Definition of Commodity in English' (Oxford Living Dictionaries of English). https://en.oxforddictionaries.com/definition/commodity, accessed 24 March 2021.

3.1 Cross-Border Data Transfer Legislation in the Context of WTO Agreements

The statement that data have value is nothing new. The financial value of personal data is high and growing. Companies are moving quickly to profit from this trend.[46] In 2011, the World Economic Forum classified personal data as a new asset class along with property, investments, cash, etc., touching all aspects of society.[47] The expression that "data are the new oil—a valuable resource of the twenty-first century"[48] sums up what market participants have long known.[49] Companies view data as a corporate asset and have invested heavily in software that facilitates the collection of data.[50] Then, the answer to the first question, "Are data a commodity?", must be yes. In the age of the Internet and digitization, there is no doubt that data are a valuable commodity.

The tradability of commodities refers to basic goods used in trade that are usually interchangeable with other goods of the same type.[51] We have arrived at a stage where personal data as a commodity can be traded publicly. In 2015, the PRC launched the Global Big Data Exchange (GBDE)—the first big data exchange platform in the world—in Guiyang, the capital of Gui Zhou Province. Over 1,500 enterprises and companies have registered as members to exchange and trade data-related assets and services.[52] The GBDE owns and operates the trading platform for big data. It offers

---

[46] Nicolaus Henke and others, 'The Age of Analytics: Competing in a Data−driven World' (McKinsey & Company December 2016). https://www.mckinsey.com/business-functions/mckinsey-analytics/our-insights/the-age-of-analytics-competing-in-a-data-driven-world, accessed 12 October 2020; Andrew McAfee and Erik Brynjolfsson, 'Big Data: The Management Revolution' (Harvard Business Review, October 2012). https://hbr.org/2012/10/big-data-the-management-revolution, accessed 12 October 2020; Jennifer Sullivan and Christopher Jones, 'How Much Is Your Playlist Worth?' (Wired News, 3 November 1999). https://www.wired.com/1999/11/how-much-is-your-playlist-worth/, accessed 12 October 2020.

[47] World Economic Forum, 'Personal Data: The Emergence of a New Asset Class—An Initiative of the World Economic Forum January 2011'. http://www3.weforum.org/docs/WEF_ITTC_PersonalDataNewAsset_Report_2011.pdf, accessed 24 August 2020.

[48] Sumeet Santani, 'Why Data Is the New Oil' (InfoSpace, 26 February 2018). https://ischool.syr.edu/infospace/2018/02/26/why-data-is-the-new-oil/, accessed 24 August 2020.

[49] Anette Gärtner, 'Building a European Data Economy—Summary Report on the Right to Data Consultation' (Reed Smith, 8 August 2017). https://www.reedsmith.com/en/perspectives/2017/08/building-a-european-data-economy-summary-report, accessed 23 August 2020.

[50] For a general discussion of the importance to corporations of customer information in the information economy, see Gartner Inc., 'Turn Your Big Data into a Valued Corporate Asset' (Forbes, 13 November 2017). https://www.forbes.com/sites/gartnergroup/2017/11/13/turn-your-big-data-into-a-valued-corporate-asset/?sh=d3ba0296ae30, accessed 15 November 2020; Andrew Sohn and Avi Kalderon, 'Managing Data as a Corporate Asset: Data Virtualization' (Dataversity, 29 May 2017). http://www.dataversity.net/managing-data-corporate-asset-data-virtualization/, accessed 12 October 2020; Diletta D' Onofrio, 'The Future Is Now: Data as an Asset in the Corporate World' (SnapLogic, 3 November 2017). https://www.snaplogic.com/blog/the-future-is-now-when-data-becomes-a-tangible-corporate-asset, accessed 15 November 2020.

[51] 'What are Tradable Commodities?' (Investopedia). https://www.investopedia.com/ask/answers/022315/what-are-tradable-commodities.asp, accessed 24 August 2021.

[52] 'China's Big Data Exchange Gains Data Access to Chicago Mercantile Exchange' (Xinhua, 12 December 2017). www.chinadaily.com.cn/a/201712/12/WS5a2f6beca3108bc8c6724003.html, accessed 23 August 2020; 'Big Data Exchange Welcomes American Partner' (China Daily,

electronic trading of big data from various sources, including social media platforms, that companies analyse for market insights and decision making.[53]

From the legal perspective, digital content—data that are produced and supplied in digital form—is now treated by several jurisdictions in the same manner as valuable commercial goods. Examples of digital content include software, games, apps, e-books, online journals and digital media such as music, film, and television. Digital content can be supplied in tangible forms, such as on a disk, or in intangible forms, such as files that are downloaded, streamed, or accessed on the web.

Therefore, the answer to the second question, "Are data tradable?", must be yes. Then, a conclusion can be drawn that data are a commodity that can be traded and can be bought and sold to make a profit.

3.1.4 Data as a Service

Offering access to data as a service (for example, access to real-time data) serves as another form of trading data. Produced and analyzed data can also be commercialized indirectly by selling data-based services (do not require the disclosure of these data) rather than selling or granting access to the data.[54]

Data are considered a service when data-based services are offered instead of data. Location-based services—Google Maps, for instance—are services that, with the help of data that companies collect and analyse, provide the end user with real-time location-relevant content or other services on a smartphone. Companies do not need to trade these data; they analyse them and then provide services based on the data that they own.[55] Location-based services can be used in various industries, such as transportation and tourism.

Another possibility for using data as a service is to collect data and offer access to the data being collected.[56] Millions of free datasets are available that are ready to be used and analysed by anyone willing to look for them, which means not selling data but offering raw data as a service. A growing number of organizations in the private and public sectors recognize the opportunities and commercial potential provided by

---

15 December 2017). http://www.chinadaily.com.cn/m/guizhou/guiyang/2017-12/15/content_3530 8468.htm, accessed 23 August 2020.

[53] 'China's Big Data Exchange Gains Data Access to Chicago Mercantile Exchange' (n 52); 'Big Data Exchange Welcomes American Partner' (n 52).

[54] Wolfgang Kerber, 'A New (Intellectual) Property Right for Non−personal Data? An Economic Analysis' (2016) Gewerblicher Rechtsschutz und Urheberrecht Internationaler Teil 989, 994.

[55] Herbert Zech, 'Data as a Tradeable Commodity—Implications for Contract Law' in Josef Drexl and others, *Proceedings of the 18th EIPIN Congress: The New Data Economy between Data Ownership, Privacy and Safeguarding Competition* (Edward Elgar Publishing September 2017) 4.

[56] Ibid., 5.

the data they possess. Therefore, they try to turn these data into data assets and insight-driven services and commercialize and monetize them.[57] For example, Google Public Data Explorer provides data from world development indicators and the OECD and human development indicators, mostly related to economic data from around the world.[58] A growing number of organizations have realized that it is not enough to think in terms of raw data as a service, letting partners or customers determine how to handle those data. They are creating more advanced and precise data-driven products and services. In the process, they transition from providers of traditional discrete manufacturing operations or 'raw data as a service' businesses into insight services providers that provide a basis for better-informed decision making, such as making support and action plans.

From the legal point of view, personal data and digital content or digital services were mentioned in the Proposal for a Directive of the European Parliament and of the Council on Certain Aspects Concerning Contracts for the Supply of Digital Content (DCD),[59] the Annex of which stipulates as follows:

> Acknowledging the increased value of personal data in modern business models, it was widely felt from the outset of the negotiations that the consumer should be entitled to the contractual remedies for lack of conformity or lack of supply not only under contracts where the consumer pays a price for the digital content or digital service but also under contracts where the consumer provides personal data to the supplier.[60]

Personal data, digital content or digital services have fundamentally been placed on the same footing as any other goods that can be bought and sold. The result is that in cross-border EU commercial transactions, digital data are treated as tradable goods and are legally protectable under contract law in the same manner as other goods. Offering data-based services and accessing data collections as a service require a higher level of professionalism than selling data as a commodity.[61]

In reality, data can be seen either as a valuable commodity which is tradeable,[62] or as part of a service, such as financial, healthcare, and telecommunications services, or as a means to deliver electronic goods, such as digital media and software applications.[63] Therefore, the GATS, for digital service, and the GATT, for electronic goods,

---

[57] Mike Davie, 'In brief: What Is Data Monetization?' (Datafloq, 14 July 2018). https://datafloq.com/read/in-brief-what-is-data-monetization/3356, accessed 1 September 2020; Marko Saarinen, 'Data Commercialization Moves to Insights Commercialization' (Fourkind, 13 June 2018). https://medium.com/value-stream-design/data-commercialization-moves-to-insights-commercialization-part-1-542fd625b00b, accessed 1 September 2020.

[58] Bernard Marr, 'Big Data: 33 Brilliant and Free Data Sources Anyone Can Use' (Forbes, 12 February 2016). https://www.forbes.com/sites/bernardmarr/2016/02/12/big-data-35-brilliant-and-free-data-sources-for-2016/?sh=2991a6adb54d, accessed 28 September 2020.

[59] 'Proposal for a Directive of the European Parliament and of the Council on Certain Aspects Concerning Contracts for the Supply of Digital Content', COM/2015/0634 final-2015/0287. https://eur-lex.europa.eu/legal-content/EN/TXT/?uri=celex%3A52015PC0634, accessed 20 August 2020.

[60] Ibid., annex.

[61] Zech (n 55) 5.

[62] For detail, please refer to Sect. 3.1.3 The Tradability of Data.

[63] Ibid.

may both apply to the cross-border transfer of data.[64] In addition, several e-commerce companies rely on data to deliver goods such as electronic devices or books across borders.[65] These goods and products will often be protected by intellectual property rights.[66] The TRIPS is technology-neutral, which means its application extends to online digital content; thus, TRIPS also applies to the cross-border transfer of data.[67]

3.1.5 Cross-Border Data Transfers: Service or Good?

Globalization in the twentieth century was defined mostly by the rapidly growing trade in goods as major multinationals created a supply chain worldwide.[68] Since then, cross-border data transfers have typically been connected with the movement of a data medium (e.g., a CD or a hard drive) or a physical product (e.g., maintenance data from exported products).[69] However, currently, globalization and international trade are going digital and becoming more concerned with data and less concerned with material goods.[70] Due to recent rapid technical development, most cross-border data transfers are completely independent from the movement of physical commodities.[71] The Internet has transformed the "very nature of many goods".[72] For instance, the music industry has witnessed the transitions from physical to digital media[73]; the album, as a format, is not as important as it used to be.[74] Modern listeners prefer to

---

[64] Andrew D. Mitchell and Jarrod Hepburn, 'Don't Fence Me In: Reforming Trade and Investment Law to Better Facilitate Cross-Border Data Transfer' (2017) 19(1) Yale Journal of Law and Technology 182, 186.

[65] Ibid., 196.

[66] Carlos A. Primo Braga, 'E—commerce Regulation in a Handbook of International Trade' in Aaditya Mattoo, Robert M. Stern, and Gianni Zanini, *Services* (1st edn, Oxford University Press 2008) 472.

[67] Mitchell and Hepburn (n 64) 186.

[68] Susan Lund, James Manyika, and Jacques Bughin, 'Globalization Is Becoming More about Data and Less about Stuff' (Harvard Business Review, 14 March 2016). https://hbr.org/2016/03/globalization-is-becoming-more-about-data-and-less-about-stuff, accessed 22 December 2020.

[69] Mannheimer Swartling, 'Data flows—Allowing Free Trade Agreements to Strengthen the GDPR,' 5 (19 October 2016). https://www.mannheimerswartling.se/globalassets/publikationer/data-flows.pdf, accessed 18 March 2021.

[70] Lund and others (n 68).

[71] Swartling (n 69) 5.

[72] Brian Hindley and Hosuk Lee-Makiyama, 'Protectionism Online: Internet Censorship and International Trade Law' (2009) ECIPE Working Paper No. 12/2009, 3. https://ecipe.org/wp-content/uploads/2014/12/protectionism-online-internet-censorship-and-international-trade-law.pdf, accessed 24 March 2021.

[73] 'IFPI Digital Music Report (2015)', 7. https://www.riaa.com/reports/digital-music-report-2015/, accessed 18 December 2020.

[74] Derrick Rossignol, 'Making One Album a Year is No Longer Enough (unless You're Adele)' (Drake, 30 November 2015). https://www.theguardian.com/music/2015/nov/30/one-album-a-year-not-enough-unless-youre-adele-drake-hotline-bling, accessed 27 December 2020.

3.1 Cross-Border Data Transfer Legislation in the Context of WTO Agreements

download services from digital retailers rather than purchase audio-visual products in a physical store.[75] In some manufacturing industries, 3-D printing has transformed the shipment of physical goods to the online transfer of a digital file that can be used to produce the good at its point of consumption.[76]

The advent of digital technology also gives rise to the so-called "convergence" phenomenon.[77] Convergence combines features selected from a variety of products, possibly from different departments or categories, into a unique, modular product.[78] Beyond the most typical convergence product, the smartphone, there has been a proliferation of other convergence devices—"from mobile devices such as tablets, watches, and automobiles, to stationary devices such as TVs, refrigerators, and home energy thermostats".[79] This trend of convergence of industries and technologies caused notably by digitization has been summarized by Fabio Ancarani and Michele Costabile as follows:

> During the last few years, competition has radically changed due to the increase of unconventional players (mainly inter-or cross-industry) that have redrawn the landscape of many industries. Boundaries are increasingly fading among hi-tech industries (for example, the ICT) as well as among hi-touch and hi-tech industries: nutriceutics (also called the "functional food" industry), edutainment, cosmeceutics and genetics diagnostics are just a sample of the emerging convergent markets.[80]

The advent of the "convergence" phenomenon affects the world of business and commerce as well as international trade because it is not easy to differentiate services from goods based on existing WTO treaty provisions. Such differentiation may result

---

[75] The most common place for people to purchase albums and songs was from digital retailers, which captured 43.7% of the 2016 U.S. album market. See Ed Christman, 'U.S. Record Industry Sees Album Sales Sink to Historic Lows (Again)—but People Are Listening More Than Ever' (Billboard, 7 June 2016). https://www.billboard.com/articles/business/7430863/2016-soundscan-nielsen-music-mid-year-album-sales-sink-streaming-growth, accessed 27 December 2020.

[76] James Manyika, Jacques Bughin, Susan Lund, Olivia Nottebohm, David Poulter, Sebastian Jauch, Sree Ramaswamy, 'Global Flows in a Digital Age: How Trade, Finance, People, and Data Connect the World Economy,' 10 (McKinsey Global Institute, April 2014). https://www.mckinsey.com/~/media/McKinsey/Featured%20Insights/Globalization/Global%20flows%20in%20a%20digital%20age/Global_flows_in_a_digital_age_Full_report%20March_2015.ashx, accessed at 25 December 2020; Sam Fleuter, 'The Role of Digital Products Under the WTO: A New Framework for GATT and GATS Classification' (2016) 17(1) Chicago Journal of International Law 153, 160.

[77] Shin-Yi Peng, 'Renegotiate the WTO Schedules of Commitments: Technological Development and Treaty Interpretation' (2012) 45(2) Cornell International Law Journal 403, 404.

[78] 'Converge Products, a Pattern Study from the Center for the Edge's Patterns of Disruption Series' (Deloitte University Press, 2016) 4. https://www2.deloitte.com/content/dam/insights/us/articles/disruptive-strategy-convergence-of-products/DUP_1465_Converge-products_vFINAL.pdf, accessed 10 March 2021.

[79] Bryan Pon, Timo Seppälä, Martin Kenney, 'One Ring to Unite Them All: Convergence, the Smartphone, and the Cloud' (13 February 2015) 15 Journal of Industry, Competition and Trade 21, 22. https://link.springer.com/content/pdf/10.1007/s10842-014-0189-x.pdf, accessed 28 March 2021.

[80] Fabio Ancarani and Michele Costabile, 'Coopetition Dynamics in Convergent Industries: Designing Scope Connections to Combine Heterogeneous Resources' in Saïd Yami and others, *Coopetition: Winning Strategies for the 21st Century* (Edward Elgar 2010) 216.

in different legal consequences because of the different depths of liberalization under the GATT and the GATS.[81] A better understanding of the classification of goods and services helps clearly describe sectors in the schedule, while unclear or ambiguous sectoral descriptions may lead to disputes.

In the *Canada Periodicals* case, accurately categorizing "split-run periodicals" as goods or services is difficult because of technological advances,[82] which drove the panel to note that:

> Overlaps between the subject matter of disciplines in GATT 1994 and in GATS are inevitable, and will further increase with the progress of technology and the globalization of economic activities.[83]

Along with advances in science and technology, services can increasingly be purchased online and offered digitally across borders.[84] Cross-border digital trade will likely become more closely associated with cross-border services[85]; however, the convergence trend caused by new technologies means that several ways of classifying industries and products, goods and services, are no longer feasible.[86] The WTO rules lag behind this trend. Strictly restricting data transfers across borders has the direct commercial effect of reducing the revenue of international online services, which raises the central question, addressed in this section, of whether the existing WTO agreements have any implications for cross-border data transfers.

3.1.6 Cross-Border Data Transfers and the GATS

3.1.6.1 The Four Modes of the GATS

The aspect of cross-border data transfer that is relevant to international trade law arises from the fact that the vast majority of international Internet services are provided as commercial services, which cannot exist without the cross-border transfer

---

[81] Mira Burri−Nenova, Christoph Beat Graber and Thomas Steiner, 'The Protection and Promotion of Cultural Diversity in a Digital Networked Environment: Mapping Possible Advances towards Coherence' in Thomas Cottier and Panagiotis Delimatsis, *The Prospects of International Trade Regulation from Fragmentation to Coherence* (Cambridge University Press April 2011) 366.

[82] WTO Panel Report, 'Canada−Certain Measures Concerning Periodicals', WTO Doc. WT/DS31/R, paras. 3.24 and 3.26 (14 March 1997). https://docs.wto.org/dol2fe/Pages/SS/direct doc.aspx?filename=Q:/WT/DS/31R.pdf&Open=True, accessed 27 December 2020.

[83] Ibid., paras. 5.18.

[84] 'WTO Trade Report 2018: The Future of World Trade: How Digital Technologies Are Transforming Global Commerce', 9 (WTO Secretariat, 3 October 2018). https://www.wto.org/english/res_e/publications_e/world_trade_report18_e_under_embargo.pdf, accessed 1 March 2021.

[85] Swartling (n 69) 5.

[86] Rostam J. Neuwirth and Alexandr Svetlicinii, 'International Trade, Intellectual Property and Competition Rules: Multiple Cases for Global "Regulatory Co−opetition"?' (2015) XIX Trade Development through Harmonization of Commercial Law 393, 396.

3.1 Cross-Border Data Transfer Legislation in the Context of WTO Agreements

of data. In the absence of a WTO agreement on data flows, actions towards cross-border data transfers are most likely to be evaluated under the GATS because GATS usually does not require the transfer of physical commodities.[87]

The first and most important determinant of whether the PRC's policies on cross-border data transfers are compatible with its undertakings under the GATS is whether the PRC has made any commitments under the relevant categories in its GATS services schedule.[88] Two relevant issues exist: the "mode" and the relevant service sectors under which data are transferred.[89]

As the first set of multilateral, legally enforceable rules that cover international trade in services,[90] the GATS itself does not explicitly define what a service is.[91] Some people hold the opinion that a definition might cause a dispute over interpretation, while others argue that it is wise to leave this definition open for the following reasons:

> Given the multitude of definition of services developed in the relevant literature – intangible, not storable, simultaneity of production and consumption, etc. – negotiators may have found it extremely difficult to distill any clear language for the purposes of the Agreement. Also, it may have been reassuring that the absence of a definition of "goods" in the GATT had apparently not caused problems in the past.[92]

Although lack of precise terminology, the GATS holds a very comprehensive view of trade in services, governing all international trade in services through four "modes of supply"[93]: Mode 1 is cross-border supply, which is defined as the production, distribution, marketing, sale and delivery of a service from the territory of one member to the territory of any other member[94]; Mode 2 is consumption abroad, which means service customers (e.g., travellers or patients) move into another country's territory to obtain a service[95]; Mode 3 is commercial presence, which involves service suppliers from one country establishing territorial presences, including through ownership or a subsidiary, in another country's territory to provide a service[96]; and Mode 4 is the presence of natural persons, which consists of persons from one country entering the territory of another country to supply a service (e.g., accountants, doctors, teachers,

---

[87] Because the GATS applies to service sectors. See 'The General Agreement on Trade in Services (GATS): Objectives, Coverage and Disciplines' (n 32).

[88] Mitchell and Hepburn (n 64) 196.

[89] Mitchell and Hepburn (n 64) 196.

[90] 'Trading into the Future, the World Trade Organization' (2nd edn, March 2001). https://www.wto.org/english/res_e/doload_e/tif.pdf, accessed 27 December 2020.

[91] Tim Wu, 'The World Trade Law of Censorship and Internet Filtering' (2006) 7(1) Chicago Journal of International Law 263, 269.

[92] Rudolf Adlung and Aaditya Mattoo, 'The GATS' in Aaditya Mattoo, Robert M. Stern, and Gianni Zanini, *A Handbook of International Trade in Services* (1st end, Oxford University Press) 49.

[93] Art. I (2) of GATS, 33 ILM 1167 (1994), see also 'Basic Purpose and Concepts' (World Trade Organization). https://www.wto.org/english/tratop_e/serv_e/cbt_course_e/c1s3p1_e.htm, accessed 16 December 2020.

[94] GATS, Art. I: 2(a).

[95] Ibid., Art. I: 2(b).

[96] Ibid., Art. I: 2(c).

and construction workers).[97] The distinction between these four modes has potential implications for determining which jurisdiction applies when a dispute arises.[98] For example, in case of a dispute, the legal regime of the service provider is most likely to be applied under Mode 2, whereas under Mode 4, the consumers' legal system may most likely be applied.

Currently, the four modes in the GATS are all related to cross-border data transfers. The dominant mode is Mode 1. Mode 1 unavoidably needs the cross-border movement of customer or business information because the services are delivered from the territory of one member to the territory of another member. In Mode 3, the customer and business data transfer from subsidiaries to offshore parent companies could still be a cross-border transfer of the data. In Mode 2, when service customers buy services in another country through an account based in their own country, information related to this transaction could be a cross-border data transfer. Mode 4 links to cross-border data transfers if employees are being transferred from a parent company in one country to a branch office in another country.

The current convergence of technologies or industries not only includes digitization and the Internet but also includes the production, storage, distribution, and consumption of variable content.[99] When addressing inconsistency claims under Article XVI (market access) and/or Article XVII (national treatment principle) of the GATS, the first step is to determine which mode the service at issue belongs to and whether the defending party has undertaken any specific commitments in the relevant service sector. However, activities under the four modes of the GATS could be linked closely in practice, it is not an easy task to make clear which mode is involved in business under certain circumstance. For example, an Englishman got sick when he came to the PRC, so he went to a hospital located in the PRC for treatment (Mode 2). This hospital, established in the PRC, was actually owned by a Japanese business group (Mode 3) and employed foreign doctors and nurses (Mode 4). Patients in this hospital can receive medical advice through the Internet from Japan-based specialists (Mode 1). Clarifying which modes are actually involved in business under certain circumstances is not simple. The classification difficulty happened in international e-commerce as well, it is a challenge to decide whether a service is provided from overseas into member's domestic (mode 1) or, vice versa, whether consumers domestically have "moved abroad" via the Internet (mode 2).[100]

There is no compulsory system about the classification issues under the GATS.[101] The GATS itself does not provide guidance on how to classify services or how

---

[97] Ibid., Art. I: 2(d).

[98] Adlung and Mattoo (n 92) 473.

[99] Rostam J. Neuwirth, 'Global Market Integration and the Creative Economy: The Paradox of Industry Convergence and Regulatory Divergence' (2015) 18 Journal of International Economic Law 21, 49.

[100] Adlung and Mattoo (n 92) 50.

[101] Ruosi Zhang, 'Covered or Not Covered: That Is the Question—Services Classification and Its Implications for Specific Commitments under the GATS', WTO Working Paper ERSD−2015–11 (7 December 2015) 1. https://www.econstor.eu/bitstream/10419/125800/1/845007270.pdf, accessed 22 October 2021.

3.1 Cross-Border Data Transfer Legislation in the Context of WTO Agreements

to describe sectors in the schedule.[102] The Scheduling of Initial Commitments in Trade in Services: Explanatory Note (MTN/GNS/164)[103] offers some detailed information on how to describe committed sectors and sub-sectors. According to the MTN/GNS/164:

> In general the classification of sectors and sub-sectors should be based on the Secretariat's revised Services Sectoral Classification List (GNS/W/120).[104] Each sector contained in the Secretariat list is identified by the corresponding United Nations Central Product Classification (CPC) number. Where it is necessary to refine further a sectoral classification, this should be done on the basis of the CPC or other internationally recognized classification (e.g. financial services annex). If a member wishes to use its own sub-sectoral classification or definitions it should provide concordance with the CPC. If this is not possible, it should give a sufficiently detailed definition to avoid any ambiguity as to the scope of the commitments.[105]

In undertaking specific commitments, determining how to map technological developments, new commercial terminology or business models into GNS/W/120 is challenging.[106] Under XXVIII (b) of the GATS, cross-border supply may include production, distribution, marketing, sale and delivery. However, not all stages belong to the same mode.[107] In addition, a uniform classification of service sectors, similar to the harmonized system used for tariff concessions under the GATT, is absent[108]; a common classification approach adopted by WTO members in their GATS schedules is the CPC,[109] a sectoral classification list that was developed by the previous GATT Secretariat during the Uruguay Round as mentioned before.[110]

---

[102] Ibid., 2.

[103] 'Scheduling of Initial Commitments in Trade in Services: Explanatory Note' (hereinafter: MTN/GNS/164) (3 September 1993). https://www.wto.org/gatt_docs/English/SULPDF/92140039.pdf, accessed 25 March 2021.

[104] The GNS/W/120 was circulated by the GATT Secretariat in 1991, it contains a 'Sectors and Subsectors' column and a 'Corresponding CPC' column which set out for every subsector of services listed in a member's schedule, its corresponding UN Central Product Classification (hereinafter: CPC) number. The CPC number then provides a detailed listing of all the categories and sub–categories of services encompassed by that number and thus included in any listed service sector in a member's schedule. See 'Services Sectoral Classification List' (hereinafter: GNS/W/120) (10 July 1991, WTO). https://www.wto.org/english/tratop_e/serv_e/mtn_gns_w_120_e.doc, accessed 25 April 2021.

[105] MTN/GNS/164, para. 16.

[106] 'Towards the WTO's Mc11: How to Move Forward on E–Commerce Discussions? South Centre Analytical Note SC/AN/TDP/2017/6' (hereinafter: Towards the WTO's Mc11), 14 (September 2017). https://www.southcentre.int/wp-content/uploads/2017/09/AN_TDP_2017_6_Towards-the-WTO%E2%80%99s-MC11-How-to-Move-Forward-on-E-Commerce-Discussions_EN.pdf, accessed 25 April 2021.

[107] Adlung and Mattoo (n 92) 50.

[108] Ruosi Zhang (n 101) 3.

[109] United Nations Statistics Division, 'Central Product Classification (CPC) Ver.2' (31 December 2008). https://unstats.un.org/unsd/classifications/Family/Detail/1073, accessed 20 December 2020.

[110] Ibid.

The current edition, CPC version 2.1 has been released on 11 August 2015.[111] CPC version 2.1 contains 10 broadly defined sectors, which are further divided into 99 sub-sectors.[112] The sectors related to the GATS include construction services; distributive trade services; accommodation, food and beverage serving services; transport services; electricity, gas and water distribution services; financial and related services; real estate services; rental and leasing services; business and production services; and community, social and personal services.[113] However, although CPC version 2.1 is the result of a scheduled review of the CPC structures and details to ensure the relevance of classifications for descriptions of current products in the economy,[114] this list failed to lead to the rapid development of technology. For example, cloud computing, which is used by service suppliers across different sectors, can be classified under the telephony and other telecommunications services (CPC versions 2.1, 841), Internet telecommunications services (CPC versions 2.1, 842), online content (CPC versions 2.1, 843) or even library and archive services (CPC versions 2.1, 845).[115] These uncertainties regarding classifications may need to await clarification on a case-by-case basis.[116]

3.1.6.2 The Technological Advances and the GATS

While a clear definition of "services" is absent from the GATS,[117] specific commitments are inscribed in the schedule on a sectoral basis. Classification is very important, as each category indicates a wholly different set of duties and/or flexibilities.[118] However, it is difficult to determine the "relevant categories" under members' commitments since the Internet and its new generation of online services, such as online gambling, did not even exist at the time most WTO members made their commitments.[119] In addition, the application of legal texts to the new technologies

---

[111] United Nations Department of Economic and Social Affairs and Statistics Division, 'Central Product Classification (CPC) Ver.2.1' ST/ESA/STAT/SER.M/77/Ver.2.1 (United Nations Publication, 11 August 2015). https://unstats.un.org/unsd/classifications/unsdclassifications/cpcv21.pdf, accessed 23 December 2020.

[112] Ibid.

[113] Ibid.

[114] Ibid.

[115] Ibid.

[116] Mitchell and Hepburn (n 64) 196.

[117] Ruosi Zhang (n 101) 1 and 2.

[118] Mira Burri, 'The Regulation of Data Flows through Trade Agreements' (2017) 48 Georgetown Journal of International Law 407, 414; see also E.G., Rolf H.Weber and Mira Burri, Classification of Services in the Digital Economy (Springer–Verlag Berlin Heidelberg 2012) 1–3; WTO Members have different levels of commitments in different modes, hence clarification is important to understand Members' existing commitments, see 'Towards the WTO's Mc11' (n 106) 14.

[119] Erixon and others (n 72) 10.

3.1 Cross-Border Data Transfer Legislation in the Context of WTO Agreements 51

and the new generation of online services was not envisaged at the time of the GATS drafting,[120] as stated below:

> When the WTO's founders wrote the GATS they had in mind a narrow category of "telecommunications services"-essentially, trade in telephone services, coupled with an additional category of "value-added" services, like "three-way calling" or "voice mail"; They had no idea that nearly every type of service under the GATS might eventually be offered over the TCP/IP protocol. In trade lingo, the framers thought of the Internet as a service sector, when, instead, it is usually a service mode.[121]

Advancements in information technology expand the number and types of services that can be traded and, in the meantime, help to create new types of services. In the *US-Gambling* case, WTO panel stated that the supply of services through electronic means is covered by Mode 1 under the GATS.[122] In the *China–Publications and Audiovisual Products* case, the question of whether a member state's commitments to the GATS include technical developments that were not expected at the time the commitments were raised. In other words, shall we interpret a WTO member's special commitments using the "ordinary meaning" at the time of its conclusion or at the time of its interpretation?[123] The PRC made both market access and national treatment commitments concerning Sound Recording Distribution Services in its GATS schedule. The PRC claimed that its commitments on distribution services were limited to products in physical form and did not cover products in digital form because the electronic distribution of sound recordings was a new phenomenon that did not exist at the time of PRC's accession to the WTO.[124] The United States cited the panel's statement in the *US-Gambling* case, stating as follows:

> The GATS does not limit the various technologically possible means of delivery under Mode 1…the GATS is sufficiently dynamic so that members need not renegotiate the agreement or their commitments in the face of ever-changing technology.[125]

In this regard, the WTO Appellate Body finally highlighted:

> We consider that the terms used in China's GATS Schedule ("sound recording" and "distribution") are sufficiently generic that what they apply to may change over time. In this respect, we note that GATS Schedules, like the GATS itself and all WTO agreements, constitute multilateral treaties with continuing obligations that WTO Members entered into for an

---

[120] Wu (n 91) 264; Ruosi Zhang (n 101) 15.

[121] Wu (n 91) 266.

[122] WTO Panel Report, 'United States—Measures Affecting the Cross–Border Supply of Gambling and Betting Services', WTO Doc. WT/DS285/R, para. 6.285 (10 November 2004). https://www.wto.org/english/tratop_e/dispu_e/285r_e.pdf, accessed 4 April 2021.

[123] Ulf Linderfalk, *On the Interpretation of Treaties—The Modern International Law as Expressed in the 1969 Vienna Convention on the Law of Treaties* (Springer Science and Business Media 2007) 73–95.

[124] WTO Panel Report, 'China—Measures Affecting Trading Rights and Distribution Services for Certain Publications and Audiovisual Entertainment Products', WTO Doc. WT/DS363/R, para.7.1159 (12 August 2009). http://trade.ec.europa.eu/doclib/docs/2009/november/tradoc_145 517.pdf, accessed 4 April 2021.

[125] Ibid., paras. 4.69 and 7.1160.

indefinite period of time, regardless of whether they were original Members or acceded after 1995.[126]

According to WTO jurisprudence, the content of generic terms, specifically "sound recording" and "distribution" in the *China-Publications and Audiovisual Products* case, vary with time. Aspects of the GATS should be considered a "living agreement" under which the scope and meaning of commitments should evolve to adapt to technological advances, particularly with regard to new forms of service delivery but also with regard to digital services within existing commitments.[127] Thus, the range of services related to cross-border data transfers, such as telecommunications-based services, is much broader than was once encompassed by the GATS; everything from education to health services can be delivered via information networks.[128]

Numerous service sectors are potentially relevant to cross-border data transfers under the GATS,[129] but interpretive guidance as well as equivalent offline predecessors are lacking.[130] Fourteen WTO members, including HKSAR (but not China itself), the EU, Japan, South Korea, and the United States, have agreed that all computer related services should be defined somewhere within the telecommunications services chapter.[131] However, WTO members themselves have not reached an agreement over the question of into which sectors within the CPC system these new online services fit. The development of a mechanism to address classification problems caused by technological and industry convergence is urgently needed.

3.1.6.3 Most Favoured Nation (MFN), Market Access and National Treatment (NT)

Similar to the GATT, the GATS functions on three levels: (1) the main body covering general principles and obligations; (2) annexes about regulations for specific

---

[126] WTO Report of the Appellate Body, 'China—Measures Affecting Trading Rights and Distribution Services for Certain Publications and Audiovisual Entertainment Products', WTO Doc. WT/DS/363/AB/R, para. 5.25 (21 December 2009). https://www.law.umich.edu/facultyhome/drwcasebook/Documents/Documents/China%20Measures%20Affecting%20Trading%20Rights-Distribution%20Services-Certain%20Publications%20AV%20Entertainment%20Products.pdf, accessed 4 April 2021, see also 'Repertory Of Appellate Body Reports—GATS' (WTO). https://www.wto.org/english/tratop_e/dispu_e/repertory_e/g1_e.htm, accessed 4 April 2021.

[127] Daniel Crosby, 'Analysis of Data Localization Measures under WTO Services Trade Rules and Commitments' (ICTSD, March 2016) 4. e15initiative.org/wp−content/uploads/2015/09/E15−Policy−Brief−Crosby−Final.pdf, accessed 29 December 2020.

[128] Wu (n 91) 266.

[129] Mitchell and Hepburn (n 64) 196.

[130] Erixon and others (n 72) 10; 'Towards the WTO's Mc11' (n 106) 14.

[131] Erixon and others (n 72) 11.

3.1 Cross-Border Data Transfer Legislation in the Context of WTO Agreements

sectors[132]; and (3) members' specific commitments.[133] The substance and structure of members' specific commitments in the GATS are discipline and schedules.[134]

Although the WTO agreements do not explicitly forbid the passage of data localization laws by the members,[135] the GATS has some provisions that establish legal obligations for members to permit the processing and transmission of data within and across borders. There are three types of obligations in the GATS: unconditional, conditional and specific.[136]

The MFN principle is unconditional because it applies automatically to all services and all members.[137] The Market Access and NT principles are specific because they apply only in cases in which members choose to include various sub-sectors in their schedule of specific commitments.[138] The members' specific commitments in Part II of the GATS are conditional because they apply only to the subsectors where the members have made specific commitments.[139]

The MFN principle is embraced by the GATT, the GATS and the TRIPS. It precludes WTO members from discriminating between their trading partners by actions such as granting a partner a special favour.[140] The MFN principle in the GATS reads as follows:

> 1…each Member shall accord immediately and unconditionally to services and service suppliers of any other Member treatment no less favourable than that it accords to like services and service suppliers of any other country. 2. A Member may maintain a measure inconsistent with paragraph 1 provided that such a measure is listed in, and meets the conditions of, the Annex on Article II Exemptions…[141]

The WTO members' unilateral decision to permit personal data transfers to specific jurisdictions risks being deemed a breach of the MFN principle under the GATS. For example, Article 45 of the GDPR permits personal data transfers to jurisdictions that the EC has decided have an "adequate level of protection". Thus far, only Andorra, Argentina, Canada (commercial organizations), the Faeroe Islands, Guernsey, Israel, the Isle of Man, Jersey, New Zealand, Switzerland, Uruguay, and

---

[132] 'Schedules of Commitments and Lists of Article II Exemptions' (WTO). https://www.wto.org/english/tratop_e/serv_e/serv_commitments_e.htm, accessed 20 December 2020.

[133] Ibid.

[134] Rachel Block, 'Market Access and National Treatment in China—Electronic Payment Services: An Illustration of the Structural and Interpretive Problems in GATS' (2014) 12(2) Chicago Journal of International Law 652, 663.

[135] Allison S. Khaskelis and Anthony L. Gallia, 'Russian Federation: Russia's Data Localization Law, a Violation of WTO Regulations?' (Mondaq, 21 January 2016). http://www.mondaq.com/russianfederation/x/460342/data+protection/Russias+Data+Localization+Law+A+Violation+Of+WTO+Regulations, accessed 20 March 2021.

[136] Block (n 134) 663.

[137] Ibid.

[138] Ibid.

[139] Ibid., 664.

[140] 'Principles of the Trading System' (WTO). https://www.wto.org/english/thewto_e/whatis_e/tif_e/fact2_e.htm, accessed 18 December 2020.

[141] GATS, Art. II (1) (2).

the United States (limited to the Privacy Shield framework) have been recognized by the EC as providing adequate protection.[142] In the absence of a relevant exemption, relaxing the jurisdictions that provide an adequate level of protection from data transfer restrictions is likely to constitute favourable treatment that is a violation of the GATS Article II (1). Then, it has the potential to be a violation of the GATS. The burden of proof to justify that treatment would then fall on the EU under either GATS Art. XIV—General Exceptions or Art. V—Economic Integration.[143]

All schedules in the GATS share the same format and are made up of four columns. The first column shows the sector or sub-sector covered by a member's schedule of commitments, while the second and third columns further stipulate the trade commitments made by each member. Two distinct sets of obligations are stipulated in Part III of the Agreement, namely, the Market Access principle (Art. XVI) and the NT principle (Art. XVII). A fourth column is about the additional commitments that do not fall under previous provisions. Article XX: 1 of the GATS requires all WTO members to list in a schedule the commitments they undertake[144] but does not prescribe any particular sector focus.[145]

GATS members may be obligated to adhere to the NT principle if they choose to include various sub-sectors in their schedule of specific commitments, which means that foreign service providers may not be treated any less favourably than domestic service providers.[146] The NT principle in Article XVII of the GATS is worded as follows:

> …each Member shall accord to services and service suppliers of any other Member, in respect of all measures affecting the supply of services, treatment no less favourable than that it accords to its own like services and service suppliers. A Member may meet the requirement of paragraph 1 by according to services and service suppliers of any other Member, either formally identical treatment or formally different treatment to that it accords to its own like services and service suppliers.[147]

It is worth noting that the NT principle is treated differently in the GATS than in the GATT. The NT principle in the GATT is a general principle, while the NT principle in the GATS applies only to those services and modes of delivery listed in each member's schedule of commitments.[148] Unless a WTO member has specifically committed to the GATS, the NT principle does not apply. In the GATS, there is no universal template. As a result, it is almost impossible to find two identical schedules

---

[142] On 30 March 2021, adequacy talks were concluded with South Korea. See 'Adequacy Decisions How the EU Determines If a Non–EU Country Has an Adequate Level of Data Protection' (European Commission (hereinafter: EC)). https://ec.europa.eu/info/law/law-topic/data-protection/international-dimension-data-protection/adequacy-decisions_en, accessed 9 April 2021.

[143] GATS, Art. II (2) (3).

[144] GATS, Art. XX: 1.

[145] Adlung and Mattoo (n 92) 53.

[146] GATS, Art. XVII: 1 and 2.

[147] Ibid.

[148] 'The General Agreement on Trade in Services (GATS): Objectives, Coverage and Disciplines' (n 32).

3.1 Cross-Border Data Transfer Legislation in the Context of WTO Agreements

of commitments.[149] The relevance of the NT obligation may need to be assessed on an ongoing, sector-by-sector and mode-by-mode basis.[150] In addition, Article XX: 2 of GATS instructs that:

> Measures inconsistent with both Articles XVI [market access] and XVII [national treatment] shall be inscribed in the column relating to Article XVI [market access]. In this case the inscription will be considered to provide a condition or qualification to Article XVII [national treatment] as well.

Therefore, the columns of members' schedules and commitments to market access and national treatment should be read together.[151] The Market Access obligations in the GATS are explained as follows:

> Each Member shall accord services and service suppliers of any other Member treatment no less favourable than that provided for under the terms, limitations and conditions agreed and specified in its Schedule. In sectors where market-access commitments are undertaken, the measures which a Member shall not maintain or adopt either on the basis of a regional subdivision or on the basis of its entire territory, unless otherwise specified in its Schedule, are defined as: (a) limitations on the number of service suppliers whether in the form of numerical quotas, monopolies, exclusive service suppliers or the requirements of an economic needs test;... (c) limitations on the total number of service operations or on the total quantity of service output expressed in terms of designated numerical units in the form of quotas or the requirement of an economic needs test;...[152]

The GATS rules could apply in principle to all commercial services.[153] However, in contrast to the GATT, in which all goods are assumed to be included unless they are explicitly exempted, members of the GATS are required to make a positive list of commitments in their schedules of specific commitments[154] and to decide which services they wish to commit to and what limitations they want to specify.[155] The GATS states members' specific commitments as follows:

> 1. In sectors where specific commitments are undertaken, each Member shall ensure that all measures of general application affecting trade in services are administered in a reasonable, objective and impartial manner...4. With a view to ensuring that measures relating to qualification requirements and procedures, technical standards and licensing requirements do not constitute unnecessary barriers to trade in services, the Council for Trade in Services shall, through appropriate bodies it may establish, develop any necessary disciplines.[156]

---

[149] Adlung and Mattoo (n 92) 48.

[150] Wu (n 91) 271.

[151] Block (n 134) 667.

[152] GATS, Art. XVI: 1 and 2(a) (c).

[153] 'The General Agreement on Trade in Services (GATS): Objectives, Coverage and Disciplines' (n 32).

[154] GATS, Art. XX: 1.

[155] Ellen Gould, 'The US Gambling Decision: A Wakeup Call for WTO Members' (2004) 5(4) Canadian Centre for Policy Alternatives 1, 3.

[156] GATS, Art. VI, 1 and 4.

Unnecessary barriers include the absence of "objective and transparent criteria"[157] or being "more burdensome than necessary to ensure the quality of the service".[158] In the *United States, China-Electronic Payment Services* case, the United States claimed that the PRC required that all payment card processing devices be compatible with UnionPay's network and that all payment cards bear the UnionPay logo no matter who had issued the card, granting UnionPay a regulation-based competitive advantage in the market for electronic payment services within the PRC, which is inconsistent with the PRC's Market Access NT commitments for electronic payment services.[159] Unnecessary barriers can take various forms, including restricting cross-border trade flows. Some domestic regulations that sound neutral – such as data localization requirements—apply to both domestic companies and foreign companies and are likely indirect barriers to trade.

Clarifying the classification of services in the GATS is essential, as was confirmed by the panel report on the *United States, China-Electronic Payment Services* case.[160] As discussed in the previous section, interpreting texts in light of changing circumstances and technologies is a problem for both domestic law[161] and international law. An empirical study has shown that the schedule of commitments related to the ICT sector has become an important issue in many WTO legal disputes.[162] There is a lack of guidance and equivalent offline predecessors for the interpretation of new services in most cases.[163] The typical practice of the WTO is to refer to Article 31 of the Vienna Convention, which provides the common-sense advice to refer to the text and various supplemental materials as needed.[164] The problem is that the meaning of circumstances that cause a treaty to be enacted, affect its content, and are attached to its conclusion is not indicated in the Vienna Convention but should be considered in practice.[165] In addition, Article 31 of the Vienna Convention says

---

[157] Ibid., Art. VI, P 4(a).

[158] Ibid., Art. VI, P 4(b).

[159] Tom Miles and Doug Palmer, 'U.S. Wins WTO Case Over China Bank Card Monopoly' (Reuters, 16 July 2012). https://www.reuters.com/article/us-usa-china-wto/u-s-wins-wto-case-over-china-bank-card-monopoly-idUSBRE86F0J020120716, accessed 4 April 2021; Duane W. Layton, Sydney H. Mintzer and Tiffany L. Smith, 'WTO Panel Rules Against China in Dispute over Electronic Payment Services' (Mayer Brown, 31 July 2012). https://www.mayerbrown.com/en/perspectives-events/publications/2012/07/wto-panel-rules-against-china-in-dispute-over-elec, accessed 4 April 2021.

[160] Panel Report, China—Certain Measures Affecting Electronic Payment Services, WT/DS413/R, para 6, para 18 and annex C−1 (16 July 2012). https://view.officeapps.live.com/op/view.aspx?src=http%3A%2F%2Fwww.wto.org%2Fenglish%2Ftratop_e%2Fdispu_e%2F413r_a_e.doc, accessed 4 April 2021.

[161] Tim Wu, 'The World Trade Law of Censorship and Internet Filtering' (2006) 7(1) Chicago Journal of International Law 263, 272.

[162] Peng (n 77) 405.

[163] Erixon and others (n 72) 10.

[164] Vienna Convention, Art. 31; Wu (n 91) 272.

[165] Richard Gardiner, *Treaty Interpretation* (OUP Oxford 2008) 343.

3.1 Cross-Border Data Transfer Legislation in the Context of WTO Agreements 57

little about what to do when the concept expressed by a word evolves and changes as a result of technological or social transformation.[166]

Regarding the WTO dispute settlement mechanism, the panel and the Appellate Body have developed several important principles for the legal interpretation and quasi-jurisprudence in the past several years. For example, the WTO dispute settlement body has adopted the principle of technological neutrality (while not necessarily depending on it for all of their conclusions),[167] which states that a member's commitments cover the sub-categories and include all means of delivery regardless of media unless otherwise specified in a member's schedule.[168] In addition, "the common intention of Members" is also considered a way to interpret the GATS commitments.[169]

3.1.6.4 The GATS Annex on Telecommunications

The GATS Annex on Telecommunications applies to all measures of members affecting access to and use of public telecommunications transport networks and services.[170] Telecommunications refers to the transmission and reception of signals by any electromagnetic means.[171] Public telecommunications transport services may consist of, inter alia:

> ...telegraph, telephone, telex, and data transmission typically involving the real-time transmission of customer-supplied information between two or more points without any end-to-end change in the form or content of the customer's information.[172]

In GNS/W/120, network services related to cross-border data transfers such as Online Information and Database Retrieval, Electronic Data Interchange, and other Online Information and/or Data Processing Services (including Transaction Processing) are listed under Telecommunication Services and Value-added Services of Communication Services. Packet-switched Data Transmission International Services and Circuit-switched Data Transmission International Services are listed under Mobile Voice and Data Services of Basic Telecommunication Services.

---

[166] Wu (n 91) 272.

[167] WTO Doc. WT/DS363/R (n 124) paras. 7.1154, 7.1160, 7.1166, 7.1248–7.1258; Peng (n 77) 427.

[168] WTO Doc. WT/DS363/R (n 124) paras. 7.1154, 7.1160, 7.1166, 7.1248–7.1258; Peng (n 77) 428.

[169] In the *United States, China—Electronic Payment Services case*, the Appellate Body and the Panel state that the 'task of identifying the meaning of a concession in a GATS Schedule, like the task of interpreting any other treaty text, involves identifying the common intention of Members'. See Petros C. Mavroidis, 'Crisis? What Crisis? Is the WTO Appellate Body Coming of Age?' in Terence P. Stewart, *Opportunities and Obligations: New Perspectives on Global and U.S. Trade Policy* (Kluwer Law International 2009) 173, 176.

[170] GATS Annex on Telecommunications, para. 2(a). See 'Annex on Telecommunications' (WTO). https://www.wto.org/english/tratop_e/serv_e/12-tel_e.htm, accessed 12 September 2020.

[171] Ibid., para. 3(a).

[172] Ibid., para. 3(b).

Transfer of Financial Information, and Financial Data Processing and Related Software by the Supplier of Other Financial Services are listed under Banking and Other Financial Services (excluding insurance and securities). Therefore, service sectors related to cross-border data transfers for the purpose of the GATS include nearly every sector in the Annex on Telecommunications. The GATS Annex on Telecommunications stipulates as follows:

> Each Member shall ensure that any service supplier of any other Member is accorded access to and use of public telecommunications transport networks and services on reasonable and non-discriminatory terms and conditions, for the supply of a service included in its Schedule.[173]

Paragraph 5(c) of the GATS Annex on Telecommunications further states that the binding obligation in every service sector where WTO members have made commitments as follows:

> Each Member shall ensure that service suppliers of any other Member may use public telecommunications transport networks and services for the movement of information within and across borders, including for intra-corporate communications of such service suppliers, and for access to information contained in data bases or otherwise stored in machine-readable form in the territory of any Member.[174]

This provision provides a context for interpreting the scope and meaning of other GATS rules and commitments concerning trade related to cross-border data flows. It also clearly obliges WTO members to ensure that the providers of all scheduled services, including Online Information and Database Retrieval, Electronic Data Interchange Services and Online Information and/or Data Processing, which fall under Telecommunication Services and Value-added Services, can be used to transfer information across borders and can access information stored in databases located in other member countries.

Based on the above provisions, WTO members may not restrict cross-border data transfers related to the scheduled services to which they have made commitments. This provision also clearly confirms that the consideration of cross-border data flows is not entirely new to the GATS; from the beginning of the GATS, the members understood that cross-border data flows are an indispensable element of all international trade in services.[175] Evidence of this is that the GATS provides that service providers have the right to use public telecommunications to transfer information within and across borders and the right to cross-border access information stored in databases.[176]

The Annex on Telecommunications specifies certain principles to ensure that a lack of progress in telecommunications negotiations will not preclude concessions

---

[173] Ibid., para. 5(a).
[174] Ibid., para. 5(c).
[175] Ibid., para. 7(a).
[176] Crosby (n 127) 7.

in other services.[177] In other words, the Annex on Telecommunications is an insurance policy for service providers who require access to basic telecommunications networks to provide enhanced or value-added services, whether financial, distribution, legal or others.[178] Although most of the GATS-related provisions were drafted before the invention of new applications (such as virtual reality, cloud computing, and AI), in theory, all of these applications are covered by the simple wording of the Annex on Telecommunications.

3.1.6.5 The PRC's GATS Commitments—Computer and Related Services

The GATS rules on Computer and Related Services may substantially limit members' regulatory space in digital trade. Computer and Related Services was a fairly new sector at the time that these rules were created and thus are largely devoid of domestic regulation.[179] The PRC has committed to the following list of sub-sectors: (a) Consultancy Services Related to the Installation of Computer Hardware, (b) Software Implementation Services, and (c) Data Processing Services. Regarding the Consultancy Services Related to the Installation of Computer Hardware, as well as Data Processing and Tabulation Services (CPC 8432) and Time-sharing Services (CPC 8433) under Data Processing Services, the PRC has listed no limitations for the first three modes of supply (cross-border, consumption abroad, and commercial presence) and remains unbound only for the presence of natural persons. Regarding the Software Implementation Services and Input Preparation Services (CPC 8431) under Data Processing Services, the PRC has listed limitations for the market access of commercial presence; only wholly foreign-owned enterprises are allowed. The domestic regulatory space in these areas is seemingly restricted by these commitments. However, the technical issue of the classification of services provides an excuse for a WTO member that does not follow its commitments. For example, the boundary between Audiovisual Services and Computer and Related Services is fuzzy. Because of cultural concerns, almost no WTO members have made commitments in these areas; thus, they remain relatively free to sustain discriminatory measures and adopt new ones in Audiovisual Services.[180]

---

[177] Marco Bronckers and Pierre Larouche, 'A Review of the WTO Regime for Telecommunications Services' in K. Alexander and others, *The World Trade Organisation And Trade In Services* (2008) 319, 325. https://ssrn.com/abstract=1995658, accessed 20 December 2020.

[178] Rohan Kariyawasam, 'A New Instrument for Digital Trade?' (ICTSD, 24 June 2015). https://e15initiative.org/blogs/a-new-instrument-for-digital-trade/, accessed 20 June 2020.

[179] Sacha Wunsch–Vincent, *The WTO, the Internet and Trade in Digital Products: EC–US Perspectives* (Hart Publishing 2006) 90–91; see also 'Computer and Related Services', WTO Doc. S/C/W/45 (WTO Secretariat, 14 July 1998). https://www.wto.org/english/tratop_e/serv_e/computer_e/computer_e.htm, accessed 20 December 2020.

[180] Mira Burri, 'The European Union, the WTO and Cultural Diversity' (2015) Cultural Governance and the European Union: Protecting and Promoting Cultural Diversity in Europe 195, 199–200. https://papers.ssrn.com/sol3/papers.cfm?abstract_id=2389603, accessed 15 March 2021;

3.1.6.6 Cross-Border Data Flows and Trade Debate

During the Uruguay Round of the WTO negotiations in 1993, the concept of "cultural exception" was introduced by the EU, led by France, aiming to treat audio-visual goods as exceptions in international treaties and agreements, especially with WTO.[181] The EU believes that culture is the product of ideas and has value beyond a strictly commercial value.[182] Conversely, the United States considers the cinema and the arts to be profit-making entertainment industries,[183] claiming that the cultural exception is a form of protectionism that harms global trade and desiring that audio-visual goods be included in the GATT to guarantee free trade.[184] GATT Article IV introduced special provisions, which essentially exempted cinematograph films from the requirement of national treatment and the prohibition of quantitative restrictions by allowing WTO members to establish screen quotas for minimum amounts of domestic origin cinema.[185] Since then, few WTO members have made any commitments in the sector of audio-visual services and therefore remain relatively free to sustain discriminatory measures and adopt new ones.[186] This situation has so far remained unchanged. For example, PRC's commitments regarding videos, sound recording distribution services, and cinema theatre services are extremely limited. Not only quantitative restrictions but also qualitative restrictions are imposed by PRC on these cultural products and services. The number foreign films imported to PRC is limited to 20 per year, and these foreign films are also subject to content examinations[187] and must comply with PRC's regulations on the administration of films.

Mira Burri, 'Trade versus Culture in the Digital Environment: An Old Conflict in Need of a New Definition' (2008) 12 Journal of International Economic Law 17, 20 and 48.

[181] Tina W. Chao, 'GATT's Cultural Exemption of Audiovisual Trade: The United States may Have Lost the Battle but not the War' (1996) 17(4) University of Pennsylvania Journal of International Economic Law 1127, 1129; Sophie des Beauvais, 'France: Ending the Cultural Exception' (World Policy, 3 November 2014). http://worldpolicy.org/2014/11/03/france-ending-the-cultural-exception/, accessed 26 March 2021; Thomas M. Murray, 'The U.S.–French Dispute over GATT Treatment of Audiovisual Products and the Limits of Public Choice Theory: How an Efficient Market Solution Was "Rent–Seeking"' (1997) 21 Maryland Journal of International Law 203, 209.

[182] Agnès Poirier, 'Why France Is Gearing Up for a Culture War with the United States' (Guardian, 7 Jun 2013). https://www.theguardian.com/commentisfree/2013/jun/07/france-culture-war-united-states, accessed 15 March 2021.

[183] Ibid.

[184] Murray (n 181) 207–208.

[185] Rostam J. Neuwirth, 'The Future of the "Culture and Trade Debate": A Legal Outlook' (2013) 47(3) Journal of World Trade 392, 399.

[186] Martin Roy, 'Audiovisual Services in the Doha Round: "Dialogue de Sourds, The Sequel"' (2005) 6 Journal of World Investment Trade 923, 941; see also J. P. Singh, 'Culture or Commerce? A Comparative Assessment of International Interactions and Developing Countries at UNESCO, WTO, and Beyond' (2007) 8 International Studies Perspectives 36, 42.

[187] Film Industry Promotion Law of the PRC (2016) (Chinese title: 電影產業促進法), Art. 14, 16, 17 and 18 (NPC Homepage, 7 November 2016). http://www.npc.gov.cn/zgrdw/npc/xinwen/2016-11/07/content_2001625.htm, accessed 24 April 2018; see also the Regulations on the Administration of Movies of the PRC 2001 (Chinese title: 電影管理條例), Chap. IV (LexisNexis, 25 November). https://hk.lexisen.com/law/law-chinese-1-29370-T.html, accessed 24 April 2021.

3.1 Cross-Border Data Transfer Legislation in the Context of WTO Agreements   61

These regulations guarantee that the Chinese government controls cultural industries and opens its cultural market gradually in a controlled manner.

This cultural exception debate has the potential to be replicated in the area of cross-border data flows, where the positions of the United States and EU diverge.[188] The culture and trade debate is complicated because it often leads to complex discussions about the relationship between the economic and non-economic value of things, that is, the value attached to something that does not have an assigned price (such as friendship, love, beauty, or the meaning of life).[189] The same is true for the cross-border data flows and trade debate since it is hard to fix a price for public policy objectives (such as privacy, national security, or public morals). New technology provides users with easy access to the information superhighway. Technological advances in global communications have brought new forms of music and movie flows through streaming and music downloads. Advances in computer-based networks will enable audiences of the PRC to receive American programming via cyberspace. Data can be considered digital content. Content is related to culture. In the digital age, the blurred lines between different domains are more blurred. Similar to the classification of products and service mentioned above, it is hard to draw a line between data and content.[190]

3.1.6.7 Exceptions to the GATS Framework

WTO members are allowed to restrict trade, even when such restriction circumvents their existing specific commitments, under certain circumstances. GATS Article XIV provides a list of general exceptions that clarifies what WTO members may and may not do, notwithstanding the rules of the GATS. The question is how to distinguish

---

[188] Mira Burri, 'Symposium—Future—Proofing Law: From Rdna to Robots the Governance of Data and Data Flows in Trade Agreements: The Pitfalls of Legal Adaptation' (November 2017) 51 U.C. Davis Law Review 65, 84; Andrada Coos, 'EU versus US: How Do Their Data Protection Regulations Square off?' (Endpoint Protection, 17 January 2018). https://www.endpointprotector.com/blog/eu-vs-us-how-do-their-data-protection-regulations-square-off/, accessed 24 April 2021; 'Europe versus the US—Who Takes Data Protection More Seriously?' (Telegraph, 20 December 2017). https://www.telegraph.co.uk/business/risk-insights/europe-us-who-takes-data-protection-more-seriously/, accessed 24 April 2021.

[189] United Nations Educational, Scientific and Cultural Organization (hereinafter: UNESCO), 'Culture, Trade and Globalization: Questions and Answers' (2000) 9. https://en.unesco.org/creativity/sites/creativity/files/culture_trade_and_globalisation.pdf, accessed 10 March 2021.

[190] There exists one of the hottest trends in the world of traditional media: data journalism. Paul Bradshaw said 'Data can be the source of data journalism, or it can be the tool with which the story is told – or it can be both. Like any source, it should be treated with scepticism; and like any tool, we should be conscious of how it can shape and restrict the stories that are created with it.' See 'What Is Data Journalism?' (Data Journalism Handbook). http://datajournalismhandbook.org/1.0/en/introduction_0.html, accessed 15 March 2021; see also Samantha Sunne, 'How Data Journalism Is Different from What We've Always Done' (American Press Institute, September 2016). https://www.americanpressinstitute.org/publications/reports/strategy-studies/how-data-journalism-is-different/, accessed 15 March 2021.

the protectionist aspects of data transfer restrictions from real policy objectives that have nothing to do with trade and investment.[191]

As previously discussed, although neither the GATT nor the GATS explicitly forbids members to adopt laws and regulations restricting cross-border data transfers, there is a strong possibility that this kind of restriction breaches the MFN principle, the Market Access principle, the NT principle, and members' commitments under the GATS Annex on Telecommunications except to the extent that the restrictions are justified under Article XIV General Exceptions of the GATS.

Therefore, in a situation in which the government of the PRC introduces restrictions on cross-border data transfers that may violate any of its obligations under the GATS, a possibility exists for deviating from such obligations by invoking an exception provision found in Article XIV of the GATS. When GATS Article XIV and similarly worded general exceptions are applied, the WTO panel or Appellate Body has substantial discretion in evaluating the legitimacy of a specific data transfer-restrictive measure.[192] Numerous factors to determine whether restrictions on cross-border data transfers are necessary to achieve the listed objectives will be assessed by the panel or Appellate Body. These include an evaluation of the necessity of the objective,[193] the contribution of the data transfer-restrictive measures to the objective and whether the objective can be categorized under the relevant paragraph of GATS Article XIV.[194] In addition, the contribution of the data transfer-restrictive measures must be weighed against its trade restrictiveness, and the importance of the interests or the value that underlie their pursuit must be considered.[195] Not just the respondent's declarations but also other pieces of evidence, such as the respondent's own systems and prevailing social, cultural, ethical and religious values, should be taken into account.[196] The most difficult aspect is evaluating a data-related measure's contribution to the objective and its trade restrictiveness.[197]

---

[191] Mitchell and Hepburn (n 64) 187.

[192] Selby (n 2) 231.

[193] 'When a measure produces restrictive effects on international trade as severe as those resulting from an import ban, it appears to us that it would be difficult for a panel to find that measure necessary unless it is satisfied that the measure is apt to make a material contribution to the achievement of its objective.' 'In order to justify an import ban under Article XX (b), a panel must be satisfied that it brings about a material contribution to the achievement of its objective.' See WTO Report of the Appellate Body, 'Brazil—Measures Affecting Imports of Retreaded Types', WTO Doc. WT/DS332/AB/R, part V. and paras. 10, 11, 25, 55, 80, 117, 124 (3 December 2007). https://www.wto.org/english/tratop_e/dispu_e/332abr_e.pdf, accessed 4 April 2021.

[194] Mitchell and Hepburn (n 64) 201.

[195] WTO Doc. WT/DS332/AB/R (n 193) paras. 210–211.

[196] WTO Doc. WT/DS363/R (n 124) para. 7.759 (quoting Panel Report, United States—Measures Affecting the Cross–Border Supply of Gambling and Betting Services, WTO Doc. WT/DS285/R (10 November 2004) para. 6.465).

[197] Mitchell and Hepburn (n 64) 201.

3.1 Cross-Border Data Transfer Legislation in the Context of WTO Agreements

The more a measure contributes to its objective, the more trade-restrictiveness is likely to be tolerated, the greater the measures restrictive effect on trade, the greater the need to demonstrate that the measure serves the objective.[198]

In the *United States Gambling* case, the defendant, the United States, depended heavily on GATS Article XIV to win the case.[199] In this case, the WTO panel adopted a two-tiered test to evaluate Article XIV of GATS for the defence.[200] According to this two-tiered approach,[201] a controversial measure adopted by WTO members first must be categorized as one of the recognized exceptions under Article XIV of the GATS, and second must meet the requirements of the introductory provisions of the Chapeau.[202]

Two elements are necessary for the successful invocation of Article XIV: first, the measures must be designed to protect public morals, to maintain public order,[203] to protect the privacy of individuals,[204] or for safety.[205]

It is notable that the public order exception can be invoked only when there is "a genuine and sufficiently serious threat to one of the fundamental interests of society",[206] and cannot be applied in a manner that would "constitute a means of arbitrary or unjustifiable discrimination between countries where like conditions prevail, or a disguised restriction on trade in services".[207] In addition, the terms "public morals" and "public order" in the context of Article XIV for members can change over time and space and depend on a range of factors, including the "prevailing social, cultural,

---

[198] Swartling (n 69) 5.

[199] Irem Dogan, 'Taking a Gamble on Public Morals: Invoking the Article XIV Exception to GATS' (2007) 32(3) Brooklyn Journal of International Law 1131, 1137.

[200] Ibid.

[201] 'General Exceptions: Article XX of the GATT 1994' (WTO). https://www.wto.org/english/tratop_e/dispu_e/repertory_e/g3_e.htm, accessed 20 December 2020.

[202] Appellate Body in Gasoline Case stipulates as follows: 'In order that the justifying protection of Article XX may be extended to it, the measure at issue must not only come under one or another of the particular exceptions paragraphs (a) to (j)-listed under Article XX; it must also satisfy the requirements imposed by the opening clauses of Article XX. The analysis is, in other words, two-tiered: first, provisional justification by reason of characterization of the measure under XX (g); second, further appraisal of the same measure under the introductory clauses of Article XX.' See WTO Report of the Appellate Body, 'United States—Standards for Reformulated and Conventional Gasoline', WTO Doc. WT/DS2/AB/R, 22 (29 April 1996). https://docs.wto.org/dol2fe/Pages/FE_Search/FE_S_S006.aspx%3FQuery%3D(%40Symbol%3D%2520wt/ds2/ab/r%2A%2520not%2520rw%2A)%26Language%3DENGLISH%26Context%3DFomerScriptedSearch%26languageUIChanged%3Dtrue, accessed 4 April 2021; see also Dr. Hans—Joachim Priess and Dr. Christian Pitschas, 'Protection of Public Health and the Role of the Precautionary Principle under WTO Law: A Trojan Horse before Geneva's Walls?' (2000) 1(24) Fordham International Law Journal 519, 536.

[203] GATS, Art. XIV (a).

[204] Ibid., Art. XIV (c) ii.

[205] Ibid., Art. XIV (c) iii.

[206] Ibid., Art. XIV (a) (footnote original) 5.

[207] General Exceptions of GATS, Art. XIV.

ethical and religious values".[208] Apart from the general principles underlying broad doctrines such as the common law or civil law, legal rules are specific to jurisdictions and based on different ideological values and social systems.[209]

In 2000, a French anti-racism association brought a case against the online portal Yahoo when it found that in the auction section of the site, Nazi memorabilia that is illegal in France was displayed on French computers.[210] Instead of requiring Yahoo to remove the Nazi memorabilia content from its auction service, the court demanded Yahoo to block access to those sections of the US version of the service by users who could reasonably be identified as located in France.[211] As the Canadian Bar Association said in the *Submission on the General Agreement on Trade in Services and the Legal Profession: the Accountancy Disciplines as a Model for the Legal Profession*:

> ...the core values are a foundation of our legal system and of our democracy. Disciplines governing trade in legal services must ensure that law societies can continue to preserve and protect these values...nothing in the disciplines will affect the right of member states or the regulators of their respective legal professions to regulate in furtherance of those values.[212]

The second element is that the measures must be considered necessary for the protection of public order and public morals.[213] The *Korean Beef* case creates a kind of less-restrictive-means test of what is "necessary"—namely, whether a less WTO-inconsistent measure is reasonably available to maintain the public order or to protect public morals.[214] In the *United States Tuna Dispute*, the panel indirectly inserted the requirement that to satisfy the criterion of "necessity", the responding party must exhaust all other options before imposing the measures.[215] In the *United States Gambling* case, the panel reiterated that members may derogate their GATS obligations under Article XIV only if they have "explored and exhausted reasonably available WTO-consistent alternatives" to those measures.[216] In the *Brazil-Retreaded Tyres* case, the Appellate Body stipulated as follows:

> In order to determine whether a measure is "necessary" within the meaning of Article XX (b) of the GATT 1994, a panel must assess all the relevant factors, particularly the extent of the

---

[208] WTO Doc.WT/DS285/R (n 122) paras. 6.465 and 6.461.

[209] Canadian Bar Association, 'Submission on the General Agreement on Trade in Services and the Legal Profession: The Accountancy Disciplines as a Model for the Legal Profession' (August 2000), 14. http://www.cba.org/Our-Work/Submissions-(1)/Submissions/2000/em-General-Agreement-em-on-Trade-in-Services-and-t, accessed 20 December 2020.

[210] Christine Duh, 'Yahoo Inc. v. LICRA' (2002) 17 Berkeley Technology Law Journal 359, 360.

[211] Ibid.

[212] Canadian Bar Association (n 209) 16–17.

[213] GATS, Art. XIV 1 (b).

[214] WTO Report of the Appellate Body, 'Korea—Measures Affecting Imports of Fresh, Chilled and Frozen Beef', WTO Doc. WT/DS169/AB/R, paras.165, 167 (11 December 2000). https://www.wto.org/english/tratop_e/dispu_e/161-169abr_e.pdf, accessed 4 April 2021.

[215] WTO Panel Report, 'United States—Restrictions on Imports of Tuna', WTO Doc. DS21/R–39S/155, para. 5.28 (3 September 1991). https://www.wto.org/english/tratop_e/dispu_e/gatt_e/91tuna.pdf, accessed 4 April 2021.

[216] WTO Doc.WT/DS285/R (n 122) para. 6.522.

3.1 Cross-Border Data Transfer Legislation in the Context of WTO Agreements

contribution to the achievement of a measure's objective and its trade restrictiveness…"[217] "To be characterized as necessary, a measure does not have to be indispensable.[218]

The exception clauses in the GATS allow controversial measures that are proven to be "necessary" for the achievement of the listed objectives. Such measures cannot account for necessity if a measure that is less restrictive to trade has the same effect.[219] All of these clauses guarantee that policies that pursue the listing objectives do not create unnecessary barriers to trade.[220]

It is believed that the PRC's policies that restrict cross-border data transfers (such as blocking foreign websites and applications) have the potential to violate its commitments under its WTO obligations because less restrictive means to achieve the same goals probably exist. However, the accessibility of the measures mentioned above to the PRC or a responding member depend heavily on technical feasibility as well as the financial and professional resources of the members.[221] The outcome also depends on the specific nature and framework of the measures and the actual situation.[222] The specific situation of each member should be taken into account when evaluating whether alternative measures exist.

The government of the PRC offers several legitimate policy objectives as justifications for its restrictions on cross-border data transfers. For example, the purpose of the Network Security Law of the PRC is to guarantee cybersecurity; safeguard cyberspace sovereignty, national security and the public interest; protect the lawful rights and interests of citizens, legal persons and other organizations; and promote the sound development of economic and social informatization.[223]

Selective filtering, which is based on keyword input from the user, frequently occurs in the PRC. Content posted on the Internet that contains sensitive words is quickly deleted by the network administrator. Chinese Internet users often use substitute words to replace censored words, and cat-and-mouse games occasionally happen between users and censors.[224] The use of alternative spellings and code words to escape the censors' attention is also common. The most controversial instance of the "Great Firewall of China" is the blocking of numerous foreign websites, apps, social media, VPNs, emails, instant messages and other online resources in the PRC. The websites that cannot be opened while using the Internet in the PRC include

---

[217] WTO Doc. WT/DS332/AB/R (n 193) para. 156.

[218] Ibid., paras. 210–211.

[219] 'Trade in the Digital Economy—A Primer on Global Data Flows for Policymakers', 5 (International Chamber of Commerce Homepage, 19 July 2016). https://iccwbo.org/publication/trade-inthe-digital-economy, accessed 19 March 2021.

[220] Ibid.

[221] Mitchell and Hepburn (n 64) 203.

[222] Ibid.

[223] Network Security Law, Art. 1.

[224] Paul Mozur, 'China's Internet Censors Play a Tougher Game of Cat and Mouse' (New York Times, 3 August 2017). https://www.nytimes.com/2017/08/03/business/china-internet-censorship.html, accessed 23 May 2021; Ben Lillie, 'China's Censorship Battle between the Cats and the Mice: Michael Anti at Tedglobal 2012' (Ted blog, 29 June 2012). https://blog.ted.com/chinas-censorship-battle-between-the-cats-and-the-mice-michael-anti-at-tedglobal-2012/, accessed 23 May 2020.

the well-known Google, Facebook, and YouTube.[225] However, it is difficult for the government of the PRC to control online information that its citizens can access and share in practice. People in the PRC can use VPNs to circumvent blocked sites and obtain access to apps such as Google, Facebook, Twitter, Tinder and others,[226] which tends to weaken the effectiveness of such bans and their justifiability under the WTO regulations. It is necessary to draw the line between legitimate regulation and protectionist intervention on a case-by-case basis, and reasonable arguments may be made on both sides.[227]

In a review of the PRC's policies of restricting cross-border data transfers, therefore, the PRC would have to show that its restrictions on cross-border data flows are necessary to achieve the objective listed in Article XIV of the GATS. When considering the importance of the objective, it is likely that the panel or Appellate Body would examine the legislature's assessment and reasoning, as stated in its restriction policies on cross-border data transfers.

It is therefore conceivable that the panel or Appellate Body would require a higher level of justification to show that (i) the PRC's restrictions on cross-border data transfers that affect international trade are necessary, and (ii) there are no less restrictive measures available to achieve the listed objectives. Apart from passing the "necessity" tests, the PRC would have the burden of proof to show that some requirements in its Network Security Law and other policies, such as the requirement of a security assessment before cross-data transfer, do not result in arbitrary or unjustified restrictions for member countries where like conditions prevail—a precondition for justifying any exception under the Chapeau.[228] It is very difficult to interpret the Chapeau to prevent the abuse of the specific exemptions provided for in Article XX.[229]

Such a review would focus both on how the law is drafted and how it is actually applied. As explained by the WTO Appellate Body, the Chapeau rules "serve to ensure that…Members use the exceptions reasonably, so as not to frustrate the rights accorded to other Members".[230] If the exceptions to public morals or national security imposed on cross-border data transfers are limited to certain WTO members, or if standards for cross-border data transfers are not applied consistently to all WTO members, either of these conditions would make it difficult to justify the restrictions under the Chapeau.

---

[225] Michael Michelini, 'List of Blocked Websites in China' (Global from Asia, 8 November 2017). https://www.globalfromasia.com/list-blocked-sites-china/, accessed 12 December 2017; Biz Carson, '9 Incredibly Popular Websites that Are Still Blocked In China' (Business Insider 23 July 2015). https://www.businessinsider.com.au/websites-blocked-in-china-2015-7, accessed 12 December 2020; Lillie (n 224).

[226] Paul Bischoff, 'What's the Best VPN for China? We tested 59 to see which work' (Comparitech, 16 February, 2021). https://www.comparitech.com/blog/vpn-privacy/whats-the-best-vpn-for-china-5-that-still-work-in-2016/, accessed 15 March 2021; Mozur (n 224).

[227] Mitchell and Hepburn (n 64) 187.

[228] Swartling (n 69) 5.

[229] WTO Report of the Appellate Body, 'United States—Import Prohibition of Certain Shrimp and Shrimp Products', WTO Doc. WT/DS58/AB/R, para. 120 (12 October 1998). https://www.wto.org/english/tratop_e/dispu_e/58abr.pdf, accessed 4 April 2021.

[230] WTO Doc.WT/DS285/R (n 122) para. 339.

3.1 Cross-Border Data Transfer Legislation in the Context of WTO Agreements

A legal review of necessity, proportionality and reasonableness is naturally an exercise in balancing different interests. The outcome will, in many cases, rely on the claim that the responding party is able to make. Thus, a WTO complaining party (in the PRC case, most likely the United States) would show the restrictiveness to trade of measures for cross-border data transfers and other data-related policies, and the PRC would have to demonstrate that, on the contrary, the service is not restricted or at least that any restrictions arising from the PRC's Network Security Law and other data-related policies are proportionate, necessary and reasonable.

One way to balance such tests of necessity, proportionality or reasonableness on the side of the existing PRC measures on cross-border data transfer restriction is to introduce generally transparent and favourable regulations and rules for cross-border data transfers between the PRC and other WTO members. That approach would possibly change the stereotyped view of the Network Security Law of the PRC and other cross-border data transfer-related regulations, i.e., that the PRC's restrictions on cross-border data transfers concerning certain data are a specific and justified exception to a broader and more general principle allowing cross-border data transfers.

Although adopting broad restriction policies on cross-border data transfers domestically, the PRC has positioned itself as a champion of globalization and economic integration internationally.[231] The "One Belt, One Road" (OBOR) initiative (Chinese title: 一带一路), otherwise known as the Belt and Road Initiative (BRI), is being advanced by PRC as a vehicle for: "promoting the economic prosperity of the countries along the Belt and Road and regional economic cooperation, strengthening exchanges and mutual learning between different civilizations, and promoting world peace and development".[232] In addition, the "Digital Silk Road"—the digital version of the BRI was highlighted at 2017 Belt and Road Forum held in Beijing.[233]

---

[231] For example, Chinese Premier Li Keqiang said, 'China proposes to advance the construction of an East Asia Economic Community so as to promote regional integration and common development'. See 'China Champions Economic Integration in East Asia despite Anti−globalization Headwinds' (Xinhua, 14 November 2017). http://www.chinadaily.com.cn/business/2017-11/14/content_34525509.htm, accessed 28 December 2020.

[232] 'Preface of Vision and Actions on Jointly Building Silk Road Economic Belt and 21st−Century Maritime Silk Road' (National Development and Reform Commission of the PRC Homepage, 28 March 2015). http://2017.beltandroadforum.org/english/n100/2017/0410/c22-45.html, accessed 29 December 2020.

[233] Huadong Guo, an academician at the Institute of Remote Sensing and Digital Earth at the Chinese Academy of Sciences, touted Information Silk Road as a digital version of the Belt and Road Initiative. See Yasir Habib Khan, 'CPEC as Digital Silk Road' (Daily Times, 7 December 2017). https://dailytimes.com.pk/154109/cpec-digital-silk-road/, accessed 28 December 2020; Elizabeth C. Economy, 'Beijing's Silk Road Goes Digital' (Asia Unbound, 6 June 2017). https://www.cfr.org/blog/beijings-silk-road-goes-digital, accessed 28 December 2020.

3.2 The Information Silk Road

The PRC is making efforts to position itself as a pioneer and supporter of the globalization and liberalization of global trade through the OBOR. The OBOR, also known as the BRI, consists of two major parts—first, the Silk Road Economic Belt,[234] stretching from Central Asia to Europe and incorporating a package of trade and infrastructure projects, and second, the 21st Century Maritime Silk Road,[235] a seabased network of shipping lanes and port development passing through Southeast Asia, Africa and Europe.

The third part of the OBOR—the Digital Silk Road, or the Information Silk Road, which has the potential to contribute substantially to both global trade and commerce—has not received as much attention as it should. The Digital Silk Road was first mentioned in the Action Plan on the BRI (Action Plan), which was published on 30 March 2015 by the State Council of the PRC.[236] The Action Plan stipulates as follows:

> We should jointly advance the construction of cross-border optical cables and other communications trunk line networks, improve international communications connectivity, and create an Information Silk Road. We should build bilateral cross-border optical cable networks at a quicker pace, plan transcontinental submarine optical cable projects, and improve spatial (satellite) information passageways to expand information exchanges and cooperation.[237]

A few months later, Lu Wei, the director of the Cyberspace Administration of the PRC, proposed that the PRC "build a digital silk road, a silk road in cyberspace".[238] The Digital Silk Road has the potential to pave the way for unprecedented trade volume in cross-border e-commerce because it will be used to support "innovation action plans for e-commerce, digital economy, smart cities and science and technology parks".[239] At the Belt and Road Forum for International Cooperation held in Beijing in May 2017, President Xi Jinping summarized the digitalization aspect of Belt and Road as follows:

> We should pursue innovation-driven development and intensify cooperation in frontier areas such as the digital economy, artificial intelligence, nanotechnology and quantum computing,

---

[234] When Chinese President Xi Jinping visited Central Asia and Southeast Asia in September and October of 2013, he raised the initiative of jointly building the Silk Road Economic Belt and the 21st−Century Maritime Silk Road. 'Action Plan on the Belt and Road Initiative' (State Council of the PRC Homepage, 30 March 2015). http://english.gov.cn/archive/publications/2015/03/30/content_281475080249035.htm, accessed 29 December 2020.

[235] Chinese Premier Li Keqiang emphasized the need to build the Maritime Silk Road oriented toward ASEAN at the China−ASEAN Expo in 2013. 'Action Plan on the Belt and Road Initiative' (n 234).

[236] 'Action Plan on the Belt and Road Initiative' (n 234).

[237] Ibid.

[238] Catherine Stupp, 'China to Europe: "We Can Build a Silk Road in Cyberspace"' (EURACTIV, 7 July 2015). https://www.euractiv.com/section/digital/news/china-to-europe-we-can-build-a-silk-road-in-cyberspace/, accessed 28 December 2020; see also Economy (n 233).

[239] Economy (n 233).

3.2 The Information Silk Road

and advance the development of big data, cloud computing and smart cities so as to turn them into a digital silk road of the 21st century.[240]

Xi described the BRI as "an open platform of cooperation to uphold and grow an open world economy".[241] The five main goals of the BRI are "policy coordination, facilities connectivity, unimpeded trade, financial integration, and people-to-people bonds".[242] Many national governments, local authorities and enterprises are already participating in the BRI in different ways.[243] The international trade infrastructure initiative is open to those in many parts of the world.[244]

At the 4th World Internet Conference in Hangzhou, held in Zhejiang Province in eastern China on 3 December 2017, the PRC and seven other countries along the Belt and Road co-launched an initiative to strengthen cooperation and enhance connectivity in the digital economy.[245] Seven countries—Saudi Arabia, Egypt, Turkey, Thailand, Laos, Serbia, and the United Arab Emirates—have publicly agreed to cooperate with the PRC in the digital economy to build an interconnected digital silk road.[246]

The PRC and these seven countries reached an agreement on extending their cooperation in the digital economy with the purpose of constructing an interconnected Digital Silk Road and creating "a community of shared interests and a shared future with win–win cooperation and common prosperity".[247] The Belt and Road Digital Economy International Cooperation Initiative includes deeper collaboration to improve broadband access and quality, digital transformation and e-commerce

---

[240] Dennis Pamlin, 'Belt and Road Initiative's "New Vision"' (China Daily, 26 November 2017). http://www.chinadaily.com.cn/world/2017-11/26/content_35017323.htm, accessed 22 December 2020.

[241] Brenda Goh and Yawen Chen, 'China Pledges $124 Billion For New Silk Road as Champion of Globalization' (Reuters, 14 May 2017). https://ca.reuters.com/article/topNews/idCAKBN18A02I-OCATP, accessed 28 December 2020.

[242] 'Action Plan on the Belt and Road Initiative' (n 234); and 'The Belt and Road Initiative' (HKTDC Research, 3 May 2018). http://china-trade-research.hktdc.com/business-news/article/The-Belt-and-Road-Initiative/The-Belt-and-Road-Initiative/obor/en/1/1X000000/1X0A36B7.htm, accessed 28 December 2020.

[243] 'List of Deliverables of the Belt and Road Forum for International Cooperation' (China Daily, 16 May 2017). http://www.chinadaily.com.cn/china/2017-05/16/content_29359377.htm, accessed 29 December 2020.

[244] 'The Belt and Road Initiative' (n 242).

[245] 'Initiative on Belt and Road Digital Economy Cooperation Launched' (Xinhua, 4 December 2017). http://www.scio.gov.cn/31773/35507/35520/Document/1612635/1612635.htm, accessed 28 December 2020.

[246] Steven Viney, Ning Pan, and Jason Fang, 'One Belt, One Road: China Heralds "Digital Silk Road"; Foresees Internet–era Power Shift Soon' (ABC News, 5 December 2017). http://www.abc.net.au/news/2017-12-05/china-presents-foundations-of-digital-silk-road-at-internet-meet/9223710, accessed 3 March 2021.

[247] Yiming Guo, 'Digital Economy Cooperation to Empower Belt, Road' (China.org.cn, 4 December 2017). http://www.china.org.cn/world/2017-12/04/content_50083923.htm, accessed 29 December 2020.

cooperation and to enable more support of Internet-based entrepreneurship and innovation.[248] It also aims to promote transparent digital economy policies, investment in the information and communications technology (ICT) sector and inter-city cooperation in the digital economy, and to establish a multi-layered communication mechanism to create a more open, orderly and safe cyberspace.[249] The Chinese authorities have used the Digital Silk Road Initiative to prove their willingness to position the PRC as a cyber-power expanding Internet services from Asia to Europe and Africa.[250]

The significance of global trade relations has been reaffirmed many times by the Chinese government.[251] Recent developments in the PRC's international trade engagements show that the PRC has positioned itself as a defender of an open world economy by seeking new models of international cooperation and global governance.[252] For example, the Digital Silk Road Initiative has exhibited the Chinese government's intention to boost the development of the overall economy and trade.

3.3 A Comprehensive Outlook on Development

The forms of national data localization restriction are various and can be categorized as direct or indirect,[253] comprehensive or sector-based, or national or provincial, to mention but a few. Direct restriction means that states explicitly require that data be located in the home country.[254] The Regulation of the Administration of the Credit Investigation Industry of the PRC (Chinese title: 征信業管理條例), for instance, clearly requires that any credit information collected within the territory of the PRC be organized, stored and processed within the PRC.[255] Compared to direct restriction, indirect restriction is more common, frequently in the form of local technology or content requirements, specific technical requirements (restrictions or mandates), disclosure of computer source codes, network monitoring, discriminatory treatment of digital products (music, videos, software, e-books) that are transmitted electronically, and a requirement that a certain security assessment be passed before the data

---

[248] Ibid.

[249] Ibid.

[250] Viney and others (n 246).

[251] In 2016 Asia Pacific Economic Cooperation (APEC) summit in Lima, Peru, President Xi Jinping said, 'No one will emerge as a winner in a trade war…pursuing protectionism is like locking oneself in a dark room'. Anna Ashton, 'Recent Developments in China's International Trade Engagement' (China Business Review, 30 May 2017). https://www.chinabusinessreview.com/recent-developments-in-chinas-international-trade-engagement/, accessed 12 December 2020.

[252] Ashton (n 251).

[253] 'Inception Impact Assessment—European Free Flow of Data Initiative within the Digital Single Market' (EC, October 2016) 2. https://ec.europa.eu/smart-regulation/roadmaps/docs/2016_cnect_001_free_flow_data_en.pdf, accessed 22 May 2020.

[254] Nigel (n 13) 21.

[255] Regulation of the Administration of the Credit Investigation Industry of the PRC (2013), Art. 24.

3.3 A Comprehensive Outlook on Development

transfer, to mention but a few. Direct restriction is mostly sector-specific instead of comprehensive. The personal data arising from the selected sectors are mainly sensitive data.

At the international level, legislation on cross-border data transfers is a multi-faceted policy issue that straddles the disciplines of Internet governance and international trade law.[256] This issue is not regulated by current international trade law in a consistent, coherent and predictable manner.[257] Methods for moving data from one jurisdiction to another are varied, complex and changing on a yearly basis (for example, Binding Corporate Rules,[258] Standard Contractual Clauses,[259] and the APEC Cross-Border Privacy Rules System.[260] More progress has been made at the bilateral level—such as United States-Korea FTA—and plurilateral levels—such as the GDPR—rather than multilateral levels—such as the WTO.[261]

In 2017, the PRC's Network Security Law was accused of damaging global trade in services by the United States in a document submitted for debate to the WTO

---

[256] Selby (n 2) 232.

[257] Mitchell and Hepburn (n 64) 182; Kriangsak Kittichaisaree and Christopher Kuner, 'The Growing Importance of Data Protection in Public International Law' (EJIL Analysis, 14 October 2015). https://www.ejiltalk.org/the-growing-importance-of-data-protection-in-public-internationonal-law/, accessed 22 May 2021; Media Buzz, 'Data Privacy Trends in Asia Pacific's Highly Fragmented Legislative Environment' (Data Protection and Security, August 2013). https://www.mediabuzz.com.sg/asian-emarketing/data-protection-security-a-regulations-week-1/2046-data-privacy-trends-in-asia-pacifics-highly-fragmented-legislative-environment, accessed 22 May 2020.

[258] Binding Corporate Rules can be defined as 'internal rules (such as a Code of Practice) followed by multinational group of corporations for international transfers of personal data within the same corporate group to entities located in countries which do not provide an adequate level of protection.' See 'Binding Corporate Rules' (EC). https://ec.europa.eu/info/law/law-topic/data-protection/international-dimension-data-protection/binding-corporate-rules-bcr_en, accessed 18 November 2020.

[259] Standard Contractual Clauses on the basis of Article 26(4) of Directive 95/46/EC is of particular relevance for transferring personal data from EU to Asia countries. The EC has the power, which was granted by the Council and the European Parliament to decide whether certain SCCs offer sufficient safeguards as required by Article 26(2), that is, 'provide adequate safeguards with respect to the protection of the privacy and fundamental rights, and freedoms of individuals and as regards the exercise of the corresponding rights'. See the Directive 95/46/EC, Art. 26(2).

[260] APEC Cross−Border Privacy Rules System (hereinafter: CBPR) adopts similar regulatory model as the GDPR. Generally speaking, the CBPR system requires enterprises to develop their own internal privacy−based rules guiding the cross−border personal data transmission under standards meeting or exceeding the APEC Privacy Framework. Organizations that choose to join in the CBPR system must submit their privacy practices and policies for evaluation by an APEC−recognized accountability agent to assess program compliance. After certification, the practices and policies will be binding on the organization and enforceable through the relevant privacy enforcement authority. The purpose of this multi−tiered model is to involve individuals, organizations, industry associations and governments within a legal framework. See 'APEC Cross−Border Privacy Rules System Policies, Rules and Guidelines', Art. 6.2(vi) and 16. https://www.apec.org/groups/committee-on-trade-and-investment/~/media/files/groups/ecsg/cbpr/cbpr-policiesrulesguidelines.ashx, accessed 30 May 2020.

[261] Mitchell and Hepburn (n 64) 182.

Services Council.[262] Although the argument was made that measures such as localized database requirements and security assessments before cross-border data transfers constitute protective measures that probably contradict the PRC's commitments to market access under Article XVI of the GATS and cross-border supply of data services as set out in the GATS Annex on Telecommunications, it is impossible to hastily conclude that the PRC is violating its commitments under its WTO obligations because the WTO treaty provisions do not explicitly forbid members to enact data localization laws.[263] The most closely related agreement—the GATS—exists as an almost comprehensive system of rules that has almost unlimited flexibility. Indeed, no policy system would be inconsistent with the GATS, as at the least, it could satisfy the exception provisions.[264] As far as the PRC is concerned, the potential violation should be determined on a case-by-case basis.

We have entered a new era of digital globalization, defined by the rapidly increasing flow of data.[265] Digital technologies that transform "flows of physical goods into digital flows"[266] are shaping the future of global trade and investment.[267] There exists an undeniable trend towards global digital trade.[268] The prosperity of global digital trade cannot exist without cross-border data transfers. Whether the PRC's cross-border data transfer restrictions, such as the localization requirements introduced by the Network Security Law, could be challenged in the international arena as a violation of its commitments under its WTO obligations is still an open question. Requiring personal data to be stored in the PRC is a default data localization rule that is very broad in scope and possibly inconsistent with international trends.[269]

---

[262] Miles (n 6).

[263] Khaskelis and Gallia (n 135).

[264] Rudolf Adlung and Aaditya Mattoo, 'The GATS' (2007). https://oxford.universitypressscholarship.com/view/10.1093/acprof:oso/9780199235216.001.0001/acprof-9780199235216-chapter-2, accessed 29 December 2020.

[265] James Manyika and others, 'Digital globalization: The New Era of Global Flows' (Mckinsey Global Institute, February 2016), 7. https://www.mckinsey.com/business-functions/digital-mckinsey/our-insights/digital-globalization-the-new-era-of-global-flows, accessed 19 December 2020.

[266] Jacques Bughin, Susan Lund, and James Manyika and others, 'Harnessing the Power of Shifting Global Flows' (McKinsey Quarterly, February 2015). https://www.mckinsey.com/business-functions/digital-mckinsey/our-insights/harnessing-the-power-of-shifting-global-flows, accessed 29 December 2020.

[267] Shamshad Akhtar, Hongjoo Hahm, Susan F. Stone, 'Asia–Pacific Trade and Investment Report 2016' (United Nations Economic and Social Commission for Asia and the Pacific, November 2016), 103. www.unescap.org/sites/default/files/publications/aptir-2016-full.pdf, accessed 28 February 2021; and 'Shaping the Future of International Trade and Investment' (World Economic Forum). https://www.weforum.org/system-initiatives/shaping-the-future-of-international-trade-and-investment, accessed 29 December 2020.

[268] Michael Vrontamitis, 'Trade Is Going Digital, Finally' (Standard Chartered, 27 April 2015). https://www.sc.com/BeyondBorders/trade-going-digital-finally/, accessed 29 December 2020.

[269] Carl E. Schonander, 'Chinese Proposed Cross−border Data Flow Rules Contradict an Emerging International Default Norm for Cross−Border Data Flows' (Linkedin, 19 April 2017). https://www.linkedin.com/pulse/chinese-proposed-cross-border-data-flow-rules-default-carl-schonander, accessed 31 March 2021.

3.3 A Comprehensive Outlook on Development

As revealed from the previous discussion, the Chinese government holds two different attitudes towards the liberalization of cross-border data transfers in the context of trade globalization. The two approaches are contradictory by nature, and together, they constitute a paradox in the PRC's data protection and trade policies: On the one hand, the government is eager to position itself as a pioneer and supporter of globalization and liberalization of global trade, while on the other hand, the government is cautious and discrete regarding the free movement of data across borders because of national security, privacy, public moral, and other concerns. The paradox is exhibited through the contradiction between two strategies being implemented simultaneously: One side involves the de facto restriction policies on cross-border data transfer in the Network Security Law and other domestic regulations, and the other side is actively entering into international FTAs as well as calling for greater international cooperation in cross-border e-commerce by advancing the concept of a digital silk road (or the Information Silk Road).[270] When the two components are combined, a paradox emerges: While restriction policies on cross-border data transfer represent a cautious approach towards the globalization of service trade in an increasingly integrated world, the ambition of the PRC on the international stage echoes with the sound of the globalization, cooperation and interoperability of international trade.

The two contradictory approaches reflect a lack of policy coherence in the field of cross-border data transfer that will inevitably lead to "policy failures".[271] The two contradictory approaches also reflect the uncertainty and ambiguity of the PRC's trade policies related to cross-border data transfer, implying that Chinese policymakers are not quite sure of the correct route for balancing trade development and data protection given the PRC's specific circumstances.

The cross-border data transfer legislation would not only have a significant impact on PRC's economy and its potential as a destination for international information flows but could also have a considerable impact on international trade. The area of trade is still widely fragmented in terms of distinctions between goods and services, the local and the global, trade and IP rights, and other so-called pairs of "trade and…problems".[272] Internet development and technological innovation exacerbate the "trade and…problems" at present. The Internet itself exists as a worldwide marketplace. The prosperity of Internet-based trade and commerce cannot exist without the cross-border data movement. However, the rapid growth of the Internet, particularly Internet-based trade and business, have largely outpaced the standard trade regulatory frameworks that cover most other forms of cross-border trade and business.[273]

---

[270] 'China Unveils Action Plan on BRI' (Xin Hua News, 28 March 2015). http://english.gov.cn/news/top_news/2015/03/28/content_281475079055789.htm, accessed 3 March 2021; see also Viney and others (n 246).

[271] Rostam J. Neuwirth, '"Novel Food for Thought" on Law and Policymaking in the Global Creative Economy' (2014) 37(1) European Journal of Law and Economics 13, 15.

[272] Peter F. Cowhey And Jonathan D. Aronson, 'Trade in Services Telecommunications' in Aaditya Mattoo, Robert M. Stern, and Gianni Zanini, *A Handbook of International Trade in Services* (1st edn, Oxford University Press 2008) 414.

[273] Erixon and others (n 72) 3.

Regarding the trends in digital convergence and technological innovation, there exists considerable uncertainty when applying WTO law to members' restrictions on cross-border data transfers. The uncertainty covers, for instance, the preliminary question of categorizing the restricted data as goods or services, or within which of the four modes of services data fall,[274] as well as the interpretation of the schedules of commitments and the problem of explicitly determining to which sectors of service members have made a special commitment.

The widespread adoption of digital technologies is changing the composition of trade in different categories of services and goods.[275] It is crucial to observe the interpretation and classification of WTO members' schedules of commitments in this ever-changing digital era, and "a clearer, better-structured and up-to-data classification, especially with regard to the sectors pertinent to cultural and the rapidly changing audiovisual and telecommunications areas, can be put high on the list of desiderate."[276]

Tensions between technological innovation and treaty interpretation are increasing, which creates new challenges for the negotiators of international trade agreements as well as the WTO Panel and Appellate Body. It is possible that the WTO Panel and the Appellate Body do not have the essential knowledge of fundamental matters, such as the efficiency of data transfer restriction policies for legitimate purposes, i.e., security and privacy; the commercial influence of data transfer restrictions; and the "technical feasibility and reliability of proposed alternative measures".[277] Furthermore, no international consensus on cybersecurity standards currently exists.[278] Therefore, the WTO Panel and the Appellate Body must depend on economic and technical evidence to develop future legal systems for exception clauses and their applicability to data transfer issues.[279] This lack of a consensus drives legislatures to consider substitute measures to strike a balance between the liberalization of cross-border data transfer and the preservation of security and consumer confidence.[280]

Services did not receive enough attention in the negotiations under the Doha Development Agenda.[281] In addition, since 1997, there has been no progress in improving the bound coverage of GATS commitments that have been made at the multilateral level. Current WTO treaty provisions have proven to lag behind technological innovation and commercial development and are not clear enough to regulate the barriers to cross-border data movement.[282] Several argumentative matters that hinder digital trade

---

[274] Mitchell and Hepburn (n 64) 206.

[275] WTO Trade Report 2018 (n 84) 9.

[276] Burri—Nenova and others (n 81) 384.

[277] Mitchell and Hepburn (n 64) 231.

[278] Ibid.

[279] Ibid.

[280] Selby (n 2) 231.

[281] Adlung and Mattoo (n 92) 4.

[282] Stephen J. Ezell, Robert D. Atkinson and Michelle A. Wein, 'Localization Barriers to Trade—Threat to the Global Innovation Economy,' 69 (Information Technology and Innovation Foundation, September 2013). www2.itif.org/2013-localizationbarriers-to-trade.pdf, accessed 18 March 2021.

3.3 A Comprehensive Outlook on Development

negotiations have emerged from more fundamental policy and cultural divergences, which make solution-finding processes difficult and protracted.[283]

The greater harmonization and convergence issues have been addressed in some WTO agreements, such as the GATS and the GATT, but they must be considered more carefully in the digital regime. In the context of international trade, cross-border data transfer calls for global cooperation, which will require national and regional policymakers to think less about ensuring that their regulatory models and norms are adopted globally and care more about achieving interoperability amongst different governance approaches.[284] To make governance approaches interoperable, it is necessary to find a common global language that clearly addresses controversial issues that are closely related to the implementation of cross-border data flows.

The free flow of data across borders and public policy objectives are essentially impossible to reconcile in the context of international trade liberalization, partly because different countries hold different cultural values and privacy perceptions.[285] The question regarding how to achieve a better balance between these two concepts is likely to be at the heart of debates in the legislative process regarding cross-border data transfers for the foreseeable future. To better address this issue, it is important to form a new, comprehensive outlook on development. This view has been summarized by Rostam J. Neuwirth as follows:

> It is necessary to also address the expected problems at the regulatory level in terms of the future governance of global trade now. This includes a discussion on the best ways to address the various effects of convergence at the regulatory level. So far, the discussion has produced useful insights, which can be framed by competing concepts of "regulatory diversity" versus "regulatory harmonization" or "regulatory competition" versus "regulatory cooperation" or "regulatory monopoly".[286]

The WTO cannot adapt to an increasingly interconnected and digital world. The WTO is a member-driven organization, and virtually all WTO decisions are made by consensus among all members and approved by the members' parliaments.[287] The WTO has more than 160 members, accounting for 98% of world trade. More than

---

[283] Burri, 'The Regulation of Data Flows through Trade Agreements' (n 118) 413.

[284] Susan Ariel Aaronson and Rob Maxim, 'Trade and the Internet: The Challenge of the NSA Revelations Policies in the US, EU, and Canada'. https://www2.gwu.edu/~iiep/assets/docs/papers/Aaronson_Maxim_Trade_Internet.pdf, accessed 5 April 2020; Susan Ariel Aaronson, 'Can Trade Policy Set Information Free?' (VOX, 22 December 2012). https://voxeu.org/article/trade-agreements-global-internet-governance, accessed 5 April 2021.

[285] Ravi Sarathy and Christopher J. Robertson, 'Strategic and Ethical Considerations in Managing Digital Privacy' (2003) 46 Journal of Business Ethics 111, 113; Sandra J. Milberg, Sandra J. Burke, H. Jeff Smith, and Ernest A. Kallman, 'Personal Information Privacy and Regulatory Approaches' (1995), 38(12) Communications of the ACM 65, 66–67.

[286] Rostam J. Neuwirth, 'The Creative Industries as a New Paradigm for Business and Law: of "Smart Phones" and "Smarter Regulation"' (17 Jun 2014) Fourth Biennial Global conference of the Society of International Economic Law (SIEL) Working Paper No. 2014/05, 15. https://papers.ssrn.com/sol3/papers.cfm?abstract_id=2450209, accessed 13 November 2020.

[287] 'The WTO in Brief' (n 25).

20 countries are seeking to join the WTO.[288] It is difficult to make progress on this issue in the near future.

3.4 Interim Remarks

The examination of the status and trends of the PRC's domestic legislation related to cross-border data transfers as well as its position regarding globalization and economic integration shows a paradox as the nation strives to maintain a balance between two seemingly contradictory attitudes towards cross-border data transfers. The "trade and… problems" also apply to the relationship between trade and cross-border data transfers. Considerable uncertainty exists when applying WTO law to members' restrictions on cross-border data transfers.

The members of the WTO have not reached an agreement on how to draw the line between restrictions on cross-border data flows that are protectionist and restrictive of trade and liberalization and those that are necessary to protect the human rights of citizens.[289] The synergism of international trade with cross-border data transfers cannot exist without a common language between the stakeholders. Thus, lacking the expansion of the WTO scope of barriers to trade to include cross-border data transfer issues, WTO members have made great efforts to go beyond the WTO by entering into bilateral and multilateral agreements.

---

[288] 'The WTO' (WTO website). https://www.wto.org/english/thewto_e/thewto_e.htm, accessed 6 January 2021.

[289] Panday Jyoti, 'Don't Trust Data Localization Exceptions in Trade Agreements to Guarantee Protection of Personal Data' (Electronic Frontier Foundation, 14 August 2017). https://www.eff.org/deeplinks/2017/08/rising-demands-data-localization-response-weak-data-protection-mechanisms, accessed 20 November 2020.

Chapter 4
The Regulation of Cross-Border Data Transfers in the Context of Free Trade Agreements

It is a truth barely worth repeating that the digital revolution has transformed the global economy…The vital commodity in this new digital economy is data, especially personal data.[1]

—Simon Chesterman

4.1 Overview

RTAs, which include FTAs and other regional preferential trading arrangements such as customs unions, are reciprocal trade agreements between two or more partners (not in the same region).[2] The number and influence of RTAs are increasing every year.[3] There are 343 RTAs in force,[4] and more than 100 FTAs in force have notified the GATT/WTO that they cover the topic of e-commerce until 1 April 2021.[5] Entering into RTAs is a popular approach chosen by many WTO members to deepen regional trade relations and reach a consensus on new trade issues. Currently, all WTO members have at least a regional trade agreement in force.[6]

---

[1] Simon Chesterman, *Data Protection Law in Singapore—Privacy and Sovereignty in an Interconnected World* (2nd edn, Academy Publishing 2018) 1.

[2] 'Regional Trade Agreements and Preferential Trade Arrangements' (WTO). https://www.wto.org/english/tratop_e/region_e/rta_pta_e.htm. 16 April 2021.

[3] 'Regional Trade Agreements' (WTO). https://www.wto.org/english/tratop_e/region_e/region_e.htm. Accessed 16 April 2021; Shujiro Urata, 'Globalization and the Growth in Free Trade Agreements' (2002) 9(1) Asia–Pacific Review 20, 21; Jo−Ann Crawford and Roberto V. Fiorentino, 'The Changing Landscape of Regional Trade Agreements', 1 WTO Discussion Paper NO 8 (2005). https://www.wto.org/english/res_e/booksp_e/discussion_papers8_e.pdf. Accessed 16 April 2021.

[4] 'List of all RTAs' (WTO). http://rtais.wto.org/UI/PublicAllRTAList.aspx. Accessed 23 April 2021.

[5] 109 RTAs in force have notified the GATT/WTO that they cover the topic of e−commerce until 1 April 2021. For detail, see the RTAs notified to the GATT/WTO by criteria in the WTO website.

[6] After the notification of the RTA between Mongolia and Japan in June 2016, all the WTO members have an RTA in force. 'Regional Trade Agreements' (WTO). https://rtais.wto.org/UI/PublicAllRTAList.aspx. Accessed 16 April 2021.

© The Author(s), under exclusive license to Springer Nature Singapore Pte Ltd. 2022
Y. Dai, *Cross-Border Data Transfers Regulations in the Context of International Trade Law: A PRC Perspective*, https://doi.org/10.1007/978-981-16-4995-0_4

Different jurisdictions and organizations hold different opinions of the scope and definition of digital trade. The narrowest definition is terming digital trade "trade in digitized products",[7] while a broader definition labels it "use of digital technologies to conduct business".[8] For discussion, in this paper, digital trade refers to trade in goods and services delivered via the Internet through cross-border data flows.[9] Awareness of the importance of digital trade can be traced back to international organizations in the late 1990s.[10] The inclusion of comparatively strong e-commerce chapters in the previous Trans-Pacific Partnership (TPP) has made digital trade a hot topic in the current global trade discussion.[11]

There is concern that certain forms of regulations, which seem to protect national security, personal privacy and consumer rights, are essentially disguised restrictions on trade that are intended to protect domestic business from overseas competitors.[12] First, restrictions on cross-border data flows may impede the essential operations of some foreign companies (such as financial services companies). For example, the "Great Firewall of China", together with other restrictive domestic regulations of multiple issues regarding cross-border data transfer, according to the 2016 National Trade Estimate Report of the United States, impose significant restrictions on a wide range of ICT products and services from the United States and other foreign countries with an obvious long-term goal of replacing foreign ICT products and services.[13]

The second barrier lies in policies on market access restrictions. For example, the 2015 Telecommunications Services Catalogue (Chinese title: 電信業務分類目錄),

---

[7] Shamshad Akhtar, Hongjoo Hahm, Susan F. Stone, 'Asia–Pacific Trade and Investment Report 2016' (United Nations Economic and Social Commission for Asia and the Pacific, November 2016), 104. https://www.unescap.org/sites/default/files/publications/aptir-2016-full.pdf, accessed 28 February 2021.

[8] Ibid.

[9] Susan Ariel Aaronson, '3 Ways to Safeguard the Future of Digital Trade' (World Trade Forum, 16 February 2016). https://www.weforum.org/agenda/2016/02/3-ways-to-safeguard-the-future-of-digital-trade/. Accessed 16 April 2021.

[10] At the Second Ministerial Conference in May 1998, ministers, recognizing that global e−commerce was growing and creating new opportunities for trade, adopted the Declaration on Global Electronic Commerce. WTO, 'Electronic Commerce'. https://www.wto.org/english/tratop_e/ecom_e/ecom_e.htm. Accessed 23 April 2021. In 1999, UNCTAD stipulates that: 'electronic commerce has the potential to be a major engine for trade and development on the global scale', see Akhtar, Hahm and Stone (n 7) 104.

[11] Rachael Stelly, 'KORUS Talks Provide Another Opportunity for Strengthening Digital Trade Rules' (Disco, 10 January 2018). http://www.project-disco.org/21st-century-trade/011018korus-talks-provide-another-opportunity-strengthening-digital-trade-rules/#.WpYXQWddCUk. Accessed 28 January 2021.

[12] Mark Wu, 'Digital Trade—Related Provisions in Regional Trade Agreements: Existing Models and Lessons for the Multilateral Trade System', 11 (ICTSD 2017). https://e15initiative.org/wp-content/uploads/2015/09/RTA-Exchange-Digital-Trade-Mark-Wu-Final-2.pdf. Accessed 22 October 2021.

[13] USTR, 'The 2016 National Trade Estimate Report' (USTR, 2016) 84. https://ustr.gov/si-tes/default/files/2016-NTE-Report-FINAL.pdf, accessed 23 February 2021.

4.1 Overview

released by the MIIT of the PRC, imposed licensing requirements for basic telecommunications services[14] and value-added telecommunications services,[15] which might increase the burden on foreign companies.[16]

Third, governments may impose digital customs duties on a packet of data. In the Geneva Ministerial Declaration on global e-commerce,[17] WTO members agreed not to impose customs duties on electronic transmissions and recognized the need to establish a comprehensive work programme to examine all trade-related issues associated with global e-commerce in the Geneva Ministerial Declaration on Global Electronic Commerce.[18] In addition, the WTO General Council adopted the Work Programme on Electronic Commerce (WTO E-commerce Programme) to "establish a comprehensive work programme to examine all trade issues relating to global electronic commerce".[19] In January 2019, 76 WTO members announced their intention to launch "negotiations on trade-related aspects of electronic commerce".[20] However, the scope of these e-commerce negotiations needs to be further defined. The WTO E-commerce Programme has not progressed much because the WTO members cannot reach consensus on a wide variety of issues. Several countries, for instance, Thailand, Canada, and Philippines are planning to extend their Value Added Tax/Goods and Services Tax laws to the consumption of cross-border digital services.[21]

Finally, governments may require software companies, network-equipment makers and other digital and electronic suppliers to disclose their source code or proprietary algorithms to their competitors or for review by national authorities.[22] In 2018, Reuters reported that Russian authorities required software companies such as McAfee, SAP, and Symantec to disclose their source code for review, which potentially jeopardizes the security of computer networks.[23]

---

[14] Telecommunications Services Catalogue of PRC (Chinese title: 電信業務分類目錄) (2015), Chap. A. (MIIT, 28 December 2015). https://www.cttic.cn/info/2376. Accessed 27 March 2021.

[15] Ibid, Chap. A and Chap. B.

[16] Because foreign companies have to establish partnerships with local companies to acquire an Internet content provider (ICP) license. 'MIIT Releases 2015 Telecoms Catalogue' (Thomson Reuters, January 2016). https://uk.practicallaw.thomsonreuters.com/6-621-8165?transitionType=Default&contextData=(sc.Default)&firstPage=true&bhcp=1. Accessed 27 March 2021.

[17] The declaration was adopted on 20 May 1998. See WTO, 'The Geneva Ministerial Declaration on Global Electronic Commerce' (25 May 1998) WT/MIN (98)/DEC/2 (98–2148). https://www.wto.org/english/tratop_e/ecom_e/mindec1_e.htm. Accessed 10 March 2021.

[18] Ibid.

[19] 'Electronic Commerce' (WTO General Council, 25 September 1998) WT/L/274, Art. 1.1. https://www.wto.org/english/tratop_e/ecom_e/ecom_e.htm. Accessed 10 March 2021.

[20] 'DG Azevêdo meets ministers in Davos: discussions focus on reform; progress on e−commerce' (WTO, 25 January 2019). https://www.wto.org/english/news_e/news19_e/dgra_25jan19_e.htm. Accessed 31 March 2021.

[21] Taxamo, 'Digital Tax Trends: International Plans to Tax the Digital Economy' (Taxamo, 27 October 2020). https://www.taxamo.com/insights/international-digital-tax-trends/. Accessed 10 March 2021.

[22] Mark Wu (n 12) 2.

[23] Dustin Volz, Joel Schectman, Jack Stubbs, 'Insight−Tech Firms Let Russia Probe Software Widely Used by U.S. Government' (Reuters, 25 January 2018). https://www.reuters.com/article/usa-cyber-russia/insight-tech-firms-let-russia-probe-software-widely-used-by-u-s-government-idUSL1N1OD2GV. Accessed 19 March 2021.

In recent years, increasing numbers of trade agreements have gradually included language preventing jurisdictions from adopting the cross-border data transfer restrictions mentioned above. The first such prohibition appears in the previous TPP,[24] for example, prevents parties from imposing customs duties on electronic transmissions,[25] and requiring the review of the source code for imported products.[26] Similar provisions are included in the modernized United States–Mexico–Canada Agreement (USMCA),[27] EU–UK Trade and Cooperation Agreement,[28] and the CPTPP.[29] In addition to trade agreements, on 19 June 2018, the European Parliament, Council and the European Commission reached a political agreement on a provisional political agreement that will allow personal data to be stored and processed across the EU without unjustified restrictions.[30]

The ability of data to freely and efficiently flow across borders, without being restricted by technical barriers or anti-competitive bottlenecks, is a precondition for the success and viability of digital trade.[31] Therefore, in recent years, many RTAs—especially FTAs—have attempted to establish a new legal landscape for cross-border data flows by compensating somewhat for the fragmented national rules on data and the availability of online information as well as overcoming the problems under WTO law.[32]

---

[24] Trans–Pacific Partnership (hereinafter: TPP), Art. 14.3 and 14.17. See 'Consolidated TPP Text' (Government of Canada). https://www.international.gc.ca/trade-commerce/trade-agreements-accords-commerciaux/agr-acc/tpp-ptp/text-texte/toc-tdm.aspx?lang=eng. Accessed 19 March 2021.

[25] Ibid, Art. 14.3.

[26] Ibid, Art. 14.17.

[27] In September 2018, the United States, Mexico, and Canada reached a new agreement called the United States–Mexico–Canada Agreement (USMCA) to replace the North American Free Trade Agreement (NAFTA). The USMCA entered into force on 1 July 2020. See 'U.S.–Mexico–Canada Agreement (USMCA)' (U.S. Customs and Border Protection). https://www.cbp.gov/trade/priority-issues/trade-agreements/free-trade-agreements/USMCA. Accessed 9 March 2021.

[28] EU–UK Trade and Cooperation Agreement (TCA), Art. DIGIT. 8 and 12, see 'Trade and Cooperation Agreement Between The European Union and The European Atomic Energy Community, of The One Part, and The United Kingdom of Great Britain and Northern Ireland, of The Other Part' (EUR–Lex). https://eur-lex.europa.eu/legal-content/EN/TXT/PDF/?uri=CELEX:22020A1231(01)&from=EN. Accessed 9 April 2021.

[29] CPTPP, Art 14.3, see 'Comprehensive and Progressive Agreement for Trans–Pacific Partnership text and resources' (New Zealand Foreign Affair and Trade). https://www.mfat.govt.nz/en/trade/free-trade-agreements/free-trade-agreements-in-force/comprehensive-and-progressive-agreement-for-trans-pacific-partnership-cptpp/comprehensive-and-progressive-agreement-for-trans-pacific-partnership-text-and-resources/. Accessed 16 March 2021.

[30] European Community, 'Digital Single Market: EU Negotiators Reach a Political Agreement on Free Flow of Non–Personal Data' (EC Press Release, 19 June 2018). https://ec.europa.eu/commission/presscorner/detail/en/IP_18_4227. Accessed 22 March 2021; EC, 'Free Flow of Non–Personal Data' (EC Policies, 10 March 2021). https://ec.europa.eu/digital-single-market/en/free-flow-non-personal-data. Accessed 22 March 2021.

[31] 'Trade in the Digital Economy—A Primer on Global Data Flows for Policymakers', 2 (International Chamber of Commerce Homepage, 19 July 2016). https://iccwbo.org/publication/trade-inthe-digital-economy, accessed 19 March 2021.

[32] James Manyika and others, 'Digital globalization: The New Era of Global Flows' (Mckinsey Global Institute, February 2016), 30–32. https://www.mckinsey.com/business-functions/digital-mckinsey/our-insights/digital-globalization-the-new-era-of-global-flows, accessed 19 December 2020.

4.2 FTAs and Cross-border Data Transfers

4.2.1 General Remarks

In the beginning, trade agreements mainly dealt with border issues such as tariffs and quotas.[33] Since the 1970s, the content of trade agreements has expanded and gradually involved domestic regulatory issues such as health and safety.[34] Henrik Horn, Petros Mavroidis and André Sapir examined 28 agreements signed by the EU and the United States between 1992 and 2008 and identified 52 policy areas in provisions in one or more RTAs, ranging from anti-corruption, money laundering, data protection, and environmental protection to nuclear safety and terrorism.[35] Currently, an increasing number of countries and regions struggle to conclude so-called "comprehensive agreements"[36] that aim to further increase trade facilitation and maximize the scope of FTAs by embracing some less typical trade issues such as IP protection and cross-border data flow facilitation.

Trade facilitation is a term for actions taken by governments to enable international trade to function smoothly. The UN Economic Commission for Europe has defined it as follows:

> Trade facilitation to encompass the systematic rationalisation of procedures and documentation for international trade, where trade procedures are the activities, practices and formalities involved in collecting, presenting, communicating and processing data required for the movement of goods in international trade.[37]

Trade liberalization has traditionally been recognized as comprising four kinds of freedom: the free movement of goods, services, capital, and persons.[38] As data become essential capital of international digital trade, a fifth freedom should be added

---

[33] Susan Ariel Aaronson and Miles D. Townes, 'Can Trade Policy Set Information Free?' (June 2014) Institute for International Economic Policy Working Paper Series, 4. https://www2.gwu.edu/~iiep/assets/docs/papers/2014WP/AaronsonIIEPWP20149.pdf. Accessed 11 March 2021; Dani Rodrik, 'What Do Trade Agreements Really Do?' (Revised February 2018) 32(2) Journal of Economic Perspectives 73, 76. https://drodrik.scholar.harvard.edu/files/dani-rodrik/files/what_do_trade_agreements_really_do.pdf. Accessed 21 April 2021.

[34] Aaronson and Townes (n 33) 4.

[35] Henrik Horn and others, 'Beyond the WTO: An Anatomy of the EU and US Preferential Trade Agreements' (2010) 33 The World Economy 1565, 1571 and 1577–1579.

[36] Aaronson and Townes (n 33) 4.

[37] Walter Goode, 'Negotiating Free−Trade Agreements: A Guide' (Commonwealth of Australia, 2005) 58. https://www.apec.org/-/media/APEC/Publications/2005/12/Negotiating-Free-Trade-Agreements-A-Guide-2005/2005_negotiating_free_trade_agreement_a_guide.pdf. Accessed 23 March 2021.

[38] Dan Ciuriak and Maria Ptashkina, 'The Digital Transformation and the Transformation of International Trade' (2018) RTA Exchange. Geneva: International Centre for Trade and Sustainable Development (ICTSD) and the Inter−American Development Bank (IDB), 1. http://e15initiative.org/wp-content/uploads/2015/09/RTA-Exchange-Digital-Trade-Ciuriak-and-Ptashkina-Final.pdf. Accessed 17 March 2021.

to the list: the free movement of data is an irresistible trend.[39] For example, the aim of the EU's Digital Single Market (DSM) Strategy is to guarantee the free movement of goods, persons, services, capital, and data.[40]

Most countries and regions in the world have different priorities for public policy objectives (e.g., privacy, national security, and environmental protection) and trade. Data and e-commerce regulations are mostly disaggregated worldwide and thus call for global collaboration.[41] Since cross-border data flows are an integral part of international trade, trade agreements have begun to regulate data.[42] Several measures have been taken to internationalize policy mechanisms for e-commerce and data flows. These measures include the EU's DSM initiative, embracing standalone chapters in trade agreements (e.g., the e-commerce chapter in the previous TPP), and adopting initiatives to strengthen the work plan at the WTO following the ministerial conference in Buenos Aires in December 2017.[43] In addition, entering into FTAs is apparently a good starting point for global collaboration on cross-border data flows.[44] In general, issues related to cross-border data flows are mainly fragmented across in the following chapters of FTAs: (1) e-commerce chapters; (2) chapters on the financial services sector; (3) chapters on economic and technical cooperation; (4) chapters on freedom, security, and justice; and (5) IP chapters.

---

[39] Communication from the Commission to the European Parliament, The Council, The European Economic and Social Committee and The Committee of The Regions—A Digital Single Market Strategy for Europe {SWD (2015) 100 final}' (EC Brussels). https://eur-lex.europa.eu/legal-content/EN/TXT/PDF/?uri=CELEX:52015DC0192&from=EN. Accessed 21 April 2021; 'Shaping the Digital Single Market' (EC) https://ec.europa.eu/digital-single-market/en/shaping-digital-single-market. Accessed 21 March 2020.

[40] 'Communication from the Commission to the European Parliament, The Council, The European Economic and Social Committee and the Committee of the Regions—A Digital Single Market Strategy for Europe {SWD (2015) 100 final}' (n 39); 'Shaping the Digital Single Market' (n 39).

[41] Mira Burri, 'Regulation of Data Flows through Trade Agreements' (2017) 48 Georgetown Journal of International Law 407, 409; UNCTAD, 'Summary of Adoption of E—Commerce Legislation Worldwide'. http://unctad.org/en/Pages/DTL/STI_and_ICTs/ICT4D-Legislation/eCom-Global-Legislation.aspx. Accessed 23 April 2021.

[42] Dan Ciuriak, 'Digital Trade–Is Data Treaty—Ready?', 1 (CIGI Papers, February 2018). https://www.cigionline.org/sites/default/files/documents/Paper%20no.162web.pdf. Accessed 16 March 2021.

[43] Ibid, 2.

[44] Neha Mishra, 'International Trade, Internet Governance and the Shaping of the Digital Economy' (June 2017) ARTNeT Working Paper Series, No. 168, Bangkok, ESCAP, 5. https://papers.ssrn.com/sol3/papers.cfm?abstract_id=2997254. Accessed 1 March 2021; Burri, 'The Regulation of Data Flows through Trade Agreements' (n 41) 417.

4.2.2 E-Commerce Chapters

4.2.2.1 The Development of E-Commerce Chapters in FTAs

The WTO rules for the development of digital trade have been outdated since many contentious issues from the WTO e-commerce programme remain.[45] This situation did not change with the Eleventh WTO Ministerial Conference in Buenos Aires.[46] Then, many WTO members turned to preferential trade agreements negotiated bilaterally, regionally or between country groups.[47] In most cases, the content of the e-commerce chapters in RTA/ FTAs can be considered WTO plus because WTO has no multilateral or plurilateral agreement in this area at present.[48] Most of the e-commerce chapters include binding commitments such as a promise that not to impose tariffs on electronic transmissions.[49]

Provisions governing e-commerce can be integrated into the main body, non-specific articles or a standalone chapter of an RTA. Provisions governing e-commerce can also be found in attached documents, such as a joint statement, letter or annex.[50]

The first FTA to address the e-commerce issue was the United States-Jordan FTA (entered into force on 15 January 2002), Article 7 of which focuses on e-commerce and applies to electronic transmissions, digitized products and electronic means of services.[51] Instead of a standalone chapter, the United States-Jordan FTA includes only limited articles about commerce, and a definition of e-commerce is absent. The Singapore-Australia FTA (SAFTA), which entered into force on 28 July 2003,

---

[45] 'Electronic Commerce' (n 19).

[46] The Eleventh Ministerial Conference (MC11) ended with a number of ministerial decisions, including e−commerce duties, and a commitment to continue negotiations in all areas. However, there was no agreement on a Ministerial Declaration. The Ministerial Conference outcome was a Chair's Statement on her own responsibility. 'Eleventh WTO Ministerial Conference', Buenos Aires, Argentina 2017. https://www.wto.org/english/thewto_e/minist_e/mc11_e/mc11_e.htm. Accessed 31 March 2021.

[47] Ciuriak and Ptashkina (n 38) 1; Mark Wu (n 12) 1.

[48] Carlos Kuriyama and Divya Sangaraju, 'Trends and Developments in Provisions and Outcomes of RTA/FTAs Implemented in 2016 by APEC Economies', 2 (APEC Policy Support Unit, October 2017). https://www.apec.org/-/media/APEC/Publications/2018/12/Trends-and-Developments-in-Provisions-and-Outcomes-of-RTA-FTAs/218_PSU_Trends-and-Developments-in-Provisions-and-Outcomes-of-RTA-FTAs.pdf. Accessed 16 March 2021.

[49] Kuriyama and Sangaraju (n 48).

[50] José−Antonio Monteiro and Robert Teh, 'Provisions on Electronic Commerce in Regional Trade Agreements', 12 WTO Working Paper ERSD−2017–11 (WTO Economic Research and Statistics Division, July 2017). https://www.econstor.eu/bitstream/10419/163426/1/894047426.pdf. Accessed 27 March 2021.

[51] United States−Jordan FTA, Art. 7.1(a) (b) (c), 'Agreement between the United States of America and the Hashemite Kingdom of Jordan on the Establishment of a Free Trade Area' (United States Department of Commerce International Trade Administration). https://tcc.export.gov/Trade_Agreements/All_Trade_Agreements/exp_005607.asp. Accessed 27 March 2020.

served as the first FTA that contains an explicit standalone chapter to address e-commerce issues.[52] The SAFTA clearly defines the terms "electronic transmission" or "transmitted electronically" and "electronic version of a document", thus covering much broader issues than previous FTAs.[53] Categories covered by the SAFTA include a commitment to transparency and the reduction of trade barriers in e-commerce as well as a moratorium on duties for digital products.[54] The SAFTA also addresses issues such as electronic authentication and electronic signature, online consumer protection, online personal data protection and paperless trading.[55] The SAFTA is a pioneer in many aspects – it not only is the first FTA to contain a standalone e-commerce chapter but also covers a broad scope of, even by current standards, pressing issues in e-commerce and offers a considerably more detailed regulation of these issues than previous agreements.[56] The SAFTA was amended in 2017, and the modified version entered into force on 1 December 2017.[57]

An indispensable precondition for the success and smooth operation of e-commerce is the free and efficient flow of information across borders. However, the scope and depth of commitments related to cross-border data transfers in different FTAs vary greatly. The FTA between the United States and South Korea (KORUS FTA), which entered into force on 15 May 2012, was the first FTA to contain language related to the free flow of data across borders.[58] Subsequently, many other FTAs have included provisions related to this issue. Therefore, the following paragraphs use 2012 as a point in time to review all FTAs that have entered into force since then with an eye towards identifying those FTAs that touch upon e-commerce-relevant issues or have provisions specifically addressing issues of cross-border data flow.

The structure of e-commerce provisions differs widely in different FTAs, even among those negotiated by the same country.[59] At present, 62 FTAs with e-commerce provisions have entered into force since 2012.[60] Among them, 56 FTAs have

---

[52] Singapore–Australia FTA, Chap. 14, 'Singapore–Australia FTA' (Australian Government Department of Home Affairs). https://dfat.gov.au/trade/agreements/in-force/safta/official-documents/Pages/default.aspx. Accessed 23 March 2021.

[53] Ibid, Chap. 14 Art. 1.

[54] Ibid, Chap. 14.

[55] Ibid.

[56] Rolf H. Weber, 'The Expansion of E–Commerce in Asia–Pacific Trade Agreements' (ICTSD, 10 September 2015). https://e15initiative.org/blogs/the-expansion-of-e-commerce-in-asia-pacific-trade-agreements/. Accessed 10 January 2021.

[57] 'Singapore–Australia FTA' (Australian Government Department of Home Affairs). https://dfat.gov.au/trade/agreements/in-force/safta/official-documents/Pages/default.aspx. Accessed 23 March 2021.

[58] WTO RTA Database Homepage. http://rtais.wto.org/ui/PublicMaintainRTAHome.aspx. Accessed 1 March 2018; see also 'KORUS FTA Final Text' (Office of the United States Trade Representative). https://ustr.gov/trade-agreements/free-trade-agreements/korus-fta/final-text. Accessed 18 March 2021.

[59] Monteiro and Teh (n 50) 12.

[60] For detail of these FTAs, see Chap. 1, footnote 17.

4.2 FTAs and Cross-border Data Transfers

established a standalone chapter; the exceptions are the PRC-Georgia FTA, EU-Ghana FTA, Chile-Thailand FTA, Turkey-Malaysia FTA, EU-Eastern and Southern Africa States FTA, and EFTA-Central America (Costa Rica and Panama) FTA.[61] E-commerce is mentioned only once in the EU-Ghana FTA.[62] In the PRC-Georgia FTA, Chile-Thailand FTA and Turkey-Malaysia FTA, e-commerce provisions are included in the economic cooperation chapter.[63] Instead of appearing in the main body of the RTA, e-commerce provisions are found in the annex of the EU-Eastern and Southern Africa States FTA, and EFTA-Central America (Costa Rica and Panama) FTA.[64] Most of these 62 FTAs address, albeit to varying degrees, some of the issues that remain from the WTO E-commerce Programme.[65]

---

[61] fter going through contents of all these 62 FTAs, I made such a conclusion. 'Search criteria: Main Topics Covered: E−Commerce' (WTO FTA database Homepage). http://rtais.wto.org/ui/PublicMaintainRTAHome.aspx. Accessed 23 April 2021.

[62] Article 44 of EU−Ghana FTA says that 'Building on the Cotonou Agreement, the Parties will cooperate to facilitate all the necessary measures leading to the conclusion as soon as possible of a global EPA between the whole West Africa region and the EC in the following: (a) trade in services and electronic commerce…', see also 'Stepping stone Economic Partnership Agreement between Ghana, of the One Part, and the European Community and its Member States, of the Other Part' (EUR−lex). https://eur-lex.europa.eu/legal-content/EN/TXT/?uri=uriserv:OJ.L_.2016.287.01.0003.01.ENG&toc=OJ:L:2016:287:TOC. Accessed 19 March 2021.

[63] E−commerce is regulated under the 'Chapter 12 Areas of Cooperation' of the PRC−Georgia FTA, 'Chapter 11 Economic Cooperation' of Chile−Thailand FTA, and 'Chapter 9 Economic and Technical Cooperation' of Turkey−Malaysia FTA. See 'Free Trade Agreement between the Government of the Republic of Chile and the Government of the Kingdom of Thailand'. http://www.sice.oas.org/Trade/CHL_THA_Final/Table_of_content_e.pdf. Accessed 12 November 2020; 'Free Trade Agreement between the Government of Malaysia and the Government of the Republic of Turkey' https://fta.miti.gov.my/miti-fta/resources/Malaysia%20-%20Turkey/MTFTA_Main_Agreement.pdf. Accessed 18 March 2021; see also 'Free Trade Agreement between The Government of the PRC and the Government of Georgia' (PRC FTA Network). http://fta.mofcom.gov.cn/georgia/annex/xdzw_en.pdf. Accessed 17 March 2021.

[64] E−commerce is mentioned only once under Annex IV of EU−Eastern and Southern Africa States FTA, which stipulates that: 'development of regional markets, harmonization of policies, strengthening of fiscal administrations and policy, macroeconomic stability, trade facilitation, harmonization of standards, enforcement and arbitration, facilitate movement of people, goods and services, and capital; and establish and invest in regional institutions and structures Activities could be:… (ii) Facilitate trade in services and right of establishment and movement of goods, services, capital and people and support to exploit fully transboundary opportunities, improve coordination, cooperation and communication including support for e−commerce…' EFTA−Central America (Costa Rica and Panama) FTA has established the framework of e−commerce in Article 1 of "Annex II Referred To In Article 1.8 Regarding Electronic Commerce". See 'Interim Agreement establishing a framework for an Economic Partnership Agreement between the Eastern and Southern Africa States, on the One Part, and the European Community and its Member States, on the Other Part' (EUR−Lex). https://eur-lex.europa.eu/legal-content/EN/TXT/?qid=1398352746247&uri=CELEX:22012A0424(01). Accessed 19 March 2021. See also 'EFTA−Central America (Costa Rica and Panama) FTA' (EFTA). https://www.efta.int/free-trade/Free-Trade-Agreement/Central-American-States. Accessed 19 March 2021.

[65] 'Work Programme on Electronic Commerce', WTO Doc. WT/L/274 (WTO General Council, 30 September 1998). https://view.officeapps.live.com/op/view.aspx?src=https%3A%2F%2Fdocsonline.wto.org%2Fdol2fe%2FPages%2FFormerScriptedSearch%2Fdirectdoc.aspx%3FDDFDocuments%2Ft%2FWT%2FL%2F274.DOC, accessed 27 March 2021.

Although the *US-Gambling* case clarified that the GATS applies to digital services, the applicability of the WTO rules and commitments to electronically traded services has not yet been confirmed at the negotiation table.[66] Some of these 62 FTAs fill this gap by confirming the applicability of the WTO rules to e-commerce. For example, when defining the terms of digital products, the Japan-Australia FTA treats digital products delivered offline and online equally without discrimination.[67] The Hong Kong, China-Georgia FTA,[68] EU-Japan FTA,[69] the CPTPP,[70] EU-Canada FTA,[71] Canada-Honduras FTA,[72] Korea, Republic of-Colombia FTA,[73] PRC-Australia FTA,[74] Canada-Korea, Republic of FTA,[75] Costa Rica-Singapore

---

[66] Sacha Wunsch–Vincent, 'Trade Rules for the Digital Age' in Marion Panizzon, Nicole Pohl and Pierre Sauvé and others, *GATS and the Regulation of International Trade in Services* (Cambridge University Press 2008) 24; Mira Burri, 'Should There Be New Multilateral Rules for Digital Trade?', 3 (International Centre for Trade and Sustainable Development (ICTSD) December 2013). http://e15initiative.org/publications/should-there-be-new-multilateral-rules-for-digital-trade/. Accessed 27 March 2021.

[67] Japan–Australia FTA, Art. 13.4, see 'Agreement between Japan and Australia for an Economic Partnership' (Ministry of Foreign Affairs of Japan). https://www.mofa.go.jp/ecm/ep/page22e_000430.html. Accessed 16 March 2021.

[68] Hong Kong, China–Georgia FTA, Chap. 9 Art.1, 'Free Trade Agreement between Hong Kong, China and Georgia' (HK Trade and Industry Department Homepage). https://www.tid.gov.hk/english/ita/fta/hkgefta/text_agreement.html. Accessed 18 March 2021.

[69] EU–Japan FTA, Art. 8.7(3), see 'Council Decision (EU) 2018/1907 of 20 December 2018 on the conclusion of the Agreement between the European Union and Japan for an Economic Partnership' (Official Journal of the European Union, 27 December 2018). http://publications.europa.eu/resource/cellar/5805924c-09a3-11e9-81b4-01aa75ed71a1.0006.01/DOC_1. Accessed 16 March 2021.

[70] CPTTP, Art. 14.4.

[71] EU–Canada FTA, Art. 16.2.1, see 'Joint Interpretative Instrument on the Comprehensive Economic and Trade Agreement (CETA) between Canada and the European Union and its Member States' (Council of the European Union). http://data.consilium.europa.eu/doc/document/ST-13541-2016-INIT/en/pdf. Accessed 16 March 2021.

[72] Canada–Honduras FTA, Art. 16.2, see 'Free Trade Agreement between Canada and the Republic of Honduras' (Asia Regional Integration Center). http://www.sice.oas.org/TPD/CAN_HND/Texts_FTA_05.11.2013/ENG/Index_Final1013_e.asp. Accessed 16 March 2021.

[73] Korea, Republic of–Colombia FTA, Art. 12.1.1, see 'Free Trade Agreement between the Republic of Colombia and the Republic of Korea' (Ministry of Trade Industry and Energy). http://www.sice.oas.org/TPD/Col_kor/Draft_Text_06.2012_e/June_2012_Index_PDF_e.asp. Accessed 16 March 2021.

[74] The PRC–Australia FTA, Art. 12.1.1.

[75] Canada–Korea, Republic of FTA, Art. 13.2.1, see 'Free Trade Agreement between Canada and the Republic of Korea' (Government of Canada). https://www.international.gc.ca/trade-commerce/trade-agreements-accords-commerciaux/agr-acc/korea-coree/fta-ale/index.aspx?lang=eng. Accessed 16 March 2021.

4.2 FTAs and Cross-border Data Transfers

FTA,[76] Malaysia-Australia FTA,[77] and United States-Panama FTA[78] all have similar provisions.

Differentiating services from goods based on the existing WTO treaty provisions is not easy; it is a question that has caused many disputes in the WTO E-commerce Programme and remains unsettled.[79] The EU-Colombia and Peru FTA, EU-Georgia FTA, EU-Ukraine FTA, EU-Moldova, Republic of FTA, and FTA between the Gulf Cooperation Council (GCC) and Singapore all have similar provisions stipulating that deliveries by electronic means or electronic transmissions are or shall be categorized as the provision of services within the scope of the chapter on cross-border supply of services.[80]

In addition, some of these 62 FTAs clearly define several concepts closely related to digital trade.[81] Moreover, several of these 62 FTAs contain provisions related to a moratorium on duties for electronic transmissions, an issue that was not touched upon by the WTO E-commerce Programme. For instance, the United States-Colombia FTA states that nothing in the e-commerce chapter shall be construed as preventing a party from imposing internal taxes or other internal charges on the domestic sale of digital products, provided that such taxes or charges are collected in a manner consistent

---

[76] Costa Rica–Singapore FTA, Art. 12.1.1, 'see Singapore–Costa Rica Free Trade Agreement' (Asia Regional Integration Center). www.sice.oas.org/Trade/CRI_SGP_FTA/Text_Apr2010_e/CRI_SGP_ToC_e.asp. Accessed 16 March 2021.

[77] Malaysia–Australia FTA, Art. 15.1, see 'Malaysia–Australia Free Trade Agreement' (Malaysia National Trade Repository). https://fta.miti.gov.my/miti-fta/resources/Malaysia-Australia/MAFTA.pdf. Accessed 16 March 2021.

[78] United States–Panama FTA, Art. 14.1.1, see 'U.S.–Panama Trade Promotion Agreement' (International Trade Administration, U.S. Department of Commerce Homepage). https://2016.export.gov/FTA/panama/. Accessed 16 March 2021.

[79] WTO Panel Report, 'Canada–Certain Measures Concerning Periodicals', WTO Doc. WT/DS31/R, paras. 3.24 and 3.26 (14 March 1997). https://docs.wto.org/dol2fe/Pages/SS/directdoc.aspx?filename=Q:/WT/DS/31R.pdf&Open=True, accessed 27 December 2020.

[80] Monteiro and Teh (n 50) 19.

[81] For instance, Eurasian Economic Union–Viet Nam FTA clearly defines the term of digital certificate, electronic commerce, electronic document, digital signature, electronic technologies, electronic authentication (Art. 13.2); Korea, Republic of–Colombia FTA defines the terms of personal data and trade administration documents (Art. 12.8); Japan–Mongolia FTA defines the terms of digital products, electronic certificate and electronic signature (Art. 9.2); the PRC–Australia FTA defines the terms of digital certificates, electronic signature, electronic version, personal information, trade administration documents, unsolicited commercial electronic message, and electronic signature (Art. 12.2); the PRC–Korea, Republic of FTA defines the terms of electronic authentication, electronic signature, data message, trade administration documents (Art. 13.8); Korea, Republic of–Viet Nam FTA defines the terms of digital certificates, electronic signature and trade administration documents (Art. 10.9).

with the agreement.[82] The Canada-Honduras FTA,[83] Canada-Ukraine FTA,[84] Korea, Republic of-Colombia FTA,[85] Korea, Republic of-Viet Nam FTA,[86] Canada-Korea, Republic of FTA,[87] Korea, Republic of-Australia FTA,[88] and Singapore-Chinese Taipei FTA[89] have regulations on this issue similar to those of the United States-Colombia FTA.

In addition, the e-commerce chapters of some FTAs, such as the Japan-Australia FTA, United States-Singapore FTA, and Singapore-Chinese Taipei FTA, ensure both the MFN principle and the NT principle for digital products trade. Discrimination is banned for digital products that are created, produced, published, stored, transmitted, contracted for, commissioned, or provided for the first time on commercial terms outside the region or whose author, performer, producer, developer, or distributor is a person of another party or a non-party.[90]

In conclusion, several issues that remain from the WTO E-commerce Programme, including definitions of concepts related to e-commerce, the applicability of the WTO rules and commitments to electronically traded services, the moratorium on duties for electronic transmissions, and classification issues (good or service?), have been compensated for by FTAs in recent years.

---

[82] United States—Colombia FTA, Art. 15.1.2, see 'Government of the United States of America and the Government of the Republic of Colombia Agreement' (International Trade Administration, U.S. Department of Commerce). https://www.federalregister.gov/documents/2019/11/20/2019-25288/agreement-between-the-government-of-the-united-states-of-america-and-the-government-of-the-republic. Accessed 16 March 2021.

[83] Canada—Honduras FTA, Art. 16.3.2.

[84] Canada—Ukraine FTA, Art. 8.2.1, see 'Text of the Canada–Ukraine Free Trade Agreement –Table of contents' (Government of Canada). https://international.gc.ca/trade-commerce/trade-agreements-accords-commerciaux/agr-acc/ukraine/text-texte/toc-tdm.aspx?lang=eng. Accessed 18 March 2021.

[85] Korea, Republic of—Colombia FTA, Art. 12.2.2.

[86] Korea, Republic of—Viet Nam FTA, Art. 10.2.2, see 'The Korea—Viet Nam Free Trade Agreement' (Vietnam Chamber of Commerce and Industry). https://wtocenter.vn/chuyen-de/12689-vkfta-full-content. Accessed 19 March 2021.

[87] Canada—Korea, Republic of FTA, Art. 13.3.2.

[88] Korea, Republic of—Australia FTA, Art. 15.1, see 'The Korea–Australia Free Trade Agreement' (Australian Government Department of Foreign Affairs and Trade). https://dfat.gov.au/trade/agreements/in-force/kafta/official-documents/Pages/full-text-of-kafta.aspx. Accessed 18 March 2021.

[89] Singapore—Chinese Taipei FTA, Art. 11.3.3, see 'Agreement between Singapore and the Separate Customs Territory of Taiwan, Penghu, Kinmen and Matsu on Economic Partnership' (ECA/FTA). http://fta.trade.gov.tw/ftapage.asp?k=2&p=9&n=456&a=329. Accessed 18 March 2021.

[90] United States—Singapore FTA, Art. 14.3; Japan—Australia FTA Art. 13.4; Singapore—Chinese Taipei FTA, Art. 11.4.

4.2.2.2 United States-Involved FTAs after 2012

The regulatory landscape for digital trade has been substantially influenced by FTAs, particularly by those in which the United States is involved.[91] The United States is the pioneer in linking cross-border data flows with trade policies. It is not only the first nation to embrace provisions related to cross-border data flows in its trade agreements but also the first to use trade policies to govern cross-border data flows.[92]

Since 2000, each FTA in which the United States is involved has contained a standalone chapter regulating e-commerce.[93] At present, four FTAs in which the United States is involved have entered into force since 2012, namely, the USMCA, the United States-Panama FTA, United States-Colombia FTA, and KORUS FTA. The KORUS FTA, which entered into force on 15 May 2012, is the first FTA to contain explicit language related to the free flow of information across borders.[94] The United States-Panama FTA also has provisions on cross-border data flows.[95] The United States is clearly the major driver of using trade agreements to facilitate and govern cross-border data flows.[96] However, both of these statements lack operability and proper deterrents to ensure the free flows of information between trading partners and lack of legitimate exception clauses for the free flow of information. The commitments made to cross-border data flows in these FTAs take the form of soft rather than hard binding.

The previous TPP changes this situation and turns the soft language of the KORUS FTA and the United States-Panama FTA on cross-border data flows into a hard rule. The previous TPP required members to guarantee the free flow of information across borders by electronic means, including personal information, for service suppliers

---

[91] Mira Burri, 'Symposium—Future—Proofing Law: From Rdna to Robots the Governance of Data and Data Flows in Trade Agreements: The Pitfalls of Legal Adaptation' (November 2017) 51 U.C. Davis Law Review 65, 99.

[92] Susan Ariel Aaronson, 'The Digital Trade Imbalance and Its Implications for Internet Governance' (April 2016) Institute for International Economic Policy Working Paper Series IIEP—WP—2016—7, 11. https://www2.gwu.edu/~iiep/assets/docs/papers/2016WP/AaronsonIIEP WP2016-7.pdf. Accessed 27 May 2021.

[93] Brian Bieron and Usman Ahmed, 'Regulating E—commerce through International Policy: Understanding the International Trade Law Issues of E—commerce' (2012) 46(3) Journal of World Trade 545, 545.

[94] Article 15.8 of the KORUS FTA says that 'the Parties shall endeavor to refrain from imposing or maintaining unnecessary barriers to electronic information flows across borders'. Annex 13—B, Sect. A. of the KORUS FTA says that 'each Party shall allow a financial institution of the other Party to transfer information in electronic or other form, into and out of its territory, for data processing where such processing is required in the institution's ordinary course of business'. See US—Korea FTA, (Office of the United States Representative). https://ustr.gov/trade-agreements/free-trade-agr eements/korus-fta/final-text. Accessed 27 March 2021.

[95] Article 14.5(c) of the United States—Panama FTA set that 'recognizing the global nature of electronic commerce, the Parties affirm the importance of... (c) working to maintain cross—border flows of information as an essential element in fostering a vibrant environment for electronic commerce'.

[96] Aaronson (n 92) 14.

and investors as part of their business activity.[97] The scope of this provision is broad and tends to cover most data that are transferred over the Internet.[98] Specifically, it imposes limits on the extent of data protection regulation that member countries can provide in their national laws.[99]

Since the previous TPP clearly prohibited data localization measures and contained a binding norm on free data flows with a potentially broad scope of application, when parties adopt data localization policies, other parties may claim that these policies are erecting barriers to Internet-related trade.[100] The renamed CPTPP incorporates, by reference, provisions from the previous TPP with the exception of some provisions to be suspended when the CPTPP enters into force.[101] In addition, the ongoing negotiations for the Trade in Services Agreement (TiSA) and the Transatlantic Trade and Investment Partnership (TTIP) have proposed personal data issues.[102] The United States, with Japan and Canada, advocates that:

> No Party may prevent a service supplier of another Party from transferring, accessing processing or storing information, including personal information, within or outside the Party's territory, where such activity is carried out in connection with the conduct of the service supplier's business.[103]

The USMCA prohibits data localization for private sector enterprises and creates explicit requirements to ensure that personal information is protected. According to the USMCA:

> 1. No Party shall prohibit or restrict the cross-border transfer of information, including personal information, by electronic means if this activity is for the conduct of the business of a covered person. 2. This Article does not prevent a Party from adopting or maintaining a

---

[97] TPP, Art. 14.11(2), 'TPP Outcomes: Trade in the Digital Age' (Australia Department of Foreign Affairs and Trade). https://dfat.gov.au/trade/agreements/not-yet-in-force/tpp/Pages/outcomes-trade-in-the-digital-age.aspx. Accessed 29 March 2021.

[98] Burri, 'The Regulation of Data Flows through Trade Agreements' (n 41) 433.

[99] For example, article 14.13 of the TPP ensures that 'no member country shall require companies 'to use or locate computing facilities in that [member country's] territory as a condition for conducting business in that territory'.

[100] Aaronson and Townes (n 33) 4.

[101] Dr Deborah Elms and Hosuk Lee–Makiyama, 'A Roadmap for UK Accession to CPTPP' (Initiative for Free Trade, October 2018), 6. http://ifreetrade.org/pdfs/UK-CPTPP.pdf. Accessed 29 March 2021; Christopher Francis Corr and others, 'The CPTPP Enters into Force: What does it mean for Global Trade?' (White and Case, 21 January 2019). https://www.whitecase.com/publications/alert/cptpp-enters-force-what-does-it-mean-global-trade. Accessed 29 March 2021.

[102] 'Trade in Service Agreement: Annex on Electronic Commerce,' Art 2 (Netzpolitik, 2016). https://netzpolitik.org/wp-upload/TISA-Annex-on-Electronic-Commerce.pdf. Accessed 29 October 2020; 'Transatlantic Trade and Investment Partnership: Proposal for Trade in Services, Investment and E–Commerce', 47–50 (2015). http://trade.ec.europa.eu/doclib/docs/2015/july/tradoc_153669.pdf. Accessed 29 October 2020.

[103] 'Draft Annex of the Trade in Services Agreement (TiSA), Annex on Electronic Commerce 3' (3 September 2013). https://wikileaks.org/tisa/document/20151001_Annex-on-Electronic-Commerce/20151001_Annex-on-Electronic-Commerce.pdf. Accessed 29 October 2020. See also 'Trade in Services Agreement: Publication' (WIKILEAKS, 14 October 2016). https://wikileaks.org/tisa/.. Accessed 29 October 2020.

4.2 FTAs and Cross-border Data Transfers

measure inconsistent with paragraph 1 that is necessary to achieve a legitimate public policy objective, provided that the measure: (a) is not applied in a manner which would constitute a means of arbitrary or unjustifiable discrimination or a disguised restriction on trade; and (b) does not impose restrictions on transfers of information greater than are necessary to achieve the objective.[104]

E-commerce issues are subject to dispute settlement mechanisms in all FTAs in which the United States has been involved since 2012. A further review of the FTAs in which the United States is involved reveals that the general dispute settlement mechanisms for e-commerce issues involve four procedures: consultation, a joint committee, a dispute settlement panel and consideration of the report.[105] However, for developing countries with less experience in the field of e-commerce, the question of whether such dispute settlement mechanisms can be directly applied to e-commerce is still unanswered.

4.2.2.3 EU-Involved FTAs

Apart from the United States, the EU is proactively pursuing to include digital trade provisions in its FTAs, but not to the same extent of the United States.[106] Until 2 April 2021, the EU-involved FTAs covering the topic of e-commerce that have entered into force since 2012 are the EU-United Kingdom FTA, EU-Viet Nam FTA, EU-Singapore FTA, EU-Japan FTA, EU-Canada FTA, EU-Ghana FTA, EU-Georgia FTA, EU-Moldova, Republic of FTA, EU-Ukraine FTA, EU-Central America FTA, EU-Colombia and Peru FTA, and EU-Eastern and Southern Africa States FTA.[107] Except for the EU-Ghana FTA and EU-Eastern and Southern Africa States FTA, the other 10 FTAs all have standalone chapters, but except for the newly signed EU-United Kingdom FTA, EU-Japan FTA and EU-Singapore FTA, provisions regarding cross-border data transfers are absent from these e-commerce chapters. The EU-United Kingdom FTA has a digital trade section (Title III: Digital Trade), as well as a whole chapter regulating data flows and personal data protection (Title III: Digital Trade Chap. 2: Data flows and personal data protection).[108] Regarding the free flow of data, the EU-Japan FTA requires both parties to re-evaluate the need to include provisions on the free flow of data in the agreement within three years of the date when the agreement enters into force, while the EU-Singapore FTA merely confirms the importance of the free flow of information on the internet.[109] The EU-United

---

[104] USMCA, Art. 19.11.
[105] United States–Jordan FTA, Art. 7.
[106] Burri (n 91) 106.
[107] 'Search Criteria: Main Topics Covered: E–Commerce' (WTO FTA database Homepage, 14 March 2019). http://rtais.wto.org/UI/PublicMaintainRTAHome.aspx. Accessed 2 April 2021.
[108] 'EU–United Kingdom FTA' (EU). https://eur-lex.europa.eu/legal-content/EN/TXT/PDF/?uri=OJ:L:2020:444:FULL&from=EN. Accessed 31 March 2021.
[109] EU–Japan FTA, Art. 8.81; EU–Singapore FTA, Art. 8.57(3).

Kingdom FTA requires parties to ensuring cross-border data flows to facilitate trade in the digital economy, data localization is forbidden.[110]

The e-commerce chapter (Chap. 6) of the EU-Colombia and Peru FTA includes a comprehensive cooperation pledge that encompasses the recognition of certificates of electronic signatures; liability of intermediary service providers; treatment of unsolicited electronic commercial communications; protection of consumers in the field of e-commerce; protection of personal data; and promotion of paperless trading.[111] In addition, it requires both parties to endeavour, insofar as possible and within their respective competences, to develop or maintain, as the case may be, personal data protection regulations.[112] However, this statement is merely promotional. No standards or benchmarks for the regulations are specified.

Measures that essentially treat domestic and foreign investors or investments as different can, theoretically, be justified upon public welfare, such as health, safety, privacy, or environmental grounds.[113] The e-commerce chapter of the EU-Georgia FTA contains specific and rather detailed provisions on the grounds of justification.[114] Article 134(2) of the EU-Georgia FTA provides exceptions to the measures that are necessary to protect public security or public morals or to maintain public order; necessary to protect human, animal or plant life or health; related to the conservation of exhaustible natural resources; and necessary for the protection of national treasures of artistic, historical or archaeological value. The language related to data protection is as follows:

> Subject to the requirement that such measures are not applied in a manner which would constitute a means of arbitrary or unjustifiable discrimination between countries where like conditions prevail, or a disguised restriction on establishment or cross-border supply of services, nothing in this Chapter shall be construed to prevent the adoption or enforcement by any Party of measures:… (e) necessary to secure compliance with laws or regulations which are not inconsistent with the provisions of this Chapter, including those relating to:… (ii) the protection of the privacy of individuals in relation to the processing and dissemination of personal data and the protection of confidentiality of individual records and accounts;…[115]

---

[110] EU–United Kingdom FTA, Article DIGIT.6 Cross–border data flows, Art.1.

[111] EU–Colombia and Peru, Art. 163.1(e), see 'Trade Agreement between the European Union and Its Member States, of the One Part, and Colombia and Peru, of the Other Part' (21 December 2012). https://eur-lex.europa.eu/legal-content/EN/TXT/PDF/?uri=CELEX:22012A1221(01)&from=EN. Accessed 18 March 2021.

[112] Ibid, Art. 164.

[113] J. Anthony VanDuzer and others, 'Integrating Sustainable Development into International Investment Agreements – A Guide for Developing Countries, Commonwealth Secretariat' (Commonwealth Secretariat, August 2012) 112. https://www.iisd.org/system/files/meterial/6th_annual_forum_commonwealth_guide.pdf. Accessed 2 April 2021.

[114] 'Association Agreement between the European Union and the European Atomic Energy Community and Their Member States, of the One Part, and Georgia, and of the Other Part' (30 August 2014) 54 Official Journal of the EU 1, 4. https://eur-lex.europa.eu/legal-content/EN/TXT/PDF/?uri=OJ:L:2014:261:FULL&from=EN. Accessed 18 March 2021.

[115] EU–Georgia FTA, Art. 134(2), see 'Association Agreement between the European Union and the European Atomic Energy Community and Their Member States, of the One Part, and Georgia, and of the Other Part' (30 August 2014) 54 Official Journal of the EU 1, 61–62. https://eur-lex.europa.eu/legal-content/EN/TXT/PDF/?uri=OJ:L:2014:261:FULL&from=EN. Accessed 18 March 2021.

4.2 FTAs and Cross-border Data Transfers

Although it lacks a standalone e-commerce chapter, the EU-Eastern and Southern Africa States FTA contains a provision similar to that of the EU-Georgia FTA under the general exception clause.[116] These non-discriminatory conditions, which aim to balance trade and privacy interests, are similar to the general exceptions clause formulated by the GATS Article XIV and the GATT Article XX. All of these provisions confirm.

> the right of Members to pursue objectives identified in the paragraphs of these provisions even if, in doing so, Members act inconsistently with obligations set out in other provisions of the respective agreements, provided that all of the conditions set out therein are satisfied.[117]

Privacy commitments are deepened in the EU-Canada FTA,[118] Article 16.6(1), which emphasizes that although the FTA is soft, both parties agree to continue addressing the issues of protecting personal information and protecting consumers and businesses from fraudulent and deceptive commercial practices in the field of e-commerce. Cooperation in data protection is framed in more concrete terms under the EU-Canada FTA.

The EU's traditional approach to cross-border trade in services follows the GATS model and uses a positive-list approach for undertaking commitments.[119] In the positive-list approach, only services that have been evaluated and approved are permitted in trade liberalization.[120] However, in the EU-Canada FTA, a negative

---

[116] EU−Eastern and Southern Africa States FTA, Art. 56(c) (ii), see 'Interim Agreement Establishing a Framework for an Economic Partnership Agreement between the Eastern and Southern Africa States, on the One Part, and the European Community and Its Member States, on the Other Part' (24 April 2012) Official Journal of the EU 1, 23. https://eur-lex.europa.eu/legal-content/EN/TXT/PDF/?uri=CELEX:22012A0424(01)&from=EN. Accessed 18 March 2021.

[117] 'WTO Analytical Index GATS—Article XIV (Jurisprudence)', Art. 1.2.1(1). https://www.wto.org/english/res_e/publications_e/ai17_e/gats_art14_jur.pdf. Accessed 15 April 2021.

[118] EU−Canada FTA has a specific provision under E−Commerce chapter that obliges the parties to 'adopt or maintain laws, regulations, or administrative measures for the protection of personal information of users engaged in electronic commerce and, when doing so, shall take into due consideration international standards of data protection of relevant international organizations of which both Parties are a member.' See 'Comprehensive Economic and Trade Agreement (Ceta) between Canada, of the One Part, and the European Union and its Member States, of the Other Part,' Art. 16.4 (14 January 2017) 60 Official Journal of the European Union. https://eur-lex.europa.eu/legal-content/EN/TXT/HTML/?uri=OJ:L:2017:011:FULL&from=EN. Accessed 15 March 2021.

[119] 'Services and Investment in EU Trade Deals Using "Positive" and "Negative" Lists' (EU, April 2016). http://trade.ec.europa.eu/doclib/docs/2016/april/tradoc_154427.pdf. Accessed 23 April 2021; Burri, 'The Regulation of Data Flows through Trade Agreements' (n 41) 426; Rachel F. Fefer, 'U.S. Trade in Services: Trends and Policy Issues Analyst in International Trade and Finance' (Congressional Research Service, 30 June 2017) 10. https://fas.org/sgp/crs/misc/R43291.pdf, accessed 12 December 2020; Markus Krajewski, 'Public Services in Bilateral Free Trade Agreements of the EU' (November 2011), 11. https://www.arbeiterkammer.at/infopool/akportal/Public_Services_in_Bilateral_Free_Trade_Agreements_of_the_EU.pdf. Accessed 15 March 2021.

[120] Martin Roy, Juan Marchetti and Hoe Lim, 'Services Liberalization in the New Generation of Preferential Trade Agreements (PTAs): How Much Further than the GATS?', 9 (WTO Economic Research and Statistics Division 2006). https://www.wto.org/english/res_e/reser_e/ersd200607_e.pdf. Accessed 15 March 2021.

list of commitments was adopted for the first time by the EU,[121] which means that unless a reservation is clearly specified, trade and investment are liberalized. Exemptions from the MFN treatment in the form of a negative list can be found in Article X.1 (2)-(4), Article X.14 and Annex I and II of the EU-Canada FTA. They are general exemptions that also apply to the NT standard, which means that the parties to the EU-Canada FTA give market access, NT and MFN status to enterprises and investors from the areas of the other parties.[122]

The negative-list approach is more liberal than the positive-list approach.[123] In addition, an Annex attached to the services chapter of the EU-Canada FTA describes an understanding regarding new services that are not classified in the UN Provisional CPC in its 1991 version, as used during the Uruguay Round negotiation.[124] This understanding stipulates that any commitments under the EU-Canada FTA do not apply to a measure in relation to new services that cannot be classified under the CPC 1991.[125] The parties must inform the other party about such new services and enter into negotiations to incorporate the new services into the scope of the agreement at the request of either party.[126] This provision manifests the EU's cautious position towards technological innovation and new services trade.

Compared to the United States, the EU template for digital trade is somewhat minimalistic.[127] The EU's position on digital trade is not proactive but defensive, particularly in trade areas where it strives to protect its policy space, such as audio-visual services and data protection.[128] The existing EU-involved FTAs seem to prioritize privacy over trade by emphasizing personal data protection rather than cross-border data transfer facilitation.[129]

---

[121] Wilhelm Schöllmann, 'Comprehensive Economic and Trade Agreement (CETA) with Canada' (European Parliamentary Research Service, January 2017) 4. http://www.europarl.europa.eu/EPRS/EPRS-Briefing-595895-Comprehensive-Economic-Trade-Agreement-Canada-rev-FINAL.pdf. Accessed 15 March 2021; European Parliamentary Research Service, 'Services and Investment in EU Trade Deals Using "Positive" and "Negative" Lists' (n 119); Burri (n 91) 106.

[122] Schöllmann (n 121).

[123] Charlotte Sieber–Gasser, *Developing Countries and Preferential Services Trade* (Cambridge University Press 2016) 116.

[124] Annex 9–B of 'Comprehensive Economic and Trade Agreement between Canada of the One Part, and the EU and its Member States, of the Other Part' (14 September 2016). http://data.consilium.europa.eu/doc/document/ST-10973-2016-ADD-3/en/pdf#page=75. Accessed June 2020.

[125] Comprehensive Economic and Trade Agreement between Canada of the One Part, and the EU and its Member States, of the Other Part, Annex 9–B (1) (4).

[126] Ibid, Annex 9–B (2) (3).

[127] Burri (n 91) 106.

[128] Ibid, 108.

[129] On 6 July 2017, the EU and Japan entered into an agreement in principle on the main elements of the EU–Japan Economic Partnership Agreement. Article 12 of the agreement (titled 'Free Flow of Data') stipulates as follows: 'the Parties shall reassess the need for inclusion of an article on the free flow of data within three years of the entry into force of this Agreement.' This shows EU's attitude towards cross–border transfer is gradually changed.'

4.2.2.4 Other FTAs

In addition to FTAs mentioned above, other FTAs have some provisions concerning e-commerce,[130] The Canada-Jordan FTA,[131] Canada-Panama FTA,[132] GCC-Singapore FTA,[133] Canada-Ukraine FTA,[134] New Zealand-Chinese Taipei FTA,[135] Costa Rica-Singapore FTA,[136] and Singapore-Chinese Taipei FTA[137] all have standalone e-commerce chapters but do not mention data protection or cross-border data transfers in their e-commerce chapters. The Turkey-Malaysia FTA has neither a standalone e-commerce chapter nor provisions regarding data protection or cross-border data transfers.[138]

4.2.3 Commitments Made on Service Sectors

Commitments made regarding service sectors, such as financial and telecommunications services as well as computer-related services, are also related to cross-border

---

[130] These FTAs include but not limited to the Costa Rica−Colombia FTA, Mexico−Panama FTA, Canada−Honduras FTA, Malaysia−Australia FTA, Korea, Republic of−Australia FTA, Canada−Korea, Republic of FTA, Japan−Australia FTA, Korea, Republic of−Viet Nam FTA, PRC−Korea, Republic of FTA, PRC−Australia FTA, Japan−Mongolia FTA, Korea, Republic of−Colombia FTA, Eurasian Economic Union−Viet Nam FTA, Singapore−Chinese Taipei FTA, New Zealand−Chinese Taipei FTA. Among them, Costa Rica−Colombia FTA, Mexico−Panama FTA, Mexico−Central America FTA, Japan−Mongolia FTA, Canada−Korea, Republic of FTA, and Canada−Honduras FTA.

[131] Chapter 3 of Canada−Jordan FTA has some provisions concerning e−commerce, see 'Canada−Jordan Free Trade Agreement' (Government of Canada). https://international.gc.ca/trade-commerce/trade-agreements-accords-commerciaux/agr-acc/jordan-jordanie/fta-ale/03.aspx?lang=eng. Accessed 18 March 2021.

[132] Chapter 15 of Canada−Panama FTA has some provisions concerning e−commerce, see 'Text of the Canada–Panama Free Trade Agreement' (Government of Canada). https://international.gc.ca/trade-commerce/trade-agreements-accords-commerciaux/agr-acc/panama/fta-ale/15.aspx?lang=eng. Accessed 18 March 2021.

[133] Chapter 7 of GCC−Singapore FTA has some provisions concerning e−commerce, see 'The Gulf Cooperation Council (GSFTA) Legal Text' (Gulf Cooperation Council (GSFTA) Legal Text). https://iccia.com/sites/default/files/tradeagreement/The20Gulf20Cooperation20Council2020GSFTA20Legal20Text_2.pdf. Accessed 18 March 2021.

[134] Chapter 8 of Canada−Ukraine FTA has some provisions concerning e−commerce.

[135] Chapter 9 of New Zealand−Chinese Taipei FTA has some provisions concerning e−commerce.

[136] Chapter 12 of Costa Rica−Singapore FTA has some provisions concerning e−commerce, see 'Costa Rica (SCRFTA) Legal Text' (SICE). http://www.sice.oas.org/Trade/CRI_SGP_FTA/Index_e.asp. Accessed 18 March 2021.

[137] Chapter 11 of Singapore−Chinese Taipei FTA has some provisions concerning e−commerce.

[138] 'Free Trade Agreement between the Government of Malaysia and the Government of the Republic of Turkey'. https://fta.miti.gov.my/miti-fta/resources/Malaysia%20-%20Turkey/MTFTA_Main_Agreement.pdf. Accessed 18 March 2021.

data transfers. For example, the Japan-Australia FTA provides detailed information about financial data transfers, stating as follows:

> Neither Party shall take measures that prevent transfers of information or the processing of financial information, including transfers of data by electronic means, or that, subject to importation rules consistent with international agreements, prevent transfers of equipment, where such transfers of information, processing of financial information or transfers of equipment are necessary for the conduct of the ordinary business of a financial service supplier. Nothing in this Article restricts the right of a Party to protect personal data, personal privacy and the confidentiality of individual records and accounts so long as such right is not used to circumvent the provisions of this Chapter and Chapters 9 (Trade in Services) and 14 (Investment).[139]

Article 10.7: Data Processing in the Financial Services Sector of the Chile-Thailand FTA has similar provisions. However, this kind of commitment appears to be a far-reaching obligation[140] because the different parties to the FTAs adopt different data privacy rules. To better enforce the FTAs, changing the domestic rules to meet the obligations of the FTAs is inevitable.

4.2.4 Economic and Technical Cooperation

Provisions of cross-border data transfers are also commonly placed in chapters on economic and technical cooperation. The parties to the Japan-Mongolia FTA recognize the importance of flows of information across borders as an essential element of a vibrant e-commerce environment.[141] The Korea, Republic of-Colombia FTA reads as follows:

> The Parties shall endeavor to establish cooperation mechanisms on issues arising from electronic commerce, which will, inter alia, address the following: ... (b) the protection of personal data; (c) the liability of providers with respect to the transmission or storage of information;... (e) the security of electronic commerce; (f) the protection of consumers in the field of electronic commerce; and...[142]

Canada's FTAs with Colombia, Honduras, Peru, and South Korea oblige the two parties to affirm the importance of joint efforts to maintain the cross-border flow of information as an essential element in facilitating and fostering a vibrant environment for e-commerce.[143]

---

[139] Japan–Australia FTA, Art. 11.6.

[140] Diane A. MacDonald and Christine M. Streatfeild, 'Personal Data Privacy and the WTO' (2014) 36 Houston Journal of International Law 625, 629–30.

[141] Japan–Mongolia FTA, Art. 9.12.5, see 'Agreement between Japan and Mongolia for an Economic Partnership' (Ministry of Foreign Affair of Japan). https://www.mofa.go.jp/a_o/c_m2/mn/page3e_000298.html. Accessed 18 March 2021.

[142] Korea, Republic of–Colombia FTA, Art. 12.6.

[143] Canada–Colombia FTA, Art. 1507; Canada–Honduras FTA, Art. 16.5; Canada–Korea, Republic of FTA, Art. 13.7; Canada–Peru FTA, Art. 1508. See 'Canada–Colombia Free Trade

4.2 FTAs and Cross-border Data Transfers

Some other FTAs address issues of cross-border data flows under the chapters on economic and technical cooperation by promoting regulatory cooperation. The Mexico-Panama FTA stipulates that cooperation activities between the two parties shall include technical assistance and the exchange of information.[144] The Chile-Thailand FTA does not have a separate chapter that regulates e-commerce. E-commerce is regulated under Chapter 11: Economic Cooperation. Similar to the EU-Colombia and Peru FTA, the e-commerce provision in the Chile-Thailand FTA includes a comprehensive cooperation pledge and provides a more detailed requirement for the field of personal data.[145] However, the language used in these FTAs is principled and lacks operability. Frequently, negotiators employ the "shall endeavour" language in their drafting of chapters on economic and technical cooperation and cross-border data transfers.

In addition, many FTAs have embraced understanding as part of the e-commerce chapters, which cover cooperation in various areas, such as the recognition of certificates of electronic signatures issued to the public, facilitation of cross-border certification services, protection of personal data, and protection of consumers in the field of e-commerce. Language emphasizing regulatory cooperation to maintain cross-border flows of information can be found in a number of RTAs between APEC members.[146]

Agreement' (Government of Canada). https://international.gc.ca/trade-commerce/trade-agreements-accords-commerciaux/agr-acc/colombia-colombie/fta-ale/index.aspx?lang=eng. Accessed 18 March 2021; see also 'Canada–Peru Free Trade Agreement' (Government of Canada). https://international.gc.ca/trade-commerce/trade-agreements-accords-commerciaux/agr-acc/peru-perou/fta-ale/index.aspx?lang=eng. Accessed 18 March 2021.

[144] 'Moreover, the Parties recognize the importance of co–operation between their customs authorities in facilitating trade and thus commit to promote it. Cooperation activities shall include technical assistance and the exchange of information. The Parties also commit to provide mutual assistance, upon request by a Party, regarding any suspicion of customs infractions. However mutual assistance can be denied inter alia to protect public order, national security or public health. Any confidential information provided by a Party under this Chapter shall be kept confidential by the other Party'. Mexico–Panama FTA, Art. 5.12–5.21; see also 'WT/REG374/1 Committee on Regional Trade Agreements—Factual presentation—Free trade Agreement between Mexico and Panama (goods and services)—Report by the Secretariat', Art. 3.40. (11 July 2017). https://docs.wto.org/dol2fe/Pages/FE_Search/FE_S_S006.aspx?Query=@Symbol=%20(wt/reg374/*)&Language=ENGLISH&Context=FomerScriptedSearch&languageUIChanged=true#. Accessed 12 November 2020.

[145] Chile–Thailand FTA, Art. 11.7.

[146] Mark Wu (n 12) 24.

4.2.5 Other Chapters

First, the chapter on personal data protection. Cross-border data transfers have raised concerns about privacy and data protection that are at a crossroads between cross-border electronic information transmission and consumer protection.[147] The FTAs in which the EU is involved, such as the EU-Moldova, Republic of FTA,[148] EU-Georgia FTA,[149] EU-Ukraine FTA,[150] and EU-Central America FTA,[151] have always included the protection of personal data in the provision of freedom, security and justice because the right to personal data is considered a fundamental right in the EU.

Second, the IP chapter. Beyond the chapters mentioned above, data protection provisions are also found in the IP chapters of several FTAs. For example, the EU-Colombia and Peru FTA protects data on certain regulated products, such as data related to the safety and efficacy of pharmaceutical products and agricultural chemical products.[152] Several United States-involved FTAs comprise provisions concerning digital rights management, such as management of country-code top-level domains,[153] and the management of rights to phonograms.[154]

All the FTAs entered into after 2012 contain soft rules. It has become a trend and a major feature of FTAs to embrace soft cooperation provisions, not only in the field of e-commerce but also in fields such as the environment and IPs. Such soft provisions leave much room for further cooperation between the parties. In terms of the legislative model, e-commerce provisions in the FTAs in which the United States is involved are dominated by hard rules and supplemented by soft rules to ensure the effective functioning of the e-commerce provisions. In particular, e-commerce dispute settlement in FTAs in which the United States is involved is endowed with mandatory features, which are obviously not accepted by most countries and means

---

[147] Monteiro and Teh (n 50) 51.

[148] EU–Moldova, Republic of FTA, Art. 13, see 'Association Agreement between the European Union and the European Atomic Energy Community and their Member States, of the one part, and the Republic of Moldova, of the other part' (Official Journal of the EU). https://eur-lex.europa.eu/legal-content/EN/TXT/PDF/?uri=CELEX:22014A0830(01)&from=EN. Accessed 12 November 2020.

[149] EU–Georgia FTA, Art. 14.

[150] EU–Ukraine FTA, Art. 15, see 'Association Agreement between the European Union and its Member States, of the one part, and Ukraine, of the other part' (EUR–Lex). https://eur-lex.europa.eu/legal-content/EN/TXT/PDF/?uri=OJ:L:2014:161:FULL&from=EN. Accessed 19 March 2021.

[151] EU–Central America FTA, Art. 34, see 'EU–Central America FTA'. https://www.efta.int/free-trade/Free-Trade-Agreement/Central-American-States. Accessed 19 March 2021.

[152] Section 6 of the EU–Colombia and Peru FTA, 'Trade Agreement between the European Union and Its Member States, of the One Part, and Colombia and Peru, of the Other Part' (21 December 2012). https://eur-lex.europa.eu/legal-content/EN/TXT/PDF/?uri=CELEX:22012A1221(01)&from=EN. Accessed 18 March 2021; United States–Panama FTA, Art. 15.4.

[153] United States–Columbia FTA, Art. 16.4, see 'Government of the United States of America and the Government of the Republic of Colombia FTA' (Office of the United States Trade Representative). https://ustr.gov/trade-agreements/free-trade-agreements/colombia-tpa/final-text. Accessed 19 March 2021.

[154] United States–Columbia FTA, Art. 16.6.

4.2 FTAs and Cross-border Data Transfers

that it is difficult for the United States FTA model to be accepted by other countries. However, FTAs in which the EU is involved focus mainly on the exchange of information and cooperation in e-commerce; they are dominated by soft provisions and are easily accepted by countries that are newcomers in the field of e-commerce. In summary, the FTAs in which the United States is involved are more aggressive, with higher standards and stronger binding force. The e-commerce provisions of the FTAs in which the EU is involved are relatively simple, granting cultural products special protection and focusing on soft cooperation mechanisms. In addition, the developing countries' FTAs are more flexible, which, to some extent, reflects their wavering legislative attitude.

4.3 FTAs and RTAs in Which the PRC Is Involved

The PRC started its efforts to negotiate FTAs after joining the WTO in 2001. Entering into FTAs is in the PRC's interest in many ways because it promotes international trade and deepens cooperation with trade partners. Because of the deficiency of the WTO in the field of digital trade, the PRC—like many other jurisdictions—has begun to take e-commerce and digital trade issues into consideration in its RTAs and FTAs in recent years. Sixteen FTAs have been concluded by the PRC thus far, with the Association of Southeast Asian Nations (ASEAN), Pakistan, Chile, New Zealand, Singapore, Peru, Costa Rica, Iceland, Switzerland, South Korea, Georgia, the Maldives, Mauritius, Cambodia, and Australia.[155] On 8 March 2021, The Chinese government has officially ratified the RCEP agreement.[156] In addition, the Central Government of Mainland China signed the Closer Economic and Partnership Arrangement (CEPA) with the government of the Special Administrative Region of Hong Kong (CEPA Hong Kong) and the government of the Special Administrative Region of

---

[155] PRC FTA Network Homepage. http://fta.mofcom.gov.cn/enarticle/chinamauritiusen/enmauritius/201910/41658_1.html, http://fta.mofcom.gov.cn/english/fta_qianshu.shtml. Accessed 1 April 2021.

[156] The Regional Comprehensive Economic Partnership (RCEP) is an FTA between the Asia–Pacific nations of Australia, Brunei, Cambodia, China, Indonesia, Japan, Laos, Malaysia, Myanmar, New Zealand, the Philippines, Singapore, Korea, Republic of, Thailand, and Vietnam. See "Regional Comprehensive Economic Partnership (RCEP) Agreement" (Ministry of Foreign Affairs of Japan, 8 February 2021). https://www.mofa.go.jp/policy/economy/page1e_kanri_000001_00007.html. Accessed 1 April 2021.

Macao (CEPA Macao) in 2003 and concluded the Cross-Strait Economic Cooperation Framework Agreement with the Chinese Taipei in 2010.[157] Moreover, the PRC has ten RTAs under negotiation,[158] and eight RTAs under consideration.[159]

4.3.1 E-Commerce Chapters

The PRC's FTAs signed before 2015 have no discrete e-commerce provisions. In recent years, the Chinese government has begun to integrate e-commerce provisions into its FTAs, trying to establish a conducive and healthy environment for the development of e-commerce. For example, specific provisions on e-commerce have been integrated into the RCEP agreement,[160] the PRC-Korea, Republic of FTA,[161] the PRC-Australia FTA,[162] the PRC-Georgia FTA,[163] the Protocol to Amend the Free Trade Agreement and the Supplementary Agreement on Trade in Services of the

---

[157] Although some scholars believe that the Economic Cooperation Framework Agreement between mainland China and Taiwan Region (Chinese title: 海峽兩岸經濟合作架構協議) is a FTA, it is not mentioned as a FTA in the Website of the PRC FTA Network—a website run by the PRC Ministry of Commerce. See PRC FTA Network Homepage. http://fta.mofcom.gov.cn/english/index.shtml. Accessed 30 March 2021, see also Pasha L. Hsieh, 'China—Taiwan Free Trade Agreement' in Simon Lester, Bryan Mercurio, Lorand Bartels, *Bilateral and Regional Trade Agreements* (Cambridge University Press 2016) 97.

[158] Free Trade Agreements under Negotiation include the PRC—GCC FTA, PRC—Japan—Korea FTA, PRC—Sri Lanka FTA, PRC—Israel FTA, PRC—Norway FTA, PRC—Moldova FTA, PRC—Panama FTA, PRC—Korea FTA second phase, PRC—Palestine FTA, PRC—Peru FTA Upgrade. See PRC FTA Network Homepage. http://fta.mofcom.gov.cn/english/index.shtml. Accessed 4 April 2021.

[159] Free Trade Agreements under Consideration include the PRC—Columbia FTA Joint Feasibility Study, PRC—Fiji FTA Joint Feasibility Study, PRC—NePal FTA Joint Feasibility Study, PRC—Papua New Guinea FTA Joint Feasibility Study, PRC—Canada FTA Joint Feasibility Study, PRC—Bengal FTA Joint Feasibility Study, PRC—Mongol FTA Joint Feasibility Study, and PRC—Switzerland Upgrade FTA Joint Feasibility Study. See PRC FTA Network Homepage. http://fta.mofcom.gov.cn/english/index.shtml. Accessed 4 April 2021.

[160] The RCEP agreement, Chap. 12.

[161] PRC—Korea, Republic of FTA, Chap. 3, see 'Free Trade Agreement between the Government of the PRC and the Government of The Republic of Korea' (PRC FTA Network Homepage). http://fta.mofcom.gov.cn/korea/annex/xdzw_en.pdf. Accessed 16 March 2021.

[162] PRC—Australia FTA, Chap. 12, see 'Free Trade Agreement between the Government of Australia and the PRC' (PRC FTA Network). http://fta.mofcom.gov.cn/Australia/annex/xdzw_en.pdf. Accessed 16 March 2021.

[163] RC—Georgia FTA, Art. 12.2, see 'Free Trade Agreement between The Government of the PRC and the Government of Georgia' (PRC FTA Network). http://fta.mofcom.gov.cn/georgia/annex/xdzw_en.pdf. Accessed 17 March 2021.

4.3 FTAs and RTAs in Which the PRC Is Involved

Free Trade Agreement between the Government of the PRC and the Government of the Republic of Chile,[164] the CEPA Hong Kong,[165] and the CEPA Macao.[166]

4.3.1.1 The CEPA Hong Kong, the CEPA Macao and the Hong Kong-Macao CEPA

The main text of the CEPA Hong Kong was signed on 29 June 2003.[167] After that, ten supplements to the CEPA Hong Kong were signed by the government of HKSAR and the CPG from 27 October 2004 to 29 August 2013 to continue deepening and expanding cooperation.[168] The CEPA Hong Kong covers three major areas: goods, services, and investment facilitation.[169] E-commerce is directly regulated under Article II: "Trade and Investment Facilitation" of Supplement V to the CEPA Hong Kong, which stipulates as follows:

> (I) The two sides will adopt the following measures to further strengthen cooperation in the area of electronic commerce: To take forward the pilot applications of mutual recognition of electronic signature certificates issued by Guangdong and Hong Kong. A working group is to be set up which will strive to submit within this year suggestions on a framework for the mutual recognition of electronic signature certificates issued by both places… (III) To promote cooperation in the area of branding between the two places, the two sides agree to add cooperation on branding into the area of trade and investment facilitation under "CEPA". Accordingly…4). Electronic business…[170]

Liberalization of trade in services is the most important arrangement of the CEPA Hong Kong.[171] The Agreement on Trade in Services under the framework of the

---

[164] 'Protocol to Amend the Free Trade Agreement and the Supplementary Agreement on Trade in Services of the Free Trade Agreement between the Government of the PRC and the Government of the Republic of Chile', Chap. 4 (PRC FTA Network). http://fta.mofcom.gov.cn/chile/xieyi/bcyds_en.pdf. Accessed 17 March 2021.

[165] 'Mainland and Hong Kong Closer Economic Partnership Arrangement (CEPA)' (Trade and Industry Department of HK Homepage). https://www.tid.gov.hk/english/cepa/index.html. Accessed 30 March 2021.

[166] 'Mainland and Macao Closer Economic Partnership Arrangement Agreement on Trade in Services' (PRC FTA Network). http://fta.mofcom.gov.cn/topic/enmacau.shtml. Accessed 18 April 2021.

[167] 'Mainland and Hong Kong Closer Economic and Partnership Arrangement' (PRC FTA Network). http://fta.mofcom.gov.cn/topic/enhongkong.shtml. Accessed 30 March 2021.

[168] Ibid.

[169] Ibid.

[170] Supplement V to CEPA Hong Kong was signed on 29 July 2008, see 'Mainland and Hong Kong Closer Economic Partnership Arrangement (CEPA) Supplement V to CEPA' (Trade and Industry Department of HK Homepage). https://www.tid.gov.hk/english/cepa/legaltext/cepa6.html. Accessed 15 March 2021.

[171] Juan Yang, 'Mainland China and Hong Kong Closer Economic Partnership Arrangement Effect Analysis' (August 2016) 5(3) Scires 67, 67. https://file.scirp.org/pdf/ChnStd_2016080414072625.pdf. Accessed 14 April 2021.

CEPA Hong Kong covers and consolidates commitments related to the liberalization of trade in services provided in the CEPA Hong Kong and its supplements.[172] It also extends the geographical coverage in the "Agreement between the Mainland and Hong Kong on Achieving Basic Liberalization of Trade in Services in Guangdong" from Guangdong to all of Mainland China for the liberalization of trade in services.[173] According to the latest supplement—a standalone subsidiary agreement made under the trade of services section in the CEPA framework—Mainland China has fully or partially opened 153 sectors to the services industry in HKSAR, including banking services, legal services, insurance services, telecommunications services, transportation services, and distribution services.[174] The agreement adopts a positive list of "Liberalization Measures under Telecommunication" and further clarifies them in a footnote as follows:

> With respect to the modes of commercial presence and cross-border services of telecommunications services sector (sub-sector), the liberalization commitments by the Mainland to Hong Kong service suppliers shall maintain the use of Positive List to set out the liberalization measures.[175]

The Agreement on Economic and Technical Cooperation of the CEPA Hong Kong[176] uses a whole chapter to regulate e-commerce and stipulates that the two parties agree to promote the development of cross-boundary e-commerce for key industries and bulk commodities, to reinforce exchanges on cross-boundary data flow between them,[177] and to set up a joint working group to study feasible policy measures

---

[172] 'Mainland and Hong Kong Closer Economic Partnership Arrangement Agreement on Trade in Services' (Trade and Industry Department of HK Homepage). https://www.tid.gov.hk/english/cepa/legaltext/files/sa27-11-2015_main_e.pdf. Accessed 15 March 2021.

[173] 'CEPA Latest News' (Office of the Government Chief Information Officer of HK Homepage). https://www.ogcio.gov.hk/en/our_work/business/mainland/cepa/. Accessed 14 March 2021; 'Mainland and Hong Kong Closer Economic Partnership Arrangement Agreement on Trade in Services' (Trade and Industry Department of HK Homepage). https://www.tid.gov.hk/english/cepa/legaltext/files/sa27-11-2015_main_e.pdf. accessed 15 March 2021; 'Agreement between the Mainland and Hong Kong on Achieving Basic Liberalisation of Trade in Services in Guangdong' (Trade and Industry Department of HK Homepage). https://www.tid.gov.hk/english/cepa/legaltext/cepa12.html. Accessed 15 March 2021.

[174] 'Mainland and Hong Kong Closer Economic Partnership Arrangement Agreement on Trade in Services Annex 1: The Mainland's Specific Commitments on Liberalisation of Trade in Services for Hong Kong' (Trade and Industry Department of HK Homepage). https://www.tid.gov.hk/english/cepa/legaltext/files/sa27-11-2015_annex1_e.pdf. Accessed 15 March 2021.

[175] 'Mainland and Hong Kong Closer Economic Partnership Arrangement (CEPA) Telecommunications Services Liberalization Measures under CEPA' (Trade and Industry Department of HK Homepage). https://www.tid.gov.hk/english/cepa/tradeservices/tel_liberalization.html. Accessed 14 March 2021.

[176] The Agreement on Economic and Technical Cooperation of the CEPA Hong Kong was signed on 28 June 2017, see 'Mainland and Hong Kong Closer Economic Partnership Arrangement Agreement on Economic and Technical Cooperation', (Trade and Industry Department of HK Homepage). https://www.tid.gov.hk/english/cepa/legaltext/cepa15.html Accessed 18 March 2021.

[177] 'Mainland and Hong Kong Closer Economic Partnership Arrangement Agreement on Economic and Technical Cooperation', Art. 14(6) (Trade and Industry Department of HK Homepage). https://www.tid.gov.hk/english/cepa/legaltext/files/cepa15_main.pdf. Accessed 18 March 2021.

4.3 FTAs and RTAs in Which the PRC Is Involved 103

and arrangements to further strengthen cooperation in the field of e-commerce.[178] However, the language is encouraging and not legally binding.

The main text of the CEPA Macao was signed on 17 October 2003.[179] MSAR and Mainland China also signed ten supplements to the CEPA Macao from 27 October 2005 to 28 December 2015.[180] These agreements are integral to the enhancement of the CEPA Macao, marking a new phase of economic and trade cooperation as well as trade exchange between Mainland China and MSAR.[181] Mainland China has progressively provided preferential treatment to MSAR on market access to the telecommunications and audio-visual information technology sectors. Both parties agreed to strengthen exchanges between them regarding cross-boundary data flow to further strengthen cooperation in the area of e-commerce.[182]

The CEPA Hong Kong and the CEPA Macao have similar provisions stipulating that notwithstanding the NT and MFN principals, one party may request information about services or service suppliers from the service suppliers of the other party only for information or statistical purposes.[183] The first party shall protect confidential commercial information from being disclosed so as not to affect the service suppliers' competitive position.[184] This paragraph shall not be construed to prevent any party from acquiring or disclosing information concerning the laws on the application of fairness and integrity.[185]

On 27 October 2017, HKSAR and MSAR signed the Hong Kong Special Administrative Region and Macao Special Administrative Region Closer Economic Partnership Arrangement (Hong Kong-Macao CEPA), which is comprehensive in scope, and the commitments therein go beyond those undertaken by HKSAR and MSAR under the WTO agreements, providing enhanced legal certainty of market access or

---

[178] Ibid, Art. 14(7).

[179] 'Mainland and Macao Closer Economic Partnership Arrangement Agreement on Trade in Services' (PRC FTA Network). https://www.wipo.int/edocs/lexdocs/treaties/en/cn-mo/trt_cn_mo.pdf. Accessed 18 April 2021.

[180] Ibid.

[181] Ibid.

[182] 'The CEPA Macao—Agreement on Economic and Technical Cooperation', Art. 13(7). 'Mainland and Macao Closer Economic Partnership Arrangement Agreement on Economic and Technical Cooperation' (PRC FTA Network). http://fta.mofcom.gov.cn/topic/enmacau.shtml. Accessed 18 April 2021.

[183] 'Mainland and Macao Closer Economic Partnership Arrangement Agreement on Trade in Services', Art. 13(2); 'Mainland and Hong Kong Closer Economic Partnership Arrangement Agreement on Trade in Services', Art. 13(2).

[184] 'Mainland and Macao Closer Economic Partnership Arrangement Agreement on Trade in Services', Art. 13(2); 'Mainland and Hong Kong Closer Economic Partnership Arrangement Agreement on Trade in Services', Art. 13(2).

[185] 'Mainland and Macao Closer Economic Partnership Arrangement Agreement on Trade in Services', Art. 13(2); 'Mainland and Hong Kong Closer Economic Partnership Arrangement Agreement on Trade in Services', Art. 13(2).

treatment to one another.[186] The agreement covers the areas of trade in goods, trade in services and a work programme on economic and technical cooperation. HKSAR and MSAR agreed to "promote trade and investment facilitation through greater transparency, standard conformity and enhanced information exchange".[187] Article 24 of the Hong Kong-Macao CEPA protects commercial information by stipulating as follows:

> One side may request information relating to services or service suppliers from the service suppliers of the other side only for information or statistical purposes. The former side shall protect confidential commercial information from leakage which may adversely affect the competitive position of the service supplier. This paragraph shall not be construed as preventing either side from acquiring or disclosing information relating to the laws on the application of fairness and integrity.

However, e-commerce provisions are absent from the Hong Kong-Macao CEPA's main text and the Hong Kong-Macao CEPA Closer Economic Partnership Arrangement Economic and Technical Cooperation Work Programme.

4.3.1.2 The Other Sixteen FTAs

Before the RCEP agreement, only the PRC-Korea, Republic of FTA and the PRC-Australia FTA contain a standalone e-commerce chapter.[188] The e-commerce regulations in these two FTAs in which the PRC is involved generally cover the following content:

First, the parties should respect the WTO treaty provisions.[189] Specifically, the PRC-Korea, Republic of FTA stipulates that both parties recognize the applicability of the WTO Agreement to measures affecting e-commerce[190] and should sustain the current practice of the WTO and not impose customs duties on electronic transmissions.[191] This provision is further explained in a footnote as follows:

---

[186] 'Hong Kong Special Administrative Region and Macao Special Administrative Region Closer Economic Partnership Arrangement (HK–Macao CEPA)' (Trade and Industry Department of HK Homepage). https://www.tid.gov.hk/english/ita/fta/hkmacao/index.html. Accessed 18 March 2021.

[187] HK–Macao CEPA, Art. 28(2).

[188] PRC–Korea, Republic of FTA, Chap. 3, see 'Free Trade Agreement between the Government of the PRC and the Government of the Republic of Korea' (PRC FTA Network). http://fta.mofcom.gov.cn/korea/annex/xdzw_en.pdf. Accessed 16 March 2021; PRC–Australia FTA, Chap. 12, see 'Free Trade Agreement between the Government of Australia and the PRC' (PRC FTA Network). http://fta.mofcom.gov.cn/Australia/annex/xdzw_en.pdf. Accessed 16 March 2021. Besides, the Protocol to Amend the Free Trade Agreement and the Supplementary Agreement on Trade in Services of the Free Trade Agreement between the Government of the PRC and the Government of the Republic of Chile has a standalone e–commerce chapter, but it's not an official FTA, the official FTA between the PRC and Chile contains no provisions regarding e–commerce. 'Free Trade Agreement between the Government of the PRC and the Government of the Republic of Chile' (PRC FTA Network). http://fta.mofcom.gov.cn/chile/xieyi/freetradexieding2.pdf. Accessed 17 March 2021.

[189] PRC–Korea, Republic of FTA, Art. 13.1; see also PRC–Australia FTA, Art 6.11.2(c).

[190] PRC–Korea, Republic of FTA, Art. 13.1.

[191] PRC–Korea, Republic of FTA, Art. 13.3.

4.3 FTAs and RTAs in Which the PRC Is Involved

The current practice will be maintained consistent with paragraph 5 of Work Programme on Electronic Commerce of the Bali WTO Ministerial Decision (WT/MIN (13)/32-WT/L/907).[192]

The PRC-Australia FTA respects the WTO rules in two aspects. First, Article 12.1(1) of the PRC-Australia FTA states that:

> 1. The Parties recognize the economic growth and opportunities provided by electronic commerce, the importance of avoiding barriers to its use and development, and the applicability of relevant WTO rules...3. The Parties shall endeavor to ensure that bilateral trade through electronic commerce is no more restricted than other forms of trade.

Then, the PRC-Australia FTA requires that neither party shall impose customs duties on electronic transmissions between the parties, consistent with the WTO Ministerial Decision of 7 December 2013 related to the Work Programme on Electronic Commerce.[193] The PRC-Korea, Republic of FTA and the PRC-Australia FTA merely confirm the existing obligations of the WTO members rather than seeking an extension of a WTO-plus obligation.[194]

Second, both the PRC-Korea, Republic of FTA and the PRC-Australia FTA embrace provisions related to personal information protection. Article 13.5 of the PRC-Korea FTA recognizes the importance of protecting personal information in e-commerce and requires that each party adopt or maintain measures to ensure the protection of the personal information of e-commerce users and share information and experience in protecting personal information in e-commerce. Article 12.8 of the PRC-Australia FTA protects online information and stipulates that:

> 1. Notwithstanding the differences in existing systems for personal information protection in the territories of the Parties, each Party shall take such measures as it considers appropriate and necessary to protect the personal information of users of electronic commerce. 2. In the development of data protection standards, each Party shall, to the extent possible, take into account international standards and the criteria of relevant international organizations.

The PRC-Australia FTA also requires that each party provide protection for e-commerce consumers that is at least equivalent to that provided for the consumers of other forms of commerce to the greatest extent possible and in a manner that it considers appropriate.[195]

In addition, the PRC-Korea, Republic of FTA regulates access to and use of public telecommunications networks or services and stipulates as follows:

> Each Party shall ensure that service suppliers of the other Party may use public telecommunications networks or services for the movement of information in its territory or across its borders in accordance with the laws and regulations of the Party, including for intra-corporate communications, and for access to information contained in databases or otherwise stored in machine-readable form in the territory of either Party or any non-Party which is a party to the WTO Agreement.[196]

---

[192] Footnote 47 of the PRC–Korea, Republic of FTA.
[193] PRC–Australia FTA, Art. 12.3(1).
[194] Mark Wu (n 12) 12.
[195] PRC–Australia FTA, Art. 12.7.
[196] PRC–Korea FTA, Art. 10.3(3).

RCEP agreement's e-commerce chapter contains provisions on cross-border transfer of information by electronic means.[197] However, the RCEP gives "its member states all the leeway that they need to adopt restrictive measures to digital trade and data flows, should they wish to do so".[198]

4.3.1.3 Electronic Authentication and Electronic Signatures

Electronic authentication technologies play an important role in enabling digital trade.[199] Both the PRC-Korea, Republic of FTA and the PRC-Australia FTA contain provisions on electronic authentication, electronic signatures, and paperless trade. In the PRC-Korea, Republic of FTA, the PRC expressly stipulated in a footnote that:

> For any electronic signature to be certified by a third party to the electronic transaction, the authentication service must be provided by a legally established authentication service provider which shall be approved by an authority accredited in accordance with domestic law.[200]

This provision explicitly requires that the government establish performance requirements for authentication technologies, consistent with domestic law or on the basis of a specific electronic certificate issued by a recognized certification authority, provided that this requirement serves a legitimate policy objective and is substantially related to achieving that objective.[201] Both the PRC-Australia FTA and the PRC-Korea, Republic of FTA have provisions stating that the parties should work towards the mutual recognition of digital certificates and electronic signatures that are issued or recognized by governments.[202] These two FTAs also stipulate that the legal validity of a signature cannot be denied simply because it is in electronic form.[203]

In addition to domestic regulatory frameworks, the PRC-Australia FTA requires the parties to embrace the provisions that are consistent with international standards,[204] such as the United Nations Commission on International Trade Law (UNCITRAL) Model Law on Electronic Commerce 1996 (Model Law 1996) and the UN Convention on the Use of Electronic Communications in International Contracts (ECC). The Model Law 1996 was created to offer a suggested pattern for national

---

[197] 'Regional Comprehensive Economic Partnership (RCEP)', Art. 12.15 (China FTA Network). http://fta.mofcom.gov.cn/rcep/rceppdf/d12z_en.pdf. Accessed 31 March 2021.

[198] Patrick Leblond, 'Digital Trade: Is RCEP the WTO's Future?' (CIGI 20th, 23 November 2020). https://www.cigionline.org/articles/digital-trade-rcep-wtos-future. Accessed 31 March 2021.

[199] Mark Wu (n 12) 1.

[200] PRC—Korea FTA, Chap. 13.

[201] Mark Wu (n 12) 16.

[202] PRC—Australia, Art. 12.6.2.

[203] PRC—Korea FTA, Art. 13.4.1.

[204] Article 12.5(1) of the PRC—Australia FTA stipulates that: 'each Party shall maintain domestic legal frameworks governing electronic transactions based on the UNCITRAL Model Law on Electronic Commerce 1996 and taking into account, as appropriate, other relevant international standards'.

legislatures to eliminate obstacles and establish a predictable legal framework for e-commerce,[205] particularly to overcome obstacles in legal provisions that may not be altered contractually by providing equal treatment for paper-based and electronic information.[206] As of March 2018, legislation based on or influenced by the Model Law 1996 had been adopted in 71 countries and regions—including the PRC, HKSAR and MSAR—in a total of 150 jurisdictions.[207]

In addition to the Model Law 1996, UNCITRAL has produced the ECC, the focus of which is to "facilitate 'paperless' means of communication by offering criteria under which they can become equivalents of paper documents".[208] The PRC has signed the ECC but not yet ratified it. The ECC can be seen as similar to the relevant international standards in Article 12.5(1) of the PRC-Australia FTA.

From the above developments, it can be seen that the e-commerce provisions under the FTAs in which the PRC is involved are gradually absorbing the relevant provisions of international treaties. This also reflects the spillover effects of multilateral rules on e-commerce on the FTAs in which the PRC is involved.

4.3.1.4 Cooperation On E-Commerce

Cooperation in e-commerce under the PRC-Australia FTA and the PRC-Korea, Republic of FTA focuses mainly, first, on sharing information and experience; second, on encouraging collaboration in research and training activities; third, encouraging business exchanges; fourth, on promoting cooperative activities and joint e-commerce projects; and fifth, on participating in regional and multilateral fora to promote the development of e-commerce in a cooperative manner.[209] Accordingly, although the declaration of cooperation on e-commerce is soft and does not define substantive obligations of the parties, it contributes substantially to strengthening the friendly exchanges and cooperation between the trading partners.

Under the cooperation provisions, it is worth noting that the PRC-Australia FTA added a new clause referring to unsolicited commercial electronic messages

---

[205] United Nations Commission on International Trade Law, 'UNCITRAL Model Law on Electronic Commerce with Guide to Enactment 1996 with additional article 5 bis as adopted in 1998'. https://uncitral.un.org/sites/uncitral.un.org/files/media-documents/uncitral/en/19-04970_ebook.pdf. Accessed 23 March 2021.

[206] Ibid.

[207] Ibid.

[208] 'United Nations Convention on the Use of Electronic Communications in International Contracts', 26 (UNCITRAL, 2007). https://www.wipo.int/edocs/lexdocs/treaties/en/uncitral-uecic/trt_uncitral_uecic.pdf. Accessed 13 March 2021.

[209] PRC–Korea, Republic of FTA, Art. 13.7; see also PRC–Australia FTA, Art. 12.10.

that states that both parties should share information on online consumer protection, including unsolicited commercial electronic messages.[210] This new clause is consistent with the previous TPP's regulations on this issue.[211]

4.3.2 Dispute Settlement

All e-commerce clauses under the PRC FTAs underscore the fact that the general dispute settlement mechanism does not apply to e-commerce disputes. The PRC-Korea, Republic of FTA specifies that neither party shall have recourse to any dispute settlement procedures under their respective RTAs with respect to any issue arising from or relating to the chapter on e-commerce. Similarly, the PRC-Australia FTA explains that the chapter on consultations and dispute settlement shall not apply to any matter arising under the e-commerce chapter. One explanation may be that e-commerce is believed to be rooted in the nature of cooperation. There is no need to introduce a mandatory dispute settlement mechanism. In addition, the PRC is a newcomer in this area and might be concerned that the application of the dispute settlement mechanism to e-commerce would be used by other countries to crack down on digital trade in the PRC.

4.3.3 Intellectual Property (IP) Chapters

The government of the PRC has been trying to improve the legislation of IP rights domestically and integrate more complicated and detailed IP provisions into its FTAs during the past few years. Early FTAs in which the PRC was involved either had relatively simple and guideline-free IP provisions or even did not have them at all. For example, there are only two items concerning IPs in the PRC-Chile FTA that was concluded in 2005.[212] IPs are mentioned only once in Article 10(1) of the PRC-Pakistan FTA that was concluded in 2006. No IP provisions exist in the

---

[210] PRC−Australia FTA, Art. 12.10(3).

[211] By far, previous TPP (now CPTPP) holds the most well−developed and advanced set of binding commitments on unsolicited commercial electronic messages. According to previous TPP, members must adopt or maintain measures regarding unsolicited electronic messages that meet specified guidelines which include (a) requiring suppliers of unsolicited electronic messages to facilitate the ability of recipients to prevent ongoing reception of those messages; (b) requiring the consent of recipients to receive commercial electronic messages; and (c) providing for the minimization of unsolicited commercial electronic messages. In addition, each member is required to provide recourse against suppliers of unsolicited commercial electronic messages that do not comply with the measures adopted or maintained, as well as to cooperate in appropriate cases of mutual concern regarding the regulation of unsolicited commercial electronic messages. See the TPP, Art. 14.4.

[212] PRC−Chile FTA, Art. 111, see 'Free Trade Agreement between the Government of the PRC and the Government of the Republic of Chile' (PRC FTA Network). http://fta.mofcom.gov.cn/chile/xieyi/freetradexieding2.pdf. Accessed 16 March 2021.

4.3 FTAs and RTAs in Which the PRC Is Involved

PRC-Singapore FTA that was concluded in 2008. With the conclusion of more FTAs in recent years, this situation has changed. The PRC-New Zealand FTA is the first PRC-involved FTA that contains a single and separate IP chapter.[213] Chapter 11 of the PRC-New Zealand FTA covers copyright and related rights, trademarks, patents, genetic resources and traditional knowledge, plant variety protection, undisclosed information, industrial designs and geographical indications.

The FTA between Switzerland and the PRC is the first to contain extensive provisions regulating specific rights and obligations rather than merely declaratory provisions regarding the protection of IP rights.[214] The PRC-Switzerland FTA has increased the transparency and convenience of IP rights protection and demonstrated the PRC's positive and open attitude towards strengthening the protection of IP rights.[215] In addition, IP issues are considered important in the PRC-Korea, Republic of FTA, the IP chapter of which includes provisions on copyrights, trademarks, patents and utility models, genetic resources, traditional knowledge and folklore, plant variety protection, undisclosed information and industrial designs.

The PRC-Australia FTA also refers to IP protection. Chapter 11 of the PRC-Australia FTA aims to promote the benefits of trade investment and innovation by establishing transparent IP systems and maintaining adequate and effective protection and enforcement mechanisms.[216] Chapter 11 contains 24 articles about patents, trademarks, copyrights, geographical indications, new species of plants, business secrets and law enforcement. This chapter also contains several new content items on the collective management of copyright.[217] Compared with other FTAs in which the PRC is involved, the PRC-Australia FTA, which contains the richest and most detailed IP content, has a higher protection level.[218] IP issues have become increasingly important in the PRC's negotiations of FTAs.[219] Regarding the relationship between IP issues and digital trade, the IP chapters of the PRC-Switzerland FTA, the PRC-Korea, Republic of FTA and the PRC-Australia FTA all refer to the World Intellectual Property Organization Internet Treaties and TRIPS Agreement. However,

---

[213] PRC−New Zealand FTA, Chap. 12, see 'Free Trade Agreement between the Government of the PRC and the Government of New Zealand' (PRC FTA Network). http://images.mofcom.gov.cn/gjs/accessory/200804/1208158780064.pdf. Accessed 16 March 2021.

[214] PRC−Switzerland FTA, Chap. 11, see 'Free Trade Agreement between the Government of the PRC and the Swiss Confederation' (PRC FTA Network). http://fta.mofcom.gov.cn/topic/enswiss.shtml. Accessed 16 March 2021.

[215] 'Head of Department of International Trade and Economic Relations Made an Interpretation on the PRC−Switzerland FTA' (Ministry of Commerce PRC, 7 August 2013). http://english.mofcom.gov.cn/article/newsrelease/policyreleasing/201308/20130800233165.shtml. Accessed 2 January 2021.

[216] PRC−Australia FTA, Art. 11.1.

[217] Ibid, Art. 11.9.

[218] 'Interpretation for the PRC−Australia Free Trade Agreement' (Ministry of Commerce PRC Homepage, 19 June 2015). http://english.mofcom.gov.cn/article/policyrelease/Cocoon/201510/20151001144954.shtml. Accessed 2 January 2021.

[219] Guangliang Zhang, 'China's Stance on Free Trade−Related Intellectual Property: A View in the Context of the China−Japan−Korea FTA negotiations' (2016) 24(1) Asia Pacific Law Review 47.

only the PRC-Korea, Republic of FTA refers to obligations to protect technological measures. No obligations related to the liability of ISPs are spelled out under the other FTAs in which the PRC involved.

4.4 Regional Comprehensive Economic Partnership

It appears that FTAs are well positioned to address the new generation of trade barriers, such as localization measures.[220] Despite these virtues, the developments of digital trade are incremental in the FTAs in which the PRC is involved. Issues related to digital trade, such as e-commerce, IPs, data protection, and financial and telecommunication services, are mostly incorporated in FTAs between the PRC and advanced countries, such as Australia and South Korea. E-commerce is undefined under the existing PRC FTAs. There are no provisions concerning culture in any FTA in which the PRC is involved. It is well known that the PRC has adopted a limited policy of openness to culture, but this policy is not stipulated in the agreements and is not even mentioned in the preambles, which inevitably leads to confusion.

To effectively solve the controversies over e-commerce and protect personal data, an appropriate method for customers to file complaints or concerns is indispensable. It is also important that the complaints or concerns reach the right place and are resolved promptly and suitably. However, dispute settlement mechanisms are inexplicably absent under the e-commerce chapter. A lack of procedural mechanisms hinders the effective implementation of the e-commerce clauses.

The PRC-Australia FTA includes unsolicited commercial electronic message provisions, but the language is limited to soft cooperation pledges to share information and are devoid of clarity and manoeuvrability. However, SC-NPC Decision provides concrete measures to deal with unsolicited commercial electronic messages.[221] This shows the disconnect between the FTAs and domestic law, which should be considered seriously by the drafters of future FTAs.

The e-commerce clauses in all FTAs in which the PRC is involved are soft and unconsolidated, which leaves flexible policy space for the cooperation of the trading parties but is not conducive to the formation of a unified Chinese FTA e-commerce model. Although the PRC's recent FTAs speak broadly to a regulatory environment

---

[220] Burri, 'The Regulation of Data Flows through Trade Agreements' (n 41) 443.

[221] Art. VII of the SC–NPC Decision stipulates that 'no organizations and individuals may, without the consent of or the request from the recipients of electronic information or with an explicit refusal from the recipients of electronic information, send commercial electronic information to their landline or mobile phones or personal e–mail boxes'... 'Citizens who discover any network information divulging their personal identities, disseminating their individual privacy or otherwise infringing upon their lawful rights and interests or who are annoyed by unwanted commercial electronic information shall have the right to require network service providers to delete relevant information or take other necessary prohibitive measures.' See 'Decision of the Standing Committee of the National People's Congress on Strengthening Information Protection on Networks' (Central People's Government of the PRC Homepage, 28 December 2019). http://www.gov.cn/jrzg/2012-12/28/content_2301231.htm. Accessed 8 March 2021.

4.4 Regional Comprehensive Economic Partnership

conducive to cross-border data flows, the language is not binding.[222] The PRC has neither included language regarding the free flow of information nor formulated and implemented a concrete and distinct strategy for digital trade in its FTAs.

These soft rules that lack concrete content make it difficult to reflect the PRC's position on digital trade. An important trade agreement called the Regional Comprehensive Economic Partnership (RCEP) is signed by ten members of the ASEAN and five partner countries—the PRC, Japan, Australia, New Zealand and South Korea on 15 November 2020.[223] The RCEP agreement includes provisions dealing with issues that are critical to digital trade, such as e-commerce, the supply of cross-border services, paperless trading, and telecommunications.[224]

It is worth noting that the RCEP's e-commerce provisions cover cross-border data transfers, data localization, the legal immunity of intermediaries and requirements concerning source code disclosure that have not been addressed in other trade mechanisms.[225] RCEP includes commitments to ensure that parties do not prevent business data and information from being transferred across borders.[226] RCEP will also include commitments to prevent countries from imposing measures that require computing facilities to be located within their own territories.[227] The RCEP has the potential to serve as an important instrument that will help the PRC consolidate its leadership role in the region.

4.5 The Defects of Existing FTAs

The international trade scenario is increasingly being changed by digital technologies and has unsurprisingly triggered regulatory responses at all levels of governance. However, due to the borderless digital environment, many solutions cannot exist

---

[222] For example, in the PRC−Korea, Republic of FTA, both parties notes the 'importance of protecting personal information in electronic commerce', and 'shall adopt or maintain measures which ensure the protection of the personal information of the users of electronic commerce and share information and experience on the protection of personal information in electronic commerce', see PRC−Korea, Republic of FTA, Art. 13.5.

[223] 'Regional Comprehensive Economic Partnership (RCEP)' (3 October 2016). https://www.dfat.gov.au/trade/agreements/not-yet-in-force/rcep. Accessed 16 December 2020.

[224] 'RCEP Outcomes Documents' (Australian Government Department of Foreign Affairs and Trade). https://www.eff.org/deeplinks/2017/07/rcep-discussions-ecommerce-gathering-steam-hyderabad. Accessed 16 December 2020.

[225] Panday Jyoti, 'RCEP Discussions on Ecommerce: Gathering Steam in Hyderabad' (Electronic Frontier Foundation, 24 July 2017). https://www.eff.org/deeplinks/2017/07/rcep-discussions-ecommerce-gathering-steam-hyderabad. Accessed 20 April 2021.

[226] These commitments will not apply to the financial services sector and also include exceptions for measures implemented for national security or other public policy reasons. See 'RCEP: Outcomes: Electronic Commerce' (Australian Government Department of Foreign Affairs and Trade). https://www.dfat.gov.au/sites/default/files/rcep-outcomes-ecommerce.pdf. Accessed 16 December 2020.

[227] These commitments will exclude the financial services sector and will be subject to exceptions that allow parties to implement measures for security and public policy reasons, see ibid.

without international cooperation.[228] In most areas, international cooperation helps governments benefit from digital trade.[229]

Restrictions on cross-border data flows have gradually become the main impediments to international digital trade. Although some domestic laws can have a global influence, domestic laws on copyright, privacy, and security do not have global legitimacy and force. Common ground on internationally accepted rules governing cross-border data flows is desirable because fragmented international and national regulations on personal data are increasing the cost of doing business and hinder innovation.[230] When negotiating bilateral, regional or multilateral trade agreements referring to cross-border data flows, policymakers should adopt language that aims to encourage interoperability among the different parties.[231] However, the international harmonization of strategies for cross-border data flows worldwide is difficult to achieve because countries have different priorities for free trade, online privacy, free speech, and national security, to mention but a few. Trade agreements can play a greater or lesser role in encouraging cooperation on minimum privacy standards.[232]

Issues related to cross-border data transfers mostly appear in the e-commerce or economic and technical cooperation chapters of FTAs. E-commerce is playing an increasingly important role in supporting economic development, especially by providing an effective way for small companies in less developed countries to reach new markets and engage in global trade.[233] There is concern that the so-called "digital divide" situation is growing wider since some societies and segments of society have little or no access to the information that is easily available to the well-off and developed countries.[234] There also exists a concern that:

---

[228] William J. Drake and Ernest J. Wilson, *Governing Global Electronic Networks: International Perspectives on Policy and Power* (MIT Press 2008) 9; see also Carlos A. Primo Braga, 'E−commerce Regulation: New Game, New Rules?' (2005) 45 Quarterly Review of Economics and Finance 541, 558.

[229] 'WTO Trade Report 2018: The Future of World Trade: How Digital Technologies Are Transforming Global Commerce', 11 (WTO Secretariat, 3 October 2018). https://www.wto.org/english/res_e/publications_e/world_trade_report18_e_under_embargo.pdf, accessed 1 March 2021.

[230] Several scholars have recognized that Internet restrictions could be trade barriers and that the world would need to develop shared rules for information flows. Tim Wu, 'The World Trade Law of Censorship and Internet Filtering' (2006) 7(1) Chicago Journal of International Law 263, 265; see also Fredrik Erixon, Brian Hindley and Hosuk Lee−Makiyama, 'Protectionism Online: Internet Censorship and International Trade Law'(2009) ECIPE Working Paper No. 12/2009, 10. https://ecipe.org/wp-content/uploads/2014/12/protectionism-online-internet-censorship-and-international-trade-law.pdf, accessed 24 March 2021.

[231] Aaronson and Townes (n 33) ii.

[232] Avi Goldfarb and Dan Trefler, 'How Artificial Intelligence Impacts International Trade' in *World Trade Report 2018* (WTO) 140. https://www.wto.org/english/res_e/publications_e/wtr18_4_e.pdf. Accessed 19 January 2021.

[233] 'E−Commerce in Developing Countries—Opportunities and Challenges for Small and Medium−sized Enterprises' (WTO 2013), 2. https://www.wto.org/english/res_e/booksp_e/ecom_brochure_e.pdf Accessed 2 May 2021.

[234] 'Process Philosophy' (Stanford Encyclopedia of Philosophy, 15 October 2012). https://plato.stanford.edu/entries/process-philosophy/. Accessed 13 November 2020.

4.5 The Defects of Existing FTAs

The "digital divide" between countries which are capitalizing on these opportunities and those which are not could become a digital chasm if the frameworks governing them do not adequately ensure the equitable distribution of benefits and overcome barriers to inclusive growth.[235]

According to the UNCTAD, there are currently 46 least-developed countries (LDCs) on the UN list[236]; so far, 35 of these have become WTO members.[237] However, none of these LDCs to date has agreed to any RTAs covering the e-commerce issue. Most of these RTAs mentioned above were concluded between developed and developing countries. It appears that developed countries and some developing countries usually have more friendly environments for the development of e-commerce and therefore gain benefits more easily, while for many LDCs, this is not yet the case because their connectivity is affected by ongoing institutional, regulatory, knowledge and skills asymmetries and limitations on physical infrastructure.[238] RTAs intensify global "asymmetric wealth distribution and rule fragmentation"[239] and, to some extent, exacerbate the imbalanced development of e-commerce markets worldwide. This situation can realistically not be expected to change in the short term and seems to be worsening because developed dominant positions in many areas of technology related to digital trade are held by certain countries.

Although digital trade-related issues have been increasingly embraced by RTAs in recent years, it should be noted that not all WTO members have strategies with regard to this issue. Many WTO members, such as the members of the European Free Trade Association, not only in developing countries but also in developed counties play roles, although not actively, as participants in the WTO E-commerce Programme but do not pursue digital trade provisions in their RTAs.[240]

The developments of FTAs in the field of digital trade are still incremental, catching up with technological progress in independent areas where business interests have been squeezed while still lacking genuine regulatory innovation.[241] Cross-border data transfer—the lifeblood of international digital trade—has only been mentioned in some FTAs. Trade agreement is in a better position than international

---

[235] 'Debating the Future of E−Commerce and Digital Trade in Buenos Aires'. https://devsol.etrade forall.org/debating-future-e-commerce-digital-trade-buenos-aires/. Accessed 31 March 2021.

[236] Least developed countries include Afghanistan, Angola, Bangladesh, Benin, Bhutan, Burkina Faso, Burundi, Cambodia, Central African Republic, Chad, Comoros, Democratic Republic of the Congo, Djibouti, Eritrea, Ethiopia, Gambia, Guinea, Guinea−Bissau, Haiti, Kiribati, Lao People's Democratic Republic, Lesotho, Liberia, Madagascar, Malawi, Mali, Mauritania, Mozambique, Myanmar, Nepal, Niger, Rwanda, Sao Tome and Principe, Senegal, Sierra Leone, Solomon Islands, Somalia, South Sudan, Sudan, Timor−Leste, Togo, Tuvalu, Uganda, United Republic of Tanzania, Yemen, Zambia. See UN list of Least Developed Countries. See 'UN List of Least Developed Countries' (UNCTAD). http://unctad.org/en/Pages/ALDC/Least%20Developed%20Countries/UN-list-of-Least-Developed-Countries.aspx. Accessed 4 April 2021.

[237] 'Least−developed Countries' (WTO). https://www.wto.org/english/thewto_e/whatis_e/tif_e/org7_e.htm Accessed 5 April 2021.

[238] 'Debating the Future of E−Commerce and Digital Trade in Buenos Aires' (n 235).

[239] Burri, 'The Regulation of Data Flows through Trade Agreements' (n 41) 444.

[240] Burri (n 91) 106.

[241] Burri, 'Should There Be New Multilateral Rules for Digital Trade?' (n 66) 1.

human right treaties to regulate cross-border data flows because trade agreements are legally binding and always have a dispute settlement mechanism. However, some FTAs, for example, the PRC-Australia FTA, PRC-Korea, Republic of FTA, and New Zealand-Chinese Taipei FTA, make it clear that the e-commerce chapter is not subject to dispute settlement provisions.[242] Meanwhile, other FTAs set up certain parts, instead of the entire chapter, to be exempt from dispute settlement provisions. For example, in the Thailand-Australia FTA and Thailand-New Zealand FTA, except for commitments regarding customs duties, the e-commerce chapter is not subject to dispute settlement.[243]

Although there are specific relevant provisions for e-commerce in these FTAs, the scope and depth of the e-commerce chapters vary.[244] It is clear that there is not yet broad-based support within the WTO membership for a comprehensive multilateral agreement to address issues of cross-border data flows.[245] As shown in the preceding sections, it is obvious that FTAs have begun to address some of the issues raised by the development of the Internet and technology, the most typical of which is e-commerce. Data protection, which strictly speaking is not a "trade" issue, is also embraced by some FTAs.[246] Data protection has the potential to be the most contentious issue with "possible spillover effects to other issue areas".[247]

Although some FTAs mandate no customs duties for e-commerce transactions and pursue deepening cooperation between the parties, other FTAs establish mutual recognition and safeguards for the free flow of data. In essence, FTAs are a kind of personalized customization approach to digital trade and hardly contribute to the free flow of data across borders in a global context.[248] Among the 62 FTAs mentioned

---

[242] PRC–Australia FTA, Art. 12.11; PRC–Korea, Republic of FTA, Art. 13.9; New Zealand–Chinese Taipei FTA, Art. 6.

[243] Australia–Thailand FTA, Art. 1109; New Zealand–Thailand FTA, Art. 10.8, see 'Australia–Thailand Free Trade Agreement' (Australia Department of Foreign Affairs and Trade). http://thailaws.com/law/e_laws/freetrade/australia/aus-thai_FTA_text.pdf. Accessed 18 March 2021; see also 'Thailand–New Zealand Closer Economic Partnership Agreement'. https://investmentpolicy.unctad.org/international-investment-agreements/treaty-files/2704/download. Accessed 31 March 2021.

[244] Monteiro and Teh (n 50) 12.

[245] WTO Members have not reached an agreement on 'where to draw the line between data protection based restrictions on data flows that are protectionist and against trade and liberalization, and those that are necessary to guarantee the rights of citizens.' See Stephen J. Ezell, Robert D. Atkinson and Michelle A. Wein, 'Localization Barriers to Trade – Threat to the Global Innovation Economy,' 69 (Information Technology and Innovation Foundation, September 2013). https://www2.itif.org/2013-localizationbarriers-to-trade.pdf, accessed 18 March 2021; Christopher Kuner, 'Regulation of Transborder Data Flows under Data Protection and Privacy Law: Past, Present and Future', OECD Digital Economy Papers No. 187, 20 (OECD publishing 2011). https://www.oecd-ilibrary.org/docserver/5kg0s2fk315f-en.pdf?expires=1604549314&id=id&accname=guest&checksum=62C9388AB859B25CE75D219D1AC46D74, accessed 4 January 2021.

[246] FTAs that EU involved always have the provisions of protection of personal data and always put this kind of provisions under the title of Freedom, Security and Justice.

[247] Burri, 'The Regulation of Data Flows through Trade Agreements' (n 41) 438.

[248] Ibid, 443.

4.5 The Defects of Existing FTAs

in the previous section, only some FTA, such as the United Kingdom—Japan FTA, USMCA, CPTPP, EU-Japan FTA, United States-Panama FTA, KORUS FTA, Costa Rica-Colombia FTA, Mexico-Panama FTA, Mexico-Central America FTA, Japan-Mongolia FTA, Canada-Korea, Republic of FTA and Canada-Honduras FTA contain explicit language concerning cross-border data flows, most of which employs the "shall endeavour" language. This kind of regulation manifests a low degree of clarity with regard to implementation and lack of enforceability. The fragmentation of the law and the compromise of regulatory consistency potentially have a negative impact on the effectiveness of e-commerce transactions.[249] It is urgent to strengthen FTA obligations related to cross-border data transfers, migrating from provisions couched in best-endeavour language to firmer commitments, thus creating obligations that are subject to dispute settlement.

In addition, regarding the relationship with other chapters, some FTAs make clear that other chapters prevail in the event of an inconsistency between the e-commerce chapter and other chapters. FTAs that make such declarations include but are not limited to the Canada-Honduras FTA,[250] Canada-Ukraine FTA,[251] and Canada-Korea, Republic of FTA.[252] The impact of the e-commerce chapter is somewhat diminished by such regulations. In conclusion, in the future, many loopholes still need to be filled in the governance of cross-border data flows in the context of FTAs.

Last but not least, with the development of technology and the rising value of cross-border data flows, the international business of data collection, storage, and processing makes individuals "more vulnerable to exploitation for profit in the private sector" beyond experiencing the invasion of privacy by their own governments.[253] The private sector, especially the giants of the Internet and technology enterprises such as Google, Apple, Alibaba, and Facebook, should be at the centre of a more holistic conversation about international regulations for data transfer, data privacy, and data ethics. They possess a significant amount of data in terms of both quantity and sensitivity. The commercial activities of these Internet and technology giants can have a significant impact on privacy and data security. However, these Internet and technology commercial giants are generally not directly bound by treaties—whether international trade treaties, international human rights treaties, or FTAs/RTAs. If these Internet and technology giants abandon their obligations to protect human rights, only the laws of their host countries can punish them, and their host countries may not have a sufficient legal framework to regulate data-related issues and protect human rights. How to make the private sector, especially those Internet and technology

---

[249] Weber (n 56).

[250] Canada–Honduras FTA, Art. 16.7: 'In the event of an inconsistency between this Chapter and another Chapter of this Agreement, the other Chapter prevails to the extent of the inconsistency.'.

[251] 607 Canada–Ukraine FTA, Art. 8.3: 'In the event of an inconsistency between this Chapter and another Chapter of this Agreement, the other Chapter prevails to the extent of the inconsistency.'.

[252] Canada–Korea, Republic of, Art. 13.8: 'In the event of an inconsistency between this Chapter and another Chapter, the other Chapter prevails to the extent of the inconsistency.'.

[253] Margaret Byrne Sedgewick, 'Transborder Data Privacy as Trade' (2017) 105 California Law Review 1513, 1516.

commercial giants, take the responsibility that they should take at the international level is another urgent but unsettled large problem.

4.6 Interim Remarks

Much still needs to be done at the international level by means of international regulatory co-operation if digital trade is to realize its potential. Areas related to digital trade-such as data privacy, encryption technology, the application of the WTO rules to digital products and trade, should be carefully considered to meet public policy objectives without restricting trade.[254] The Doha negotiations remain stagnant and, as a result, the WTO faces difficulties in handling the multifaceted and highly technical areas. Therefore, countries are increasingly turning to RTAs for relief and the further development of the framework governing trade in data.[255] RTAs have filled the gaps in WTO's regulatory scope by creating rules and norms in the fields of digital trade, especially in the fields of e-commerce, in the past few decades.[256] In fact, issues related to digital trade are providing most of the impetus for the seeking of RTAs and are currently becoming an essential part of RTAs.[257]

The recent trend in FTAs is to include a standalone e-commerce chapter affirming the application of the WTO trade rules (the MFN principle, the NT principle and Market Access) to the cross-border electronic delivery of services and digital products and regulating some of the remaining issues not covered by the WTO e-commerce rules. Other rules concerning online consumer protection, electronic authentication and electronic signature, and cross-border data flows have also been embraced by FTAs in recent years.

The tensions inherent in trade agreements highlighted by existing RTAs will spill over to the digital realm.[258] One of the tricky problems that cause concern among treaty makers in the field of data is how to balance the relationship between the apparently divergent goals of fostering liberalization and greater international cooperation in international trade by entering into RTAs, on the one hand, and the much broader goals of domestic personal data protection legislation, which are not limited to facilitating trade but also include protection of cybersecurity, national security, public morals and privacy, on the other.

---

[254] Julia Nielsen and Rosemary Morris, 'E−Commerce and Trade: Resolving Dilemmas' (OECD Observer). http://oecdobserver.org/news/archivestory.php/aid/421/E-commerce_and_trade:_resolving_dilemmas.html. Accessed 7 March 2020.

[255] There are 343 RTAs in force have been notified to the WTO until March 2021. See WTO RTA Database, http://rtais.wto.org/UI/PublicAllRTAList.aspx. Accessed 2 April 2021.

[256] Mishra (n 44) 19–20.

[257] Burri, 'The Regulation of Data Flows through Trade Agreements' (n 41) 409; see also Mishra (n 44) 6.

[258] Mark Wu (n 12) 29.

4.6 Interim Remarks

FTAs do not contribute to the free flow of information across the globe.[259] The so-called "spaghetti-bowl" effect, which is a result of the growing number of FTAs and their occasional overlap, has been discussed for years.[260] Although the issue may be overstated, FTAs at some point are believed to create barriers for traders and administrators and to increase the cost of trading.[261] In addition, FTAs may significantly undermine the value and impact of multilateralism[262] as well as the role played by international law in general.[263] Moreover, the influence of FTAs is limited since FTAs apply only to the signatory parties[264]; thus, FTAs risk "further entrenching economic inequalities and widening the digital divide".[265] The existing legal frameworks, whether at the global level, such as the WTO, or the bilateral or multilateral level, such as RTAs and FTAs, are insufficient to handle the exponential growth and complexity of trans-border data flow.[266]

---

[259] Burri, 'The Regulation of Data Flows through Trade Agreements' (n 41) 444.

[260] Christoph Antons and Reto M. Hilty, 'Introduction: IP and the Asia–Pacific "Spaghetti Bowl" of Free Trade Agreements' in Christoph Antons, Reto M. Hilty and others, *Intellectual Property and Free Trade Agreements in the Asia–Pacific Region* (Springer 2015); Maria Panezi, 'The WTO and the Spaghetti Bowl of Free Trade Agreements Four Proposals for Moving Forward' (CIGI, September 2016). https://www.cigionline.org/sites/default/files/pb_no.87.pdf. Accessed 23 March 2021; Masahiro Kawai and Ganeshan Wignaraja, 'Tangled Up In Trade? The "Noodle Bowl" of Free Trade Agreements in East Asia' (VOX, 15 September 2009). http://voxeu.org/article/noodle-bowl-free-trade-agreements-east-asia. Accessed 23 March 2021.

[261] Goode (n 37) 5.

[262] Andrew G. Brown and Robert M. Stern, 'Free Trade Agreements and Governance of the Global Trading System' (2011) 34 World Economic Forum 331, 349–350. https://pdfs.semanticscholar.org/3640/7b0d0698f580871aa8f25ab2c25355a6daf5.pdf. Accessed 23 March 2021.

[263] Nico Krisch, 'The Decay of Consent: International Law in an Age of Global Public Goods' (2014) 108 American Journal of International Law 1, 2–7.

[264] Weber (n 56).

[265] 'Debating the Future of E–Commerce and Digital Trade in Buenos Aires' (n 235).

[266] Christopher Kuner, *Transborder Data Flows and Data Privacy Law* (Oxford University Press 2013) 167.

Chapter 5
Cross-Border Data Transfers Regulations in the Context of International Trade Law-Challenges and Perspective

In the same way, as we cannot any longer only think of paper books in a world with e-books, or CDs in a world where it is possible to stream music, we cannot think of roads, bridges and tunnels only as physical constructions. We need to include all-new sustainable ways that can provide the service the old infrastructure used to provide.[1]

—Dennis Pamlin

5.1 The Necessity of Cross-Border Data Transfers

From an economic and trade point of view, data stand as the lifeblood of the modern global economy.[2] Data-fueled technologies have the potential to promote dramatic increases in innovation, productivity gains, and economic growth.[3] The widespread use of data analytics in almost every industries has streamlined business practices and improved efficiency and made the data movement even more important.[4] Almost all businesses now use services that involve data transfers, and many of these transfers cross borders.[5]

---

[1] Pamlin (n 407).

[2] Cory Nigel, 'Cross−Border Data Flows: Where Are the Barriers, and What Do They Cost?' 1 (Information Technology and Innovation Foundation, May 2017). http://www2.itif.org/2017-cross-border-data-flows.pdf, accessed 16 March 2021.

[3] Michael E. Porter and James E. Heppelmann, 'How Smart, Connected Products Are Transforming Competition' (Harvard Business Review, November 2014). https://hbr.org/2014/11/how-smart-connected-products-are-transforming-competition#comment-section, accessed 24 October 2020.

[4] Daniel Castro and Alan McQuinn, 'Cross−Border Data Flows Enable Growth in All Industries' (Information Technology & Innovation Foundation, February 2015). http://www2.itif.org/2015-cross-border-data-flows.pdf, accessed 24 October 2020.

[5] 'Business Without Borders: The Importance of Cross−Border Data Transfers to Global Prosperity' (United States Chamber of Commerce and Hunton and Williams LLP), 1. https://www.huntonprivacyblog.com/wp-content/uploads/sites/28/2014/05/021384_BusinessWOBorders_final.pdf, accessed 1 March 2021(n 185) 1.

© The Author(s), under exclusive license to Springer Nature Singapore Pte Ltd. 2022
Y. Dai, *Cross-Border Data Transfers Regulations in the Context of International Trade Law: A PRC Perspective*, https://doi.org/10.1007/978-981-16-4995-0_5

Global e-commerce totalled US$ 27.7 trillion in 2016, up from US$ 19.3 trillion in 2012.[6] Increasing cross-border data flows currently create more economic value than the traditional flows of traded goods.[7] The international dimension of flows in data, goods and foreign direct investment, has amplified the current global GDP by approximately 10% compared with what would have occurred in a world without any such flows.[8] Data flows represent an estimated $2.8 trillion of this added value.[9] Globalization has entered a new era defined by cross-border data flows that transfer information, ideas, and innovation.[10]

From a human rights point of view, the communication landscape is experiencing a rapid, and profound transformation[11] accompanied by the advance of the Internet. The Internet provides unprecedented scope for interactive communication using multiple devices located in different jurisdictions.[12] The freedom to communicate across borders is a basic human right recognized by Article 19 of the Universal Declaration of Human Rights (UDHR) and Article 19 of the International Covenant on Civil and Political Rights (ICCPR), both of which confirm that everyone should enjoy the freedom to receive and impart information and ideas, regardless of frontiers. This kind of freedom belongs to the right to freedom of opinion and expression.[13]

In addition, the UN Human Rights Council makes it clear in the "Promotion, Protection and Enjoyment of Human Rights on the Internet" that:

> …on freedom of expression on the Internet, 1. Affirms that the same rights that people have offline must also be protected online, in particular freedom of expression, which is applicable regardless of frontiers and through any media of one's choice, in accordance with articles 19 of the Universal Declaration of Human Rights and the International Covenant on Civil and Political Rights;…3. Calls upon all States to promote and facilitate access to the Internet and international cooperation aimed at the development of media and information and communications facilities in all countries;…5. Decides to continue its consideration of the promotion, protection and enjoyment of human rights, including the right to freedom of expression, on the Internet and in other technologies, as well as of how the Internet can be

---

[6] 'WTO Trade Report 2018: The Future of World Trade: How Digital Technologies Are Transforming Global Commerce', 5 (WTO Secretariat, 3 October 2018). https://www.wto.org/english/res_e/publications_e/world_trade_report18_e_under_embargo.pdf, accessed 1 March 2021.

[7] James Manyika and others, 'Digital globalization: The New Era of Global Flows' (Mckinsey Global Institute, February 2016), 2. https://www.mckinsey.com/business-functions/digital-mckinsey/our-insights/digital-globalization-the-new-era-of-global-flows, accessed 19 December 2020.

[8] Ibid., 1.

[9] Ibid.

[10] Ibid.

[11] 'Freedom of Expression, Media and Digital Communications Framework—Key Issues' (EC, 2012). http://vtsns.edu.rs/wp-content/uploads/2020/03/Freedom-of-expression.pdf, accessed 31 October 2020.

[12] Ibid., 7.

[13] Anne W. Branscomb, 'Global Governance of Global Networks: A Survey of Transborder Data Flow in Transition' (1983) 36 Vanderbilt Law Review 985, 1030–31.

5.1 The Necessity of Cross-Border Data Transfers

an important tool for development and for exercising human rights, in accordance with its programme of work.[14]

The EU Strategic Framework and Action Plan on Human Rights and Democracy has similar provisions.[15] Moreover, Article I 2(a) of the Constitution of the UN Educational, Scientific and Cultural Organization requires the organization to "promote the free flow of ideas by word and image". In addition, the Agreement on the Importation of Educational, Scientific and Cultural Materials 1950 aimed to facilitate "the free flow of books, publications and educational, scientific and cultural materials"[16]; therefore, the contracting states agreed to not impose customs duties or other charges on or in relation to the importation of such materials.[17] Freedom of expression is currently a crucial area in which to facilitate access to information, the exchange of views and opinions and the free flow of data across borders. However, Large-scale direct and indirect data localization requirements have been adopted into the domestic law of many countries.

5.2 Challenges Facing Legislatures

5.2.1 Fragmentation of the Legal System[18]

Half of the Asian data privacy statutes explicitly require consent from the data subject before data collection and data processing.[19] Several countries, such as

---

[14] 'The Promotion, Protection and Enjoyment of Human Rights on the Internet' (UN Human Rights Council, 22 June 2016). https://www.article19.org/data/files/English_22.pdf, accessed 19 March 2021.

[15] The EU Strategic Framework and Action Plan on Human Rights and Democracy gives a high priority to freedom of expression, saying 'the EU will continue to promote freedom of expression, opinion, assembly and association, both on-line and offline'. See 'EU Strategic Framework and Action Plan on Human Rights and Democracy', 2 (Council of the EU, 25 June 2012). https://www.consilium.europa.eu/uedocs/cms_data/docs/pressdata/EN/foraff/131181.pdf, accessed 19 May 2021.

[16] The Preamble of Florence Agreement, 'Agreement on the Importation of Educational, Scientific and Cultural Material' (UNESCO, 17 June 1950). https://eur-lex.europa.eu/legal-content/EN/TXT/?uri=CELEX%3A21979A0531%2801%29, accessed 19 March 2021.

[17] Ibid.

[18] '5.1 Fragmentation of the Legal System' is based on Yihan Dai, 'Data Protection Laws—One of the Most Important Sources of Competitive Advantage in the Context of International Trade' (2021) 4(1) Journal of Data Protection & Privacy.

[19] Graham William Greenleaf, *Asian Data Privacy Laws: Trade and Human Rights Perspectives* (1st edn, Oxford University Press 2014) 487.

the United Kingdom,[20] Russia,[21] Brazil,[22] Canada,[23] and France[24] have placed increasing restrictions on the cross-border flow of data. The PRC, in its Network Security Law, for the first time, expressly requires that the personal information and important data of Chinese citizens that are collected, generated and produced by operators of CII be stored in servers located in Mainland China.[25] To transfer data outside the country, including to HKSAR, MSAR, and Taiwan region, operators must receive government permission and undergo a security review.[26] If transfers of data offshore are necessary for operational reasons, a security assessment must be conducted by designated agencies, unless otherwise regulated by law.[27]

Over 60 countries have adopted data protection or privacy laws that regulate cross-border data flows on the Internet, but these data protection or privacy laws have different objectives, different rationales, different levels of legal reach, different default positions, and different approaches.[28] Although the motivations for these

---

[20] According to the United Kingdom's Companies Act 2006, 'if accounting records are kept at a place outside the United Kingdom, accounts and returns…must be sent to, and kept at, a place in the United Kingdom, and must at all times be open to such inspection. See 'Companies Act of United Kingdom', Chap. 46 (2006). http://www.legislation.gov.uk/ukpga/2006/46/pdfs/ukpga_200 60046_en.pdf, accessed 9 November 2020.

[21] In 2015, Russia enacted a Personal Data Law that mandates that data operators who collect personal data about Russian citizens must 'record, systematize, accumulate, store, amend, update and retrieve' data using databases physically located in Russia. 'Russia's Personal Data Localization Law Goes into Effect' (Duane Morris, 2015). https://www.duanemorris.com/alerts/russia_personal_data_localization_law_goes_into_effect_1015.html, accessed 9 November 2020.

[22] 'In 2016, Brazilian government agencies, including the Secretary of Information Technology of the Ministry of Planning, Development, and Management, included forced data localization as a requirement for public procurement contracts involving cloud-computing services.' Cory Nigel, 'Cross–Border Data Flows: Where Are the Barriers, and What Do They Cost?' 21 (Information Technology and Innovation Foundation, May 2017). http://www2.itif.org/2017-cross-border-data-flows.pdf, accessed 16 March 2021; see also 'USTR Request for Public Comments to Compile the National Trade Estimate Report (NTE) on Foreign Trade Barriers', 6 (27 October 2016). www.itic.org/public-policy/ITI2017NTEPublicComments.pdf, accessed 9 November 2020.

[23] Two Canadian provinces, British Columbia and Nova Scotia, have implemented laws mandating that personal data held by public bodies such as schools, hospitals, and public agencies be stored and accessed only in Canada unless certain conditions are fulfilled. Fred H. Cate, 'Provincial Canadian Geographic Restrictions on Personal Data in the Public Sector Submitted to the Trilateral Committee on Transborder Data Flows', 5–7 (2008). https://www.huntonak.com/images/content/3/3/v2/3360/cate_patriotact_white_paper.pdf, accessed 9 November 2020.

[24] Article 68 of the France Data Protection Act stipulates that a data controller cannot transfer personal data to a state that is not an EU member state if it does not provide a sufficient level of protection of individuals' privacy. Myria Saarinen, Julie Ladousse, and others, 'Data Protection in France: Overview' (Thomson Reuters, 1 February 2017). https://ca.practicallaw.thomsonreuters.com/6-502-1481?transitionType=Default&contextData=(sc.Default)&firstPage=true, accessed 9 February 2021.

[25] Network Security Law of the PRC, Art. 73.

[26] Ibid.

[27] Ibid.

[28] Christopher Kuner, 'Regulation of Transborder Data Flows under Data Protection and Privacy Law: Past, Present and Future', OECD Digital Economy Papers No. 187, 20. (OECD

5.2 Challenges Facing Legislatures

restrictions are diverse and, in some cases, multidimensional, the core motivations lie in privacy protection, economic and political reasons, and national security concerns. Cross-border data transfers often encompass cross-sectional issues of data protection and privacy law, e-commerce law, and law related to cyberspace (such as cybercrime law or cybersecurity law). Therefore, these laws of several nations and regions must be considered together because they are interrelated in protecting the privacy of personal data sent over the Internet.[29] However, existing data protection systems are highly fragmented and regulated in different ways at the global, regional and national levels.[30]

First, the right to protect personal data is explicitly considered a fundamental human right by EU law such as the GDPR[31] and the Charter of Fundamental Rights of the EU.[32] While, in other jurisdictions, for example, the PRC and the APEC forum, the right to the protection of personal data is not explicitly considered a fundamental human right. The Constitution of the PRC does not grant the right to privacy or the right to the protection of personal information as fundamental human rights. The General Provisions of the Civil Law set the basic rules for the protection of personal information. Although it can be interpreted as recognizing the right to the protection of personal information as a fundamental civil right, the General Provisions of the Civil Law do not explicitly adopt the concept of "personal information right". In the APEC Privacy Framework, privacy and data protection are less related to "human rights" and "fundamental rights" since these two words are not used at all.[33] In legal systems that do not consider the right to the protection of personal data a fundamental

---

publishing 2011). https://www.oecd-ilibrary.org/docserver/5kg0s2fk315f-en.pdf?expires=1604549314&id=id&accname=guest&checksum=62C9388AB859B25CE75D219D1AC46D74, accessed 4 January 2021.

[29] Bu–Pasha Shakila, 'Cross–Border Issues under EU Data Protection Law with Regards to Personal Data Protection' (2017) 26(3) Information and Communications Technology Law 213, 214; John P Carlin, James M Koukios, David A Newman and Suhna N Pierce, 'Data Privacy and Transfers in Cross–border Investigations' (Global Investigations Review, 9 August 2017). https://globalinvestigationsreview.com/insight/the-investigations-review-of-theamericas-2018/1145431/data-privacy-and-transfers-in-cross-border-investigations, accessed 26 March 2021.

[30] 'Data Protection Regulations and International Data Flows: Implications for Trade and Development' UNCTAD/WEB/DTL/STICT/2016/1/iPub, xi (United Nations Publication, 2016). http://unctad.org/en/PublicationsLibrary/dtlstict2016d1_en.pdf, accessed 29 March 2021.

[31] Article 1(2) and 1 (3) of the GDPR stipulate that 'This Regulation protects fundamental rights and freedoms of natural persons and in particular their right to the protection of personal data. (3) The free movement of personal data within the Union shall be neither restricted nor prohibited for reasons connected with the protection of natural persons with regard to the processing of personal data.'

[32] Article 8(1) of the Charter of Fundamental Rights of the EU stipulates that: '1. Everyone has the right to the protection of personal data concerning him or her. 2. Such data must be processed fairly for specified purposes and on the basis of the consent of the person concerned or some other legitimate basis laid down by law. Everyone has the right of access to data which has been collected concerning him or her, and the right to have it rectified.'

[33] Christopher Kuner, *Transborder Data Flows and Data Privacy Law* (Oxford University Press 2013) 62.

right, its status depends on the type of legal basis on which protection rests in a particular case—for instance, federal law, state law, case law, and administrative regulations.[34]

Second, the extent of the data protection provided by legislation varies worldwide.[35] In addition to the PRC, many countries have enacted legislation designed to protect individuals from inappropriate and unwanted uses of their personal data. However, the extent to which different countries and regions provide data protection differs. According to the UNCTAD, 128 out of 194 countries have enacted laws to protect data and privacy.[36] Sixty-six percent of UN countries have enacted data protection legislation, while 10% of UN countries have developed draft legislation for data protection.[37] Nineteen percent of UN countries do not have data protection legislation in place.[38] It is not possible to obtain data on 5% of UN countries. In this area, Asia and Africa have similar levels of adoption, with less than 40% of countries having a law in place.[39] The prerequisite for doing business online is having an electronic transaction law that recognizes that paper transactions are legally equivalent to electronic transactions. Of the 158 countries that have adopted such laws, 68 are developing countries or transition economies and 30 are LDC.[40] A total of 154 countries have enacted cybercrime legislation.[41] However, more than 13 countries do not have such legislation in place.[42] Regarding online consumer protection legislation, it is not possible to obtain data on as many as 57 countries, suggesting that online consumer protection is not fully addressed. Out of the 134 countries for which data exist, 110 have implemented consumer protection legislation that relates to e-commerce.[43]

Third, existing data protection systems vary greatly at the national level. Comprehensive data protection and privacy laws have been adopted by over 130 countries or independent jurisdictions and territories worldwide to protect the personal data held

---

[34] Ibid.

[35] UNCTAD/WEB/DTL/STICT/2016/1/iPub (n 30).

[36] 'Data Protection and Privacy Legislation Worldwide' (United Nations Conference on Trade and Development (hereinafter: UNCTAD), 2 April 2020). https://unctad.org/en/Pages/DTL/STI_and_ICTs/ICT4D-Legislation/eCom-Data-Protection-Laws.aspx, accessed 4 April 2021.

[37] Ibid.

[38] Ibid.

[39] Ibid.

[40] 'E-transactions Legislation Worldwide' (UNCTAD, 2 April 2020). https://unctad.org/en/Pages/DTL/STI_and_ICTs/ICT4D-Legislation/eCom-Transactions-Laws.aspx, accessed 4 April 2021.

[41] 'Cybercrime Legislation Worldwide' (UNCTAD, 2 April 2020). https://unctad.org/en/Pages/DTL/STI_and_ICTs/ICT4D-Legislation/eCom-Cybercrime-Laws.aspx, accessed 4 April 2021.

[42] Ibid.

[43] 'Online Consumer Protection Legislation Worldwide' (UNCTAD). https://unctad.org/en/Pages/DTL/STI_and_ICTs/ICT4D-Legislation/eCom-Consumer-Protection-Laws.aspx, accessed 4 April 2021.

5.2 Challenges Facing Legislatures

by private and public bodies.[44] The laws that apply to personal data in these countries and independent jurisdictions not only apply to data held in a physical form but also extend to data held in electronic forms, covering all or nearly all subject areas.[45] Some other countries, do not have a comprehensive data protection law in place but have sector-specific laws or regulations pertaining to data protection. In some jurisdictions, there may not even be any data protection measures at all.[46]

Fourth, the strength of jurisdictions' measures regarding data localization differ.[47] Greece, Brunei, the PRC, Indonesia, Nigeria, Russia and Vietnam are considered countries that have strong data localization laws because they all have laws that comprise explicit data localization requirements.[48] The EU is considered to have de facto data localization laws in place because there are few explicit data localization mandates in the EU.[49] The EU laws that create barriers to cross-border data transfers effectively act as data localization requirements.[50] Belarus, India, Kazakhstan, Malaysia, and South Korea are considered to have partial data localization laws because a wide range of data localization measures, including regulations requiring the consent of individuals before transferring their data across borders, and regulations applying only to certain domain names, are in place.[51] Argentina, Brazil, Columbia, Peru, and Uruguay are considered to have mild data localization laws in place because they restrict cross-border data transfers under certain conditions.[52] Australia, Canada, New Zealand, Turkey, Venezuela are considered to have sector-specific data localization laws in place because their data localization laws apply to specific sectors, including healthcare, telecommunications, finance, and national security.[53]

Fifth, the approaches to cross-border data transfers diverge in different legal frameworks. Some jurisdictions adopt approaches based on the "adequacy" of the data protection in foreign jurisdictions, requiring that the legal regime in the country importing the data have an "adequate", "sufficient", or "comparable" level of protection in place for data containing personal information or a system that is "equivalent" to that of the country exporting the data.[54] Some jurisdictions adopt approaches based

---

[44] David Banisar, 'National Comprehensive Data Protection/Privacy Laws and Bills 2020' (15 December 2020). https://ssrn.com/abstract=1951416, accessed 5 April 2021.

[45] Ibid.

[46] Yves Poullet and J. Marc Dinant, 'The Internet and Private Life in Europe: Risks and Aspirations' in Andrew T. Kenyon and Megan Richardson, *New Dimensions in Privacy Law—International and Comparative Perspectives* (Cambridge University Press 2006) 63–64.

[47] Igor Runets, 'Meeting the Challenge of Data Localization Laws'he Challenge of Data Localization Laws' (Linkedin, 27 September 2016). https://www.linkedin.com/pulse/meeting-challenge-data-localization-laws-igor-runets/, accessed 4 January 2021.

[48] Ibid.

[49] Ibid.

[50] Ibid.

[51] Ibid.

[52] Ibid.

[53] Ibid.

[54] Kuner (n 28) 20.

on the "person's consent", requiring the prior consent of the data subject before his or her personal information can be transmitted across borders.[55] For example, Korea requires obtaining consent from the data subjects if data transfers across borders occur in the context of a third party provider.[56] Other jurisdictions, such as Australia, adopt approaches based on the "accountability principle", requiring that the agency or organization that transfers personal information about an individual to a recipient (other than the agency, organization or the individual) who is outside the country remains accountable for that personal information.[57] Currently, increasing numbers of jurisdictions combine these three approaches together. Approaches based on the accountability principle allow the "adequacy" of data protection in foreign jurisdictions to be considered in making decisions about whether the transfer of personal data abroad is appropriate[58] or require that data be transferred only if the recipient adheres to the same level of data protection as the transferring entity and the consent of data subjects is obtained.[59] For example, Japan, under its amended the Act on the Protection of Personal Information (APPI), stipulates as follows:

> Prior consent of data subjects specifying the receiving country is required for transfers to third parties in foreign countries except if the transfer is to (i) a receiver having a data protection system which is equivalent to the system required under the APPI, or (ii) a receiver located in a country that is designated by the Committee as providing an adequate level of protection.[60]

Since different jurisdictions and organizations take vastly different approaches to regulating cross-border data transfers, it is challenging to evaluate the true compliance cost of some methods, namely, actual compliance costs and the more abstract costs of investing in innovation and diversification in the regulated sector.[61]

---

[55] For example, the GDPR, Art. 7.

[56] Jin Hwan Kim, Brian Tae-Hyun Chung and others, 'Data protection in South Korea: Overview' (Thomson Reuters Practical Law, 1 July 2015). https://content.next.westlaw.com/Document/I1d81ec834f2711e498db8b09b4f043e0/View/FullText.html?contextData=(sc.Default)&transitionType=Default&firstPage=true&bhcp=1, accessed 11 December 2020.

[57] For example, Australian Privacy Principles, Art. 8.1.

[58] Kuner (n 28) 20.

[59] Eric A. Packel and Patrick H. Haggerty, 'Cross-border Data Transfers: Cutting through the Complexity' (Lexology, 14 November 2014). https://www.lexology.com/library/detail.aspx?g=4ae7c510-e6cd-4eac-8bb0-b266794b6170, accessed 9 November 2020.

[60] 'Data Protection Laws of the World-Japan' (DLA PIPER, Last modified 24 Jan 2017). https://www.dlapiperdataprotection.com/index.html?c=JP&c2=&t=transfer, accessed 11 November 2020; 'The Amendment to the Act on the Protection of Personal Information—Impact on Foreign Financial Institutions' (Deloitte, 17 May 2017). https://www2.deloitte.com/jp/en/pages/legal/articles/dt-legal-japan-regulatory-update-17may2017.html, accessed 21 March 2021; Norbert Gehrke, 'Japan's Act on Protection of Personal Information Comes into Effect on May 30' (Medium, 6 May 2017). https://medium.com/tokyo-fintech/japans-act-on-protection-of-personal-information-comes-into-effect-on-may-30-dd7c7d476ec4, accessed 21 March 2021; Sicelo Kula, 'Japanese Personal Information Protection Act (PIPA)—a Heads up' (Mechalsons, 31 January 2017). https://www.michalsons.com/blog/personal-information-protection-act-pipa/24252, accessed 21 March 2021.

[61] Joaquin Blaya, 'Patient Privacy in a Mobile World—a Framework to Address Privacy Law Issues in Mobile Health' (GHDonline, 25 June 2013). https://www.trust.org/contentAsset/raw-data/03172beb-0f11-438e-94be-e02978de3036/file, accessed 9 November 2020.

5.2 Challenges Facing Legislatures

In addition, there are significantly different obligations concerning the processing of personal data among different jurisdictions. For example, Article 5.2 of the GDPR requires data controllers "to demonstrate that personal data are processed in a transparent manner in relation to the data subject". These transparency requirements under the GDPR are "throughout the life cycle of processing".[62] However, transparency is not a requirement for processing personal data in the PRC. Zhima Credit (Sesame Credit)—led by the Alibaba Group—uses data such as individuals' purchasing data from Alibaba's services to develop a credit score.[63] Such credit scoring likely violates the GDPR transparency rules.[64] Certain services based on personal data that are offered in one country may violate the laws of another.

Finally, several regulations, such as the GDPR, are legally binding, while others such as the OECD Privacy Guidelines[65] and the APEC Privacy Framework,[66] are not legally binding. Some initiatives, such as international human rights treaties and instruments adopted by UN bodies, have been enacted at the global level, while others, such as the APEC Privacy Framework, have been enacted at the regional level. There also exists a third kind of regulation, namely, the Council of Europe Convention 108, which is quite difficult to categorize; this council was originally enacted on an European (regional) scale but is now open to states outside of Europe.[67]

There is no global convention or treaty specifically dealing with issues of cross-border data transfers. Fragmentation and market barriers are emerging around the requirements for privacy and cross-border data flows, which makes international interoperability an increasingly serious challenge.[68] The diversity of international and regional data protection directives, treaties, guidelines, and other instruments, as well as "the difficulty of agreeing on the form of the legal framework, selecting the

---

[62] Müge Fazlioglu, 'Transparency and the GDPR: Practical Guidance and Interpretive Assistance from the Article 29 Working Party' (Iapp, 14 December 2017). https://iapp.org/news/a/transparency-and-the-gdpr-practical-guidance-and-interpretive-assistance-from-the-article-29-working-party/, accessed 9 March 2021.

[63] 'Zhima Credit' (Alipay). www.xin.xin/#/home, accessed 9 March 2019.

[64] 'Personal data shall be: processed lawfully, fairly and in a transparent manner in relation to the data subject ("lawfulness, fairness and transparency")'. See GDPR Art. 5(1) a.

[65] OECD, 'OECD Guidelines governing the Protection of Privacy and Transborder Flows of Personal Data' (2013) oecd.org/sti/ieconomy/2013-oecd-privacy-guidelines.pdf accessed 29 October 2020.

[66] APEC, 'APEC Privacy Framework' (2005). apec.org/Groups/Committee-on-Trade-and-Investment/~/media/Files/Groups/ECSG/05_ecsg_privacyframewk.ashx, accessed 4 November 2020.

[67] So far, one non-member of the Council of Europe, namely Uruguay, has enacted the Convention. See Council of Europe, 'Convention for the Protection of Individuals with regard to Automatic Processing of Personal Data, Treaty open for signature by the Member States and for accession by non-Member States' conventions.coe.int/Treaty/Commun/ChercheSig.asp?NT=108&CM=&DF=&CL=ENG accessed 4 November 2020.

[68] 'New China Data Privacy Standard Looks More Far-reaching than GDPR' (CSIS, 29 January 2018). https://www.csis.org/analysis/new-china-data-privacy-standard-looks-more-far-reaching-gdpr, accessed 14 January 2021.

standards on which such an instrument would be based, determining the scope of the instrument, and agreeing on an international organization to coordinate the work" impede the process of reaching an agreement on a single international framework.[69]

A standard or uniform way to comply with cross-border transfer obligations is lacking even among the EU's 27 member states, let alone among the more than 60 countries with data protection laws that restrict cross-border transfers.[70] Each comprehensive data protection and privacy law has provisions regarding cross-border data transfers, and the diversity of laws makes it virtually impossible for companies to select a single safeguard to protect data in the process of cross-border data transfers.[71] As countries and regions continue to develop new regulations and enter into new RTAs/FTAs, companies have to constantly educate themselves on the evolving nuances of laws related to data protection in every jurisdiction, specifically as those laws relate to transferring data in and out of the countries in question.[72]

The diversity of laws and the complexity of the regulatory requirements has led to poor compliance with the regulation of cross-border data transfers, which makes it harder for individuals to know which laws apply to their data processing, and complicates the lives of regulators by forcing them to deal with other regulatory systems; additionally, all of these problems give rise to legal issues related to the enforcement of cross-border data transfers.[73] When there are infringements on personal data, data subjects must know who is to blame, which laws to apply, and how to solve the problem. The answers to these questions may be complicated because of the multi-jurisdictional nature of cross-border data transfers and the complex applicability of one or more sets of national rules.[74] More work is needed to simplify the conditions for international data transfers.[75]

As international trade gradually becomes digital, the cross-border data transfer restrictions imposed by national laws are attracting the attention of international trade rule makers. It appears that these nationally mandated requirements and restrictions are acts of "spectacularly literal self-absorption"[76]; however, this kind of action may

---

[69] Kuner (n 28) 20.

[70] Miriam Wugmeister, Karin Retzer and Cynthia Rich, 'Global Solution for Cross-border Data Transfers: Making the Case for Corporate Privacy Rules' (2007) 38 Georgetown Journal of International Law 449, 461.

[71] Ibid.

[72] Dan Whitaker, 'The Challenge of Complying with China's New Cybersecurity Law' (Cybersecurity Law & Strategy, May 2017). https://uk.consilio.com/resource/challenge-complying-chinas-new-cybersecurity-law/, accessed 4 January 2021.

[73] Kuner (n 33) 147.

[74] Wugmeister and others (n 70) 469.

[75] 'First Report on the Implementation of the Data Protection Directive (95/46/EC)', 19 (15 May 2003). https://eur-lex.europa.eu/LexUriServ/LexUriServ.do?uri=COM:2003:0265:FIN:EN:PDF, accessed 12 November 2020.

[76] Manuel E. Maisog, 'Making the Case against Data Localization in China' (IAPP, 20 April 2015). https://iapp.org/news/a/making-the-case-against-data-localization-in-china/, accessed 5 March 2021.

5.2 Challenges Facing Legislatures

have "an impact that ripples quickly and resolutely outward into other countries".[77] Cross-border data transfer regulation is an example of the pluralistic legal framework that cannot be analysed under a single regulatory theory.[78] Cross-border data transfer regulation is not limited to one specific area of law but is related to many areas of law, including human rights law, trade law, contract law, labour law, and international public and private law; all of these laws must be taken into consideration in sufficient detail.[79] In the digital environment, domestic regulations cannot be neatly isolated and often have worldwide spill-over effects.[80] Ultimately, data localization is largely a global issue.[81] Although the emergence of regional or bilateral trade agreements as the vital component in data protection regulation is a new trend, its future remains unclear.[82]

5.2.2 Cross-Border Data Transfers and Emerging Concerns

Christopher Kuner summarizes nine developments that have changed the landscape for cross-border data flows in his book "Transborder Data Flows and Data Privacy Law" as follows:

> ...the increased globalization of the world economy; the growing economic importance of data processing; the social and cultural importance of online activity; the ubiquity of cross-border data flows; increase in data transfer by states and data sharing between them; interaction between the public and private sectors in the processing of personal data; the changing role of geography; greater direct involvement of individuals in trans-border data flows; glowing danger to the privacy of individuals.[83]

In addition to what Kuner mentions above, there are other new and fast-growing business models and technologies that also contribute to the new landscape of cross-border data flows.

First, cloud computing. The term "cloud computing" is defined by the National Institute of Standards and Technology as follows:

> ...a model for enabling ubiquitous, convenient, on-demand network access to a shared pool of configurable computing resources (e.g., networks, servers, storage, applications and services)

---

[77] Ibid.

[78] Kuner (n 33) 23.

[79] Ibid., 21.

[80] Mira Burri, 'Symposium—Future—Proofing Law: From Rdna to Robots the Governance of Data and Data Flows in Trade Agreements: The Pitfalls of Legal Adaptation' (November 2017) 51 U.C. Davis Law Review 65, 119.

[81] Maisog (n 76).

[82] For example, the TPP was finally abandoned by the United States in November 2016.

[83] Kuner (n 33) 2–4.

that can be rapidly provisioned and released with minimal management effort or service provider interaction.[84]

Most businesses currently use cloud-computing to streamline business processes and maintain relevancy in the current rapidly evolving business environment.[85] Cloud computing providers may need to collect personal data from customers to provide services to them.[86] Data can be managed and stored on external service providers (in "the cloud") remotely through the Internet instead of locally.[87] Making use of cloud services requires service providers and users to transfer data through the cloud.[88] The external service providers are often located in different jurisdictions.[89] Cloud-based providers must ensure that their data are stored and processed in compliance with all relevant laws[90] while ensuring data confidentiality and integrity.[91]

Using cloud services, individuals can download data from all over the world without leaving their own community.[92] The free movement of data across borders is the precondition for the operation and development of cloud computing.[93] Cloud computing makes it difficult to define the roles of the actors in cross-border data transfers—who is the data controller and who is the data processor—thus increasing the difficulty of implementing the existing laws.[94] The development of cloud computing

---

[84] Peter Mell and Tim Grance, 'The NIST Definition of Cloud Computing' (US Department of Commerce, September 2011) 2. https://csrc.nist.gov/publications/detail/sp/800-145/final, accessed 20 March 2021.

[85] Moritz Godel, Alexander Joshi and others, 'Facilitating Cross-border Data Flow in the Digital Single Market' (EU 2016) 1. http://ec.europa.eu/newsroom/document.cfm?doc_id=41185, accessed 20 October 2020; see also Beniamino Di Martinoa, Giuseppina Cretellaa, Antonio Espositoa, 'Cloud Forward: From Distributed to Complete Computing, Towards a Legislation-aware Cloud Computing Framework' (2015) 68 Procedia Computer Science 127, 128. https://doi.org/10.1016/j.procs.2015.09.229, accessed 20 March 2021.

[86] Renee Berry and Matthew Reisman, 'Policy Challenges of Cross-Border Cloud Computing' (May 2012) 4 Journal of International Commerce & Economics 1, 13. https://usitc.gov/journals/policy_challenges_of_cross-border_cloud_computing.pdf, accessed 20 March 2021.

[87] Steve Ranger, 'What is cloud computing? Everything you need to know about the cloud explained' (ADENT, 13 December 2018). https://www.zdnet.com/article/what-is-cloud-computing-everything-you-need-to-know-about-the-cloud/, accessed 1 November 2020; and Kommerskollegium, 'E-commerce-New Opportunities, New Barriers a Survey of E-Commerce Barriers in Countries Outside the EU' (National Board of Trade, November 2012), 16. https://www.wto.org/english/tratop_e/serv_e/wkshop_june13_e/ecom_national_board_e.pdf, accessed 20 March 2021.

[88] John Harauz, Lori M. Kaufman and Bruce Potter, 'Data Security in the World of Cloud Computing' (4 August 2009) 7(4) IEEE Security & Privacy 61, 62.

[89] Kommerskollegium (n 87) 16.

[90] Berry and Reisman (n 87) 1, 13.

[91] Harauz, Kaufman and Potter (n 88) 62.

[92] Galway Project and Centre for Information Policy Leadership, 'Data Protection Accountability: the Essential Elements a Document for Discussion' (October 2009), 2. https://www.ftc.gov/sites/default/files/documents/public_comments/privacy-roundtables-comment-project-no.p095416-544506-00059/544506-00059.pdf, accessed 13 November 2020.

[93] Kommerskollegium (n 87) 16.

[94] For example, the distinction between data 'controller' and data 'processor' lies at the heart of the Directive 95/46/EC, these two concepts are very important when applying the Directive

5.2 Challenges Facing Legislatures

has stimulated governments' concern about their information sovereignty. Some jurisdictions have begun to construct cloud computing in their own jurisdictions.[95]

Second, AI. In a generation, AI will transform some of the largest categories of international trade in goods (such as self-driving cars) and international trade in services (such as financial services).[96] Data are essential in developing AI capabilities.[97] Without data, we cannot make full use of AI, high-performance computing, and other technological advances. These technologies can help us improve healthcare, education, transportation networks, and energy conservation.[98]

Cross-border data flows matter to AI because AI relies on large data sets for predictive analysis and insights.[99] For AI to realize its full potential, it is better to present the data on a global level than on a national level. AI will learn more if it receives data from ten countries instead of one.[100] In addition, the availability of cross-border data flows informs AI in a way that transforms and promotes its ability to solve problems on a larger scale.[101] Large amounts of data flow in cyberspace occur across borders. These data are flowing among individuals, companies, and governments every day as part of the operation of the Internet and the associated technologies.[102] A high percentage of these data transfers is used to fuel AI applications such as

---

95/46/EC, as it determines who will be responsible for complying with EU data protection rules, which Member State laws apply, which data protection authorities take charge of the operations of data processing and how do data subjects exercise their rights. See Bridget Treacy, 'Working Party Confirms "Controller" and "Processor" Distinction' (2010) 10(5) Privacy & Data Protection 3, 3.

[95] Kuner (n 33) 31. For example, most European governments are already investing in cloud infrastructures. Matthew Coates, James (Jimmy) Harris and others, 'A New Era For European Public Services Cloud Computing Changes the Game', 5 (Accenture 2013). https://www.accenture.com/t20150527T211057__w__/fr-fr/_acnmedia/Accenture/Conversion-Assets/DotCom/Documents/Local/fr-fr/PDF_4/Accenture-New-Era-European-Public-Services-Cloud-Computing-Changes-Game.pdf, accessed 30 May 2020.

[96] Avi Goldfarb and Dan Trefler, 'How Artificial Intelligence Impacts International Trade' *in World Trade Report 2018* (WTO) 140. https://www.wto.org/english/res_e/publications_e/wtr18_4_e.pdf. Accessed 19 January 2021.

[97] Dan Ciuriak and Maria Ptashkina, 'The Digital Transformation and the Transformation of International Trade' (2018) RTA Exchange. Geneva: International Centre for Trade and Sustainable Development (ICTSD) and the Inter−American Development Bank (IDB), VI. http://e15initiative.org/wp-content/uploads/2015/09/RTA-Exchange-Digital-Trade-Ciuriak-andPtashkina-Final.pdf. Accessed 17 March 2021.

[98] Natasha Lomas, 'Europe Eyes Boosting Data Re-use and Funds for AI Research' (Riptari, 25 April 2018). https://techcrunch.com/2018/04/25/europe-eyes-boosting-data-re-use-and-funds-for-ai-research/, accessed 20 March 2021; Bobby Hellard, 'EU Outlines Plans to Promote More Data-sharing to Fuel Innovation' (ITPRO, 26 April 2018). http://www.itpro.co.uk/big-data/31002/eu-outlines-plans-to-promote-more-data-sharing-to-fuel-innovation, accessed 20 March 2021.

[99] Barry Devlin, 'AI and Predictive Analytics: Myth, Math, or Magic?', (TDWI, 10 February 2020). https://tdwi.org/articles/2020/02/10/adv-all-ai-and-predictive-analytics-myth-math-or-magic.aspx, accessed 19 October 2020.

[100] Ibid., 22.

[101] Ibid.

[102] Susan Ariel Aaronson, 'Data Minefield? How AI Is Prodding Governments to Rethink Trade in Data' (Centre for International Governance Innovation, 3 April 2018). https://www.cigionline.org/articles/data-minefield-how-ai-prodding-governments-rethink-trade-data, accessed 19 March 2021.

Siri, Alexa, Waze and Google searches.[103] Many AI applications and devices, such as language translation apps (Google Translate), navigation apps (Google Map), digital personal assistants (Siri), ride-sharing apps (Uber) and IBM's AI-powered supercomputers, depend on cross-border data flows for training.[104]

Therefore, AI-based companies desire a loose regulatory framework in their own country that allows them to collect and deploy large amounts of data, which creates a race to the bottom among regulators.[105] The empirical evidence suggests that there is a trade-off between privacy regulation and innovation.[106] No country can regulate AI alone because it is based on cross-border data flows.[107] In addition, AI often requires industry standards that, without international cooperation, will fragment world markets.[108]

Third, change of language and the way of thinking because of technological innovation. In the 1970s, the term "cross-border data flows" was typically understood as point-to-point data transfers, such as the exchange of internal company management information and responses to customers' service requirement.[109] By contrast, many cross-border data flows currently involve multiple partners (i.e. persons, organizations) communicating through online social networks (Facebook, Twitter), instant messaging apps (WhatsApp, line, WeChat), search engines (Google), and cloud computing (Google Drive).[110] Clearly defining the roles of the actors involved in cross-border data transfers is difficult.

Under the GDPR, the data controller is defined as "the natural or legal person, public authority, agency or other body which, alone or jointly with others, determines the purposes and means of the processing of personal data;"[111] data processor is defined as "a natural or legal person, public authority, agency or other body which processes personal data on behalf of the controller".[112] Differentiating data controller from the data processor is significant because these two have different responsibilities under the GDPR.[113] However, in practice, the boundary between data controller and processor is blurred as the number of collaborative business models increase, the dynamic characteristics of the relationships between customers and suppliers expand,

---

[103] Ibid.

[104] Ibid.

[105] Goldfarb and Trefler (n 96) 140.

[106] Goldfarb and Trefler (n 96) 140.

[107] Ibid.

[108] Goldfarb and Trefler (n 96) 140.

[109] Akira Ariyoshi, and others, 'Capital Control: Country Experience with Their Use and Liberalization' (International Monetary Fund, 17 May 2000). http://www.imf.org/external/pubs/ft/op/op190/index.htm, accessed 18 March 2021.

[110] Kuner (n 33) 2.

[111] GDPR, Art. 4.7.

[112] Ibid., Art. 4.8.

[113] According to Article 28 of the GDPR, 'Where processing is to be carried out on behalf of a controller, the controller shall use only processors providing sufficient guarantees to implement appropriate technical and organizational measures in such a manner that processing will meet the requirements of this Regulation and ensure the protection of the rights of the data subject.'

5.2 Challenges Facing Legislatures

cloud computing emerges and the use of web 2.0 models grow.[114] The controller versus processor dilemma is here to stay because facts change over time, which was well summarized as follows:

> Data is freely shared and duplicated more than ever before. The specific responsibilities of individuals, government, corporations, and the network of friends, partners, and other third parties who may come into possession of personal data have yet to be worked out. The technological trajectory, however, is clear: more and more data will be generated about individuals and will persist under the control of others.[115]

Some multinational organizations acknowledge that cultural and linguistic differences can lead to misunderstanding. For example, what Americans see as innocent documents, such as customer lists, weather reports or pricing spreadsheets, can in some cases, for example, in the PRC, be considered state secrets.[116]

Finding a common language that clearly differentiates among some controversial concepts that are closely related to the implementation of cross-border data flows, though difficult to achieve in practice, is essential.[117] These concepts include but are not limited to those of "personal data and personal information", "data privacy and data security", "data controller and data processor", "cross-border data flows", or "services and goods" under international trade law.

In the field of data, this common language should be transparent and established by determining the values inhering in information privacy that should constrain and structure technological and legal relations.[118] To maintain users' trust in the global Internet, cross-border data transfers must be not only free and open but also consider public policy objectives.[119] Negotiators should find a common language as to the degree to which they are willing to seek common ground while reserving differences.[120]

5.3 A Proposed Approach: Plurilateral Trade Agreements

There are currently two contradictory phenomena in the world, the growing globalization of the economy and society (much of which is achieved through the Internet

---

[114] Treacy (n 94) 3.

[115] Podesta and others, 'Big Data: Seizing Opportunities, Preserving Values Interim' (Executive Office of the President, May 2014), 9. https://obamawhitehouse.archives.gov/sites/default/files/docs/big_data_privacy_report_5.1.14_final_print.pdf, accessed 24 March 2021.

[116] Whitaker (n 72).

[117] Rostam J. Neuwirth, 'Essentially Oxymoronic Concepts' (2013) 2(2) Global Journal of Comparative Law 147, 149.

[118] Lawrence Lessig, *Code and Other Laws of Cyberspace* (1st edn, Basic Books 1999) 142–163.

[119] Andrew D. Mitchell and Jarrod Hepburn, 'Don't Fence Me In: Reforming Trade and Investment Law to Better Facilitate Cross-Border Data Transfer' (2017) 19(1) Yale Journal of Law and Technology 182, 229.

[120] Mira Burri, 'Regulation of Data Flows through Trade Agreements' (2017) 48 Georgetown Journal of International Law 407, 448.

and online communication) and the growth of the controls and restrictions on means (i.e., personal data flows) necessary to achieve it.[121] The greater harmonization and convergence issue has been addressed in some WTO agreements, such as the GATS and the GATT, but it must be considered more carefully in the digital regime.

We are living in an interconnected global digital society where the services of different operating systems are essentially universal. One critical question is which law should be applied since the Internet world has no physical boundaries.[122] From the perspective of approximate justice based on truth, a high-coherence legal system is superior to a low-coherence legal system.[123] The difference is that the latter is more fragmented and inconsistent than the former.[124] The legal divergence and increasing conflict between data use and privacy protection partly obstruct the process of identifying coherent solutions. However, this does not mean that nothing can be changed.

In a multilateral trading system, inter-jurisdictional competition may remain the dominant regulatory model, and the focus of regulatory competition will shift to better coordination between different regulatory areas.[125] At the regional level, the EU's legal framework is modified to force regulators to strengthen cooperation.[126] A voluntary cooperation mechanism between data protection regulators is being developed by organizations such as the APEC and the OECD. Due to the limited application, there is an urgent need to build "legal interoperability" between different systems of cross-border data flow regulation over a much broader range.

Data protection and cross-border data transfers are contentious issues. This kind of contentious issue often impedes digital trade negotiations and stems from more fundamental policy and cultural divergences. To use the WTO terminology, the issues can be categorized as various "trade and…pairs",[127] which make solution-finding processes different and protracted.[128] Different countries hold different cultural values and privacy perceptions.[129] The diversity of values greatly influences how

---

[121] Kuner (n 33) 186.

[122] Shakila (n 29) 213.

[123] Rostam J. Neuwirth, *Law in the Time of Oxymora: A Synaesthesia of Language Logic and Law* (Routledge 2018) 225.

[124] Ibid.

[125] Rostam J. Neuwirth, 'Global Market Integration and the Creative Economy: The Paradox of Industry Convergence and Regulatory Divergence' (2015) 18 Journal of International Economic Law 21, 46.

[126] 'Free Flow of Non-Personal Data: Parliament Approves EU's Fifth Freedom' (EC, 4 October 2018). www.europarl.europa.eu/news/en/press-room/20180926IPR14403/free-flow-of-non-personal-data-parliament-approves-eu-s-fifth-freedom, accessed 15 October 2020.

[127] Andrew T. F. Lang, 'Reflecting on "Linkage": Cognitive and Institutional Change in the International Trading System' (2007) 70 Modern Law Review 523, 523–49.

[128] Burri, 'The Regulation of Data Flows through Trade Agreements' (n 120) 413.

[129] Ravi Sarathy and Christopher J. Robertson, 'Strategic and Ethical Considerations in Managing Digital Privacy' (2003) 46 Journal of Business Ethics 111, 113; Sandra J. Milberg, Sandra J. Burke, H. Jeff Smith, and Ernest A. Kallman, 'Personal Information Privacy and Regulatory Approaches' (1995), 38(12) Communications of the ACM 65, 66–67.

privacy is appreciated and treated in a given country. This, in turn, determines the data protection legislation that a country may introduce and whether a country has effective laws and regulations to protect data.[130] Take the EU as an example:

> The European Union's adoption of Europe-wide governmental regulation over protecting consumer data privacy may be interpreted as a reaction to the excesses of various oppressive regimes in the earlier part of the twentieth century, especially during World War Two, and the continuing fear of the misuse of personal data by corporate and government entities.[131]

The United States, in contrast, has been more inclined to industry self-regulation because of the "country's history of entrepreneurial behavior and laissez-faire capitalism".[132]

New and unpredictable developments are on the way, and the way of handling problems today may not be sufficient for tomorrow's task.[133] Several sensitive issues must be taken into account in the process of negotiating regional or bilateral digital trade regulations. These sensitive issues include national security, privacy and cultural values. Coherence—in the sense of unity but not uniformity—may be considered a "precondition for an approximation of truth in the sense of justice" in the field of law.[134] A common language is needed to build a global legal framework for the future.[135] Negotiators can pursue coherence by finding a common language as to:

> The degree to which they are willing to skirt their differences and leave the interpretation of these concepts to future WTO adjudicators to elucidate through case law versus needing to spell out these concepts in detail so as to prevent the exception from swallowing the rule.[136]

Much of the discussion within and outside the WTO, as well as in the literature on trade and cross-border data transfers, has focused on trade in services and its regulation.[137] This argument is reinforced by the current trend of "servicification", whereby

---

[130] Sarathy and Robertson (n 129) 115–116, 122–123; Milberg and others (n 129) 68–69.

[131] Tiwalade Adelola, Ray Dawson, and FiratBatmaz, 'Privacy and Data Protection in E-commerce the Effectiveness of a Government Regulation Approach in Developing Nations, Using Nigeria as a Case', 235. http://ieeexplore.ieee.org/document/7038812/?reload=true, accessed 24 March 2021.

[132] Sarathy and Robertson (n 129) 111, 115.

[133] Peter J. Guffin, Kyle J. Glover, and others, 'Whose Governing Privacy? Regulation and Protection in a Digital Era: Foreword' (2014) 66 Maine Law Review 369, 369.

[134] Neuwirth (n 123) 225 and 233.

[135] Neuwirth (n 123) 202.

[136] Mark Wu, 'Digital Trade—Related Provisions in Regional Trade Agreements: Existing Models and Lessons for the Multilateral Trade System', 29 (ICTSD 2017). http://e15initiative.org/wp-content/uploads/2015/09/RTA-Exchange-Digital-Trade-Mark-Wu-Final-2.pdf. Accessed 22 February.

[137] Mira Burri and Thomas Cottier, *Trade Governance in the Digital Age: World Trade Forum* (Cambridge University Press 2012) 420; Kommerskollegium, 'No Transfer, No Trade—the Importance of Cross-Border Data Transfers for Companies Based in Sweden' (1st end, National Board of Trade, January 2014). https://unctad.org/meetings/en/Contribution/dtl_ict4d2016c01_Kommerskollegium_en.pdf, accessed 30 March 2021; 'Business Without Borders: The Importance of Cross–Border Data Transfers to Global Prosperity' (United States Chamber of Commerce and Hunton and Williams LLP), 2. https://www.huntonprivacyblog.com/wp-content/uploads/sites/28/2014/05/021384_BusinessWOBorders_final.pdf, accessed 1 March 2021; Joshua P. Meltzer, 'International Data Flows and Privacy the Conflict and Its Resolution' Policy Research Working Paper

there is an increase in the use, production, and sale of services.[138] However, no RTAs to date have dealt exclusively with the services sector.[139] In addition, compared to the Doha Round, in which the 160 members participated, the number of participants in the negotiation of RTAs is limited.[140] RTAs are not the only way to advance beyond the commitments made in the WTO and achieve deeper integration than what has been achieved by older multilateral agreements. The WTO provides another mechanism, the conclusion of plurilateral trade agreements under Article II.3 of the Marrakesh Agreement Establishing the World Trade Organization, which allows members to move forward on an agenda of common interest. The agreement states that:

> The agreements and associated legal instruments included in Annex 4 (hereinafter referred to as "Plurilateral Trade Agreements") are also part of this Agreement for those Members that have accepted them and are binding on those Members. The Plurilateral Trade Agreements do not create either obligations or rights for Members that have not accepted them.

This provision has provided a pathway towards the possibility of sectoral or issue specific plurilateral trade agreements amongst interested WTO members only, versus the multilateral approach based on an agreement embraced by all WTO members. This approach offers the opportunity for WTO members to agree to certain disciplines that apply to signatory countries and regions only. Compared to RTAs, which must encompass broad issues related to trade in goods or trade in services, the plurilateral agreement can focus on a specific area.

The TiSA is a plurilateral initiative for service liberalization and rulemaking being discussed by 23 like-minded countries and regions amongst a coalition called "Really Good Friends of Services".[141] The TiSA has adopted a hybrid approach of commitments: NT commitments are scheduled using a negative list approach, while market access commitments are scheduled using a positive list approach.[142] Under the TiSA, NT will in principle be applied across the board, and signatory countries and regions

---

8431, 97-99 (World Bank Group, May 2018). http://documents.worldbank.org/curated/en/751621525705087132/pdf/WPS8431.pdf, accessed 12 March 2021.

[138] Emilie Anér and Magnus Rentzhog, 'Everybody Is in Services: The Impact of Servicification in Manufacturing on Trade and Trade Policy', 2 (2012). https://slidetodoc.com/everybody-is-in-services-servicification-and-trade-policy/, accessed 24 November 2020; Rainer Lanz and Andreas Maurer, 'Services and Global Value Chains—Some Evidence on Servicification of Manufacturing and Services Networks' (WTO 2015). https://www.wto.org/english/res_e/reser_e/ersd201503_e.htm, accessed 24 November 2020.

[139] WTO Regional Trade Agreements Information System. https://rtais.wto.org/UI/PublicMaintainRTAHome.aspx, accessed 1 April 2021.

[140] Ibid.

[141] 'An international "Trade in Services Agreement" (TiSA)? Why this Proposed Free Trade Agreement (FTA) in Services Is Dangerous to Democracy, Development, and the Public Interest, and Must Be Stopped!' (June 2017). https://www.handelskampanjen.no/files/documents/Memo-Proposed_TISA_June_2017_OWINFS.pdf, accessed 15 November 2020; 'Public Services International Brief on the Trade in Services Agreement (TiSA)' (July 2013). https://www.world-psi.org/sites/default/files/documents/research/en_psi_tisa_policy_brief_july_2013_final.pdf, accessed 15 March 2021.

[142] 'TiSA Factsheet', 11 (EC, 26 September 2016). http://trade.ec.europa.eu/doclib/html/154971.htm, accessed 15 November 2020.

5.3 A Proposed Approach: Plurilateral Trade Agreements

might agree to so-called standstill clauses and ratchet clauses unless other provisions are made. In standstill clauses, members have to list all the barriers as they are at the moment of making the commitments, and after that, they cannot introduce any new barriers.[143] Ratchet clauses effectively prevent the government from reversing achieved liberalization floors made by previous governments once a sector is liberalized.[144]

Discussions on data flows are envisaged by the TiSA.[145] The TiSA develops a negotiation framework that will lay the foundation for future international rules dealing with sensitive issues, such as cross-border data flows and culture services, as it has developed alternative architectures and scheduling practices in trade in service. Since the application of RTAs is limited to specific regions and counties while "the business community has a preference for rules on a global level",[146] the TiSA is likely to play a supporter role that will alleviate the so-called "spaghetti-bowl" effect of RTAs as well as help to establish globally harmonized frameworks.[147] The TiSA could play a significant role in the setting of global rules for cross-border data transfers, as it is a creative and flexible approach. Moreover, the TiSA is in a better position to strike a balance between the free flow of data across borders and public policy objectives in the context of international trade liberalization because the TiSA would bind only those WTO members that are ready to make the concessions.[148] Entering into Plurilateral Trade Agreements such as TiSA is a good way of seeking common ground while reserving differences.

5.4 Interim Remarks

Laws and institutions cannot catch up with the current development of data-fueled technologies and the convergence of industry. The convergence of industry and technology not only leads to the difficulty of classification but also poses serious challenges to determining the range of multilateral disciplines. The existing international trade rules do not protect cross-border data transfers in a consistent, coherent and predictable manner[149]; the existing legal international trade frameworks are insufficient to handle the exponential growth and complexity of cross-border data flows, regardless of whether they exist at the global level (WTO) or at the bilateral or

---

[143] Ibid., 10.
[144] Ibid.
[145] Ibid., 5.
[146] Nakatomi Michitaka, 'Services Negotiation and Plurilateral Agreement: TiSA and Sectoral Approach', 5 (September 2014). https://www.rieti.go.jp/jp/publications/pdp/14p023.pdf, accessed 15 November 2020.
[147] Ibid., 16.
[148] Burri, 'The Regulation of Data Flows through Trade Agreements' (n 120) 439.
[149] Mitchell and Hepburn (n 119) 182.

multilateral level (RTAs).[150] The diversity of law and the complexity of the regulatory requirements have led to poor compliance with the regulation of cross-border data transfers, which hampers individuals' rights to know which law governs their data-related rights and obligations, increases the burden of regulators by forcing them to cope with other regulatory systems, and brings about legal issues regarding cross-border enforcement.[151] Cross-border data transfer regulation is an example of the pluralistic legal framework that cannot be analysed under a single regulatory theory.[152] Cross-border data transfer is not limited to one specific area of law; it is related to many areas of law, including human rights, trade, contract, labour, and international public and private. All these areas of law must be taken into consideration in sufficient detail.[153]

The greater harmonization and convergence issue has been addressed in some WTO agreements, such as the GATS and GATT, but it must be considered more carefully in the digital regime. In the context of international trade liberalization, cross-border data transfers call for cooperation globally, which will require national and regional policymakers to think less about ensuring that their regulatory models and norms are adopted globally and more about achieving interoperability among different governance approaches.[154] To make governance approaches interoperable, it is necessary to find a common global language that clearly addresses some controversial issues that are closely related to the implementation of cross-border data flows. The conclusion of plurilateral trade agreements is a good starting point to build bridges between different systems of data protection and cross-border data flow regulations.

---

[150] Kuner (n 33) 167.

[151] Kuner (n 33) 147.

[152] Kuner (n 33) 23.

[153] Kuner (n 33) 21.

[154] Susan Ariel Aaronson and Rob Maxim, 'Trade and the Internet: The Challenge of the NSA Revelations Policies in the US, EU, and Canada'. https://www2.gwu.edu/~iiep/assets/docs/papers/Aaronson_Maxim_Trade_Internet.pdf, accessed 5 April 2021; Susan Ariel Aaronson, 'Can Trade Policy Set Information Free?' (VOX, 22 December 2012). https://voxeu.org/article/trade-agreements-global-internet-governance, accessed 5 April 2021.

Chapter 6
Conclusion

...greater coherence in law, and legal thinking in particular, may be able to resolve many serious global problems that humanity face. The reason is that when facing complexity, the difficulty of the task is not to identify the correct means for the solution of each single problem; instead, the difficulty lies in the solution of each single problem through a coordinated and coherent approach.[1]

—Rostam J. Neuwirth

Data privacy is a fundamental issue in today's information age.[2] In Helen Nissenbaum's book *Privacy in Context: Technology, Policy, and the Integrity of Social Life*, she gives an account of privacy in terms of the expected flows of personal information, modelled on the construct of "context-relative informational norms", which is defined by Nissenbaum as:

> ...depending on the function of the types of information in question, the respective roles of the subject, the sender and recipient of the information and the principles under which the information is transmitted from the sender to the recipient.[3]

Nissenbaum argues that information should be distributed and protected according to the norms of different social environments—whether the office, hospital, shopping mall, university, or among family and friends. Nissenbaum also claims that, when people complain and protest about privacy violations, what they are truly concerned about is not the act of sharing information itself but the inappropriate sharing of information.[4] Privacy protection means ensuring proper flows of personal information, both online and offline, and also means that disruptions in information flows,

---

[1] Rostam J. Neuwirth, *Law in the Time of Oxymora: A Synaesthesia of Language Logic and Law* (Routledge 2018) 229.

[2] Johannes Gehrke, Edward Lui and Rafael Pass, 'Towards Privacy for Social Networks: A Zero-Knowledge Based Definition of Privacy' (28–30 March 2011) Proceeding TCC' 11 Proceedings of the 8th Conference on Theory of Cryptography, 432–449. http://www.cs.cornell.edu/~luied/zkPrivacyFinal.pdf, accessed 31 March 2021.

[3] Helen Nissenbaum, *Privacy in Context: Technology, Policy, and the Integrity of Social Life* (Stanford University Press 2010) 127.

[4] Ibid., 2.

powered by information technology and digital media, can be equally disturbing, both online and offline.[5]

The PRC's experience in the field of data legislation is of interest for at least three reasons. First, the Chinese government is eager to position itself as a pioneer and supporter of the globalization and liberalization of trade, while, on the other hand, the government is cautious and discrete regarding the free movement of data across borders because of national security, privacy, and other concerns. While the cross-border data restriction policies represent a cautious approach towards the globalization of trade in services in an increasingly integrated world, the ambition of the PRC on the international stage emphasizes globalization, cooperation, and interoperability of international trade.

Second, the goals of the PRC's data-related legislation differ widely from those of other jurisdictions. The EU long approached data protection through the lens of human rights in general and the right to privacy in particular.[6] In US privacy legislation, state security agencies are committed to a "collect everything" approach to electronic surveillance.[7] The PRC's data-related legislation tries to boost sales,[8] safeguard security (national and network security), meet the legitimate needs of business, intentionally leave a viable space for technological innovation—especially the development of new technology that is nourished by data, and discount the rights of individuals as less important. Moreover, recent developments in PRC legislation mainly focus on personal data in cyberspace rather than all personal data.

Finally, the PRC enjoys the competitive advantage of its data-related legislation in the context of international trade. The Chinese government has begun to integrate e-commerce provisions into FTAs, trying to establish a conducive and healthy environment for the development of e-commerce (for example, in the RCEP agreement, the PRC-Korea, Republic of FTA and the PRC-Australia FTA). However, it should be noted that the hard commitments in these FTAs have not exceeded those already made to the WTO.[9]

The PRC's online strategy and data-related legislation have partly cleared the way for domestic companies to develop a fast-growing, technologically advanced "parallel universe" in which domestic companies operate in the same field as familiar

---

[5] Helen Nissenbaum, 'A Contextual Approach to Privacy Online' (2011 Fall) 140(4) Journal of the American Academy of Arts and Sciences 33, 45.

[6] John Robinson, 'The Snowden Disconnect: When the Ends Justify the Means' (2014). http://dx.doi.org/10.2139/ssrn.2427412, accessed 13 December 2020.

[7] Ibid.

[8] Paul De Hert and Vagelis Papakonstantinou, 'The Data Protection Regime in China, In–depth Analysis' (19 November 2015) 1(4) Brussels Privacy Hub Working Paper 1, 26. http://www.europarl.europa.eu/RegData/etudes/IDAN/2015/536472/IPOL_IDA(2015)536472_EN.pdf, accessed 29 March 2021.

[9] Dan Ciuriak and Maria Ptashkina, 'The Digital Transformation and the Transformation of International Trade' (2018) RTA Exchange. Geneva: International Centre for Trade and Sustainable Development (ICTSD) and the Inter–American Development Bank (IDB), 3. http://e15initiative.org/wp-content/uploads/2015/09/RTA-Exchange-Digital-Trade-Ciuriak-and-Ptashkina-Final.pdf. Accessed 17 March 2021.

western companies.[10] The PRC's tech scene is booming in this parallel universe.[11] Some of these domestic companies that benefit from this parallel universe are world-class market leaders: Tencent's WeChat, Weibo, Alibaba, and Baidu.

"Data is the new oil, and China is the new Saudi Arabia", says AI expert Kai-Fu Lee.[12] At the end of December 2020, nearly 1 billion Chinese people are now actively using the Internet,[13] which is greater than the entire population of the United States. Among them, almost 986 million people are mobile users.[14] As the impetus to collect, apply and share personal data grows, the laws of the PRC related to data protection determine the level of development of the data-fueled industry. The Chinese government holds a positive and facilitative attitude towards Internet-related issues, as it recognizes the role played by the Internet and its related technologies, which, among other benefits, increases the country's economic competitiveness.[15] From the central government to local governments, many incentive measures and preferential policies related to the Internet have been adopted or promulgated.[16]

Data protection laws are critical for the functioning of modern businesses. For companies, the ability to harness personal data is essential for the development of the digital economy; for countries, data protection laws are one of the most important sources of competitive advantage in the context of international trade, especially for the PRC, which is extremely data-rich because of its large population and the substantial number of active Internet users.[17] The widespread use of ICT and the Internet

---

[10] Emily Rauhala, 'America Wants to Believe China Can't Innovate. Tech Tells a Different Story' (Washington Post, 19 July 2016). https://www.washingtonpost.com/world/asia_pacific/america-wants-to-believe-china-cant-innovate-tech-tells-a-different-story/2016/07/19/c17cbea9-6ee6-479c-81fa-54051df598c5_story.html?noredirect=on&utm_term=.e008b42cc8ee, accessed 17 September 2020.

[11] Ibid.

[12] Kai-Fu Lee, 'Joins "Squawk Box" to Discuss His New Book, "AI Superpowers", and the U.S.-China Trade Tensions' (CNBC, 24 September 2018). https://www.cnbc.com/video/2018/09/24/data-china-tech-trade-war-artificial-intelligence.html, accessed 17 October 2020.

[13] Palash Ghosh, 'China Now Has Almost 1 Billion Internet Users' (Forbes, 10 February Ghosh, 2021). https://www.forbes.com/sites/palashghosh/2021/02/04/china-now-has-almost-1-billion-internet-users/?sh=cf1a56026d91, accessed 6 March 2021.

[14] Lai Lin Thomala, 'Number of mobile internet users in China 2021–2020' (Statista, 10 February 2021). https://www.statista.com/statistics/273973/number-of-mobile-internet-users-in-china/, accessed 6 April 2021.

[15] Jihong Chen, 'China' in Robert Bond, *Getting the Deal Through: E-Commerce 2019* (August 2018). https://www.wildy.com/isbn/9781789150179/getting-the-deal-through-e-commerce-2018-paperback, accessed 10 September 2020.

[16] The cities of Xiang Yang (襄阳), Chong Qing (重庆), Xin Xiang (新乡), Jing Men (荆门), Shen Zhen (深圳), Bao Tou (包头), Shan Tou (汕头), Zhan Jiang (湛江), Zun Yi (遵义), to mention but a few and the Zheng Jiang Province of the PRC have enacted their own Internet Plus Strategy. See also 'State Council's Guidance on Actively Promoting the "Internet plus" Action' (Chinese title: 國務院關於積極推進 "互聯網+" 行動的指導意見) (Ministry of Commerce of the PRC, 26 August 2015). http://www.mofcom.gov.cn/article/b/g/201508/20150801092189.shtml, accessed 26 March 2021.

[17] Thomala (n 14); see also Ghosh (n 13).

give rise to new business models and more technological innovation.[18] Additionally, a large amount of personal data needs to be used and processed, which arouses users' concerns about their privacy and is one reason that governments claim to restrict cross-border data transfers.[19] However, the belief that cross-border data transfers would greatly raise the risk of privacy infringements is not supported for several reasons.

First, compared to personal data stored in physical forms, the massive amount of personal information stored in digital forms is much simpler and more inexpensive to access, duplicate, remove, and transfer. In other words, privacy and data security do not depend on the country in which the information is stored.

Second, cross-border data transfers increase the choice of information providers available to consumers and businesses, letting them select service providers with the best privacy and security practices in the world.[20] Third, there is a risk that the regulation of cross-border data flows may be used by governments not to promote human rights but to thwart them.[21] For example, some governments prevent data from being transferred to another country with a higher standard of privacy protection to protect informational sovereignty.[22]

In addition, data localization requirements sometimes make it easier for governments to implement surveillance on their own citizens.[23] Data localization requirements also provide more opportunities for governments to claim jurisdiction over the data stored in their jurisdictions.[24]

Fourth, another concern is that the transfer of data to another country has the potential to prevent citizens from a more sophisticated national legal system.[25] Such a concern mainly occurs in regimes that have stricter data protection laws, such as the EU. The truth is that, although tougher domestic data protection laws exist, the

---

[18] 'Data Protection Regulations and International Data Flows: Implications for Trade and Development' UNCTAD/WEB/DTL/STICT/2016/1/iPub, xi (United Nations Publication, 2016). http://unctad.org/en/PublicationsLibrary/dtlstict2016d1_en.pdf, accessed 29 March 2021.

[19] Kommerskollegium, 'No Transfer, No Trade—the Importance of Cross-Border Data Transfers for Companies Based in Sweden' (1st end, National Board of Trade, January 2014). https://unctad.org/meetings/en/Contribution/dtl_ict4d2016c01_Kommerskollegium_en.pdf, accessed 30 March 2021.

[20] Usman Ahmed and Anupam Chander, 'Information Goes Global: Protecting Privacy, Security, and the New Economy in a World of Cross−border Data Flows', E15Initiative, Geneva: International Centre for Trade and Sustainable Development (ICTSD) and World Economic Forum (2015), 1. http://e15initiative.org/wp-content/uploads/2015/09/E15-Digital-Chander-and-Ahmed-Final.pdf, accessed 24 May 2021.

[21] Christopher Kuner, Transborder Data Flows and Data Privacy Law (Oxford University Press 2013) 120.

[22] Ibid.

[23] Tatevik Sargsyan, 'Data Localization and the Role of Infrastructure for Surveillance, Privacy, and Security' (2016) 10 International Journal of Communication 2221, 2223.

[24] Ibid., 2224.

[25] Kuner (n 21) 166.

threats to personal data and privacy are usually domestic.[26] In Germany, everyone must be formally registered with the police at all times.[27] In both Germany and France, inspectors have the power to arrive at your door to investigate whether you have an unlicensed television.[28] Furthermore, countries can still insist that their public order, privacy protection, and security requirements be followed by foreign jurisdictions wherever they transfer, store or process data. It is common in cross-border outsourcing arrangements that outsourcing providers promise to protect personal data by complying with local standards.[29]

Finally, cross-border digital trade builds on the foundation of users' trust.[30] The willingness of individuals and companies to share their data is fundamental to the data-driven economy.[31] The privacy of individuals should be well protected to elicit the confidence of users.[32] Protecting the privacy of data subjects is critical to accomplishing the purposes of cross-border data transfers.[33] For example, health studies are increasingly conducted at the international level, "with results being compared and matched to achieve greater statistical significance".[34] Therefore, the international transfer of personal information is quite important in the area of health research for the future of all people.[35] The existence and efficacy of privacy, and data security measures will influence the decision of potential research participants to contribute their samples and data,[36] thus influencing whether health research can be smoothly conducted.

---

[26] Matthias Bauer Hosuk and others, 'The Costs of Data Localization: Friendly Fire on Economic Recovery,' 3 (ECIPE, 2014). https://ecipe.org/wp-content/uploads/2014/12/OCC32014__1.pdf, accessed 20 March 2021.

[27] James Q. Whitman, 'The Two Western Cultures of Privacy: Dignity versus Liberty' (Whitman, 2004) 113 Yale Law Journal 1153, 1158.

[28] Ibid., 1158–1159.

[29] Ahmed and Chander (n 20) 1.

[30] Susan Ariel Aaronson and Miles D. Townes, 'Can Trade Policy Set Information Free?' (June 2014) Institute for International Economic Policy Working Paper Series, 9. https://www2.gwu.edu/~iiep/assets/docs/papers/2014WP/AaronsonIIEPWP20149.pdf. Accessed 11 March 2021; UNCTAD/WEB/DTL/STICT/2016/1/iPub (n 18).

[31] Michael Mandel, 'The Economic Impact of Data: Why Data Is Not like Oil' (PPI, 7 November 2017). https://www.progressivepolicy.org/wp-content/uploads/2017/07/PowerofData-Report_2017.pdf, accessed 9 November 2020.

[32] 'Report on what's the Big Deal with Data?' 18 (Software Alliance, 21 October 2016). https://data.bsa.org/wp-content/uploads/2015/12/bsadatastudy_en.pdf, accessed 24 October 2020.

[33] Xiaoyan Zhang, 'Cracking China's Cybersecurity Law,' (China Law and Practice, 19 January 2017). http://www.chinalawandpractice.com/sites/clp/2017/01/19/cracking-chinas-cybersecurity-law/?slreturn=20171008234213, accessed 24 October 2020.

[34] Jennifer Stoddart, Benny Chan and Yann Joly, 'Harmonizing Privacy Laws to Enable International Biobank Research: The EU's Adequacy Approach to Privacy and International Data Sharing in Health Research' (2016) 44 Journal of Law, Medicine & Ethics 143, 146.

[35] Ibid.

[36] A Canadian survey conducted on a random sample of adults revealed that government privacy impact assessments had a positive influence on 46% of survey respondents with regards to how they feel about participating in health research. See Teschke and others, 'Public Opinions about Participating in Health Research' (2010) 101 Canadian Journal of Public Health 159, 163.

Overall, privacy and cross-border data transfers are not independent issues but are closely related to each other. The EU Council of Europe Convention 108,[37] OECD Guidelines on the Protection of Privacy and Transborder Flows of Personal Data,[38] and the APEC Privacy Framework,[39] are motivated by both economic and privacy protection concerns. In addition, the relationship between privacy and personal information is complicated; these issues do intersect, but not all personal information can be considered private. Cross-border data transfers involve issues of economic efficiency, trade promotion and fundamental human rights protection. The emphasis of national and international legislation should not only focus on protecting against risks but also focus on maximizing the benefit of cross-border data transfers.[40] The issues of privacy and cross-border data transfers do not conflict in the context of international trade. Protecting the privacy of data subjects is critical to accomplishing the purposes of cross-border data transfers.[41]

Existing data protection systems are highly fragmented,[42] and will be difficult to harmonize the objectives of data protection laws with those of international trade liberalization in the near future. The most important law governing this issue are usually adopted at the domestic level. As data, particularly personal data, are now the most valuable assets of the digital age, the regulation of personal data shall be at the heart of policymaking to ensure the goal of a "sustainable" development and competitive development of trade, science and technology, and society. Countries need to address concerns with regard to consumer protection, data security and

---

[37] According to the preamble of the Convention for the Protection of Individuals with regard to Automatic Processing of Personal Data: 'considering that it is desirable to extend the safeguards for everyone's rights and fundamental freedoms, and in particular the right to the respect for privacy, taking account of the increasing flow across frontiers of personal data undergoing automatic processing; Reaffirming at the same time their commitment to freedom of information regardless of frontiers; Recognizing that it is necessary to reconcile the fundamental values of the respect for privacy and the free flow of information between peoples'. See 'Convention for the Protection of Individuals with regard to Automatic Processing of Personal Data' (Council of Europe, 28 January 1981). https://www.coe.int/en/web/conventions/full-list/-/conventions/treaty/108, accessed 24 October 2020.

[38] According to the preface of the OECD Guidelines on the Protection of Privacy and Transborder Flows of Personal Data: 'the development of automatic data processing, which enables vast quantities of data to be transmitted within seconds across national frontiers, and indeed across continents, has made it necessary to consider privacy protection in relation to personal data. …On the other hand, there is a danger that disparities in national legislation could hamper the free flow of personal data across frontiers; these flows have greatly increased in recent years and are bound to grow further with the widespread introduction of new computer and communications technology. Restrictions on these flows could cause serious disruption in important sectors of the economy, such as banking and insurance.'

[39] According to the preamble (1) of the APEC Privacy Framework: 'APEC economies realize that a key part of efforts to improve consumer confidence and ensure the growth of electronic commerce must be cooperation to balance and promote both effective information privacy protection and the free flow of information in the Asia Pacific region.'

[40] Kuner (n 21) 186.

[41] Zhang (n 33) 22.

[42] UNCTAD/WEB/DTL/STICT/2016/1/iPub (n 18) xii.

6 Conclusion

privacy that arise with digital trade in a way that is not more trade-distorting than necessary to achieve these public policy objectives. Countries' personal data protection laws must be strengthened to better achieve public policy objectives and improve citizens' legal protection through constitutional law, human resource law, competition law, consumer law, intellectual property law, to mention but a few. From the angle of a sustainable and perhaps also peaceful development of individual societies and the world as a whole, a balanced level of protection and freedom to transfer data is needed. The careful implementation of personal data protection laws and intelligent application of such laws will allow counties to unlock the benefits of technological innovation and digital trade given that these kinds of regulations rely heavily on credible enforcement. Improved domestic data protection laws must be compatible with countries' international obligations, especially their WTO obligations. Additionally, WTO law must first be improved. International trade law and domestic data protection law should be drafted and enacted in close cooperation.

References

Primary Resource

Act on the Protection of Personal Information of Japan
Agreement on the Importation of Educational, Scientific and Cultural Materials
Agreement on Trade-Related Aspects of Intellectual Property Rights
APEC's Privacy Framework
Basic Law of the Hong Kong Special Administrative Region of the PRC
Basic Law of the Macao Special Administrative Region of the PRC
Charter of Fundamental Rights of the European Union
Civil Code of the PRC (Chinese title: 中華人民共和國民法典)
Common European Sales Law
Companies Act of United Kingdom
Constitution of the PRC (Chinese name: 中華人民共和國憲法)
Constitution of the United Nations Educational, Scientific and Cultural Organization
Convention for the Protection of Individuals with Regard to Automatic Processing of Personal Data
Counterterrorism Law of the PRC (Chinese name: 中華人民共和國反恐怖主義法)
Criminal Law of the PRC (Chinese title: 中華人民共和國刑法)
Cross-Strait Economic Cooperation Framework Agreement with Taiwan Region (Chinese title: 海峽兩岸經濟合作架構協議)
Data Security Law of the PRC (數據安全法)
Decision of the Standing Committee of the National People's Congress on Strengthening Information Protection on Networks (Chinese title: 全國人民代表大會常務委員會關於加強网络信息保護的決定)
Draft of the Measures on Security Assessment of Cross-border Data Transfer of Personal Information and Important Data (Chinese title: 個人信息和重要數據出境安全評估辦法 (徵求意見稿))
Draft of Information Security Technology – Guidelines for Cross-Border Transfer Security Assessment (Chinese title: 信息安全技術 數據出境安全評估指南 (草案))
E-Commerce Law of the PRC (Chinese title: 中華人民共和國電子商務法)
Film Industry Promotion Law of the PRC (Chinese title: 電影產業促進法)
France Data Protection Act
FTAs with e-commerce provision entering into force since 2012 (including namely the PRC – Mauritius FTA, United Kingdom – Japan FTA, United Kingdom - Ecuador and Peru FTA, United Kingdom - CARIFORUM States FTA, United Kingdom - Central America FTA, United

© The Editor(s) (if applicable) and The Author(s), under exclusive license to Springer Nature Singapore Pte Ltd. 2022
Y. Dai, *Cross-Border Data Transfers Regulations in the Context of International Trade Law: A PRC Perspective*, https://doi.org/10.1007/978-981-16-4995-0

Kingdom – Chile FTA, United Kingdom - Côte d'Ivoire FTA, United Kingdom – Georgia FTA, United Kingdom - Korea, Republic of FTA, United Kingdom – Ukraine FTA, United Kingdom – Moldova, Republic of FTA, United Kingdom – Singapore FTA, United Kingdom - Viet Nam FTA, EU - United Kingdom FTA, United Kingdom – Colombia FTA, EU - Viet Nam FTA, Indonesia – Australia FTA, United States-Mexico-Canada Agreement, Peru – Australia FTA, EU-Singapore FTA, Hong Kong, China-Australia FTA, Hong Kong, China-Georgia FTA, EU-Japan FTA, the Comprehensive and Progressive Agreement for Trans-Pacific Partnership, PRC-Georgia FTA, Turkey-Singapore FTA, EU-Canada FTA, Canada-Ukraine FTA, EU-Ghana FTA, Eurasian Economic Union-Viet Nam FTA, Costa Rica-Colombia FTA, Korea, Republic of-Colombia FTA, Japan-Mongolia FTA, Pacific Alliance, PRC-Australia FTA, PRC-Korea, Republic of FTA, Korea, Republic of -Viet Nam FTA, Chile-Thailand FTA, Turkey-Malaysia FTA, Mexico-Panama FTA, Japan-Australia FTA, Canada-Korea, Republic of FTA, Korea, Republic of -Australia FTA, Canada-Honduras FTA, EU-Georgia FTA, EU-Moldova, Republic of FTA, EFTA-Central America (Costa Rica and Panama) FTA, EU-Ukraine FTA, Singapore-Chinese Taipei FTA, New Zealand-Chinese Taipei FTA, Gulf Cooperation Council (GCC)-Singapore FTA, EU-Central America FTA, Costa Rica-Singapore FTA, Canada-Panama FTA, EU-Colombia and Peru FTA, Malaysia-Australia FTA, United States-Panama FTA, Canada-Jordan FTA, Mexico-Central America FTA, United States-Colombia FTA, EU-Eastern and Southern Africa States FTA and Korea, Republic of- United States FTA)

General Agreement on Tariffs and Trade

General Agreement on Trade in Services

General Principles of the Civil Law of the PRC (Chinese title: 中華人民共和國民法通則)

General Provisions of the Civil Law of the PRC (Chinese title: 中華人民共和國民法總則)

Hong Kong Special Administrative Region and Macao Special Administrative Region Closer Economic Partnership Arrangement

Information Security Technology—Guideline for Personal Information Protection within Information System for Public and Commercial Services (Chinese title: 信息安全技術–公共及商用服務信息系統個人信息保護指南)

Interim Measures for the Administration of the Basic Data of Individual Credit Information (Chinese Title: 個人信用信息基礎資料庫管理暫行辦法)

International Covenant on Civil and Political Rights

Law of the PRC on Commercial Banks (Chinese title: 中華人民共和國商業銀行法)

Law of the PRC on Guarding State Secrets (Chinese title: 中華人民共和國保守國家秘密法)

Law of the PRC on Resident Identity Cards (Chinese title: 中華人民共和國居民身份證法)

Law of the PRC on the People's Bank of China (Chinese title: 中華人民共和國中國人民銀行法)

Law of the PRC on the Protection of Minors (Chinese title: 中華人民共和國未成年人保護法)

Law of the PRC on the Protection of the Rights and Interests of Women (Chinese title: 中華人民共和國婦女權益保障法)

Law on Practicing Doctors of the PRC (Chinese title: 中華人民共和國執業醫師法)

Law on the Protection of Consumer Rights and Interests of the PRC (Chinese title: 中華人民共和國消費者權益保護法)

Lawyers Law of the PRC (Chinese title: 中華人民共和國律師法)

Legislation Law of the PRC (Chinese title: 中華人民共和國立法法)

Lottery Regulations (Chinese title: 彩票管理條例)

Mainland and Hong Kong Closer Economic Partnership Arrangement (Chinese Title: 內地與香港關於建立更緊密經貿關係的安排)

Mainland and Macao Closer Economic Partnership Arrangement (Chinese Title: 內地與澳門關於建立更緊密經貿關係的安排)

Measures for the Administration of Electronic Banking Business (Chinese Title: 電子銀行業務管理辦法)

Measures for the Administration of Population Health Information (Trial) (Chinese Title: 人口健康信息管理辦法(試行))

Multilateral Agreements on Trade in Goods

References

Network Security Law of the PRC (Chinese title: 中華人民共和國網絡安全法)
North American Free Trade Agreement
Notary Law of the PRC (Chinese title: 中華人民共和國公證法)
Notice by the Cyberspace Administration of China of Requesting Public Comments on the Measures for the Security Assessment for Cross-border Transfer of Personal Information (Exposure Draft)' (Chinese title: 國家互聯網信息辦公室關於《個人信息出境安全評估辦法 (徵求意見稿)》公開徵求意見的通知)
Notice of the Supreme People's Court, the Supreme People's Procuratorate and the Ministry of Public Security on Legally Punishing Criminal Activities Infringing upon the Personal Information of Citizens 2013 (Chinese title: 最高人民法院、最高人民檢察院、公安部關於依法懲處侵害公民個人信息犯罪活動的通知2013)
Notice of Ministry of Industry and Information Technology on Clearing and Regulating Internet Network Access Service Market (Chinese title: 工業和信息化部關於清理規範互聯網網絡接入服務市場的通知)
Notice of the Cyberspace Administration of China on Assessment of Cross-border Data Transfer of Personal Information and Important Data (Chinese title: 國家互聯網信息辦公室關於《個人信息和重要數據出境安全評估辦法 (徵求意見稿)》公開徵求意見的通知)
Notice of the People's Bank of China on Issuing the Industry Standards on the Information Security Standards for Credit Reporting Institutions (Chinese title:中國人民銀行關於發佈《征信機構信息安全規範》行業標準的通知)
Notice of the PRC on Improving Work Related to the Protection of Personal Financial Information by Banking Financial Institutions (Chinese title: 中國人民銀行關於銀行業金融機構做好個人金融信息保護工作的通知)
Notice of the Supreme People's Court on Issuing Opinions on Several Issues Concerning the Implementation of the General Principles of the Civil Law of the People's Republic of China (For Trial Implementation) [Partially Invalid] (Chinese title: 最高人民法院印發《關於貫徹執行<中華人民共和國民法通則>若干問題的意見(試行)》的通知 [部分失效])
OECD Guidelines on the Protection of Privacy and Transborder Flows of Personal Data
Opinions of the Office of the Central Leading Group for Cyberspace Affairs on Strengthening Cybersecurity Administration of Cloud Computing Services for Communist Party and Government Agencies (Chinese Title:中央網絡安全和信息化領導小組辦公室關於加強黨政部門雲計算服務網絡安全管理的意見)
Outline of the 13th Five-year Plan for National Economic and Social Development of the PRC (Chinese title: 中華人民共和國國民經濟和社會發展第十三個五年規劃綱要)
Passport Law of the PRC (Chinese title: 中華人民共和國護照法)
Personal Information Protection Law of the PRC (個人數據保護法)
Proposal for a Directive of the European Parliament and of the Council on Certain Aspects Concerning Contracts for the Supply of Digital Content
Proposal for a Regulation of the European Parliament and of the Council on a Common European Sales Law
Provisions of the Supreme People's Court on Several Issues Concerning the Application of Law in the Trial of Cases involving Civil Disputes over Infringements upon Personal Rights and Interests through Information Networks (Chinese title: 最高人民法院關於審理利用信息網絡侵害人身權益民事糾紛案件適用法律若干問題的規定)
Provisions on Administration of Online Publishing Services (Chinese Title: 網絡出版服務管理規定)
Provisions on Employment Services and Employment Management (Chinese title: 就業服務與就業管理規定)
Provisions on Protection of the Personal Information of Telecommunications and Internet Users (Chinese title: 電信和互聯網用戶個人信息保護規定)
Provisions on the Management of Social Insurance Archives (Chinese title: 社會保險業務檔案管理規定 (試行))

Public Security Administration Punishments Law of the PRC (Chinese title: 中華人民共和國治安管理處罰法)
Regional Comprehensive Economic Partnership
Regulation (EU) 2016/679 of the European Parliament and of the Council of 27 April 2016 on the protection of natural persons with regard to the processing of personal data and on the free movement of such data, and repealing Directive 95/46/EC (General Data Protection Regulation)
Regulation of the Administration of Credit Investigation Industry of the PRC (Chinese title: 征信業管理條例)
Regulation on Map Management (Chinese Title: 地圖管理條例)
Regulation on Supervision and Administration of Informatization of Insurance Organization (Draft for Comments) (Chinese name: 保險機構信息化監管規定 (徵求意見稿))
Regulations on the Administration of Movies of China (Chinese title: 電影管理條例)
Several Provisions on Regulating the Market Order of Internet Information Services (Chinese title: 規範互聯網信息服務市場秩序若干規定)
Social Insurance Law of the PRC (Chinese title: 中華人民共和國社會保險法)
Standards for Assessment of Personal Information Protection of Internet Enterprises (Chinese Title: 互聯網企業個人信息保護測評標準)
State Council's Guidance on Actively Promoting the "Internet plus" Action (Chinese Title: 國務院關於積極推進"互聯網+"行動的指導意見)
Statistics Law of the PRC (Chinese title: 中華人民共和國統計法)
Supreme People's Court Regulations Concerning Some Questions of Applicable Law in Handling Civil Dispute Cases Involving the Use of Information Networks to Harm Personal Rights and Interests (Chinese title: 最高人民法院關於審理利用信息網絡侵害人身權益民事糾紛案件適用法律若干問題的規定)
Telecommunications Services Catalogue of the PRC (Chinese Title: 電信業務分類目錄)
Temporary Measures for Internet Information Services Market (Chinese title: 互聯網信息服務市場秩序監督管理暫行辦法 (徵求意見稿))
Tort Liability Law of the PRC (Chinese title: 中華人民共和國侵權責任法)
Trans-Pacific Partnership Agreement
UNCITRAL Model Law on Electronic Commerce 1996
United Nations Central Product Classification
United Nations Convention on the Use of Electronic Communications in International Contracts
Universal Declaration of Human Rights

Secondary Resource

Burri, M., & Cottier, T. (Eds.). (2012). *Trade governance in the digital age: World trade forum.* Cambridge University Press.
Burri, M., & Weber, R. H. (2012). *Classification of services in the digital economy.* Springer.
Bygrave, L. A. (1957–2010). *Privacy protection in a global context.* Stockholm Institute for Scandinavian Law.
Chesterman, S. (2018). *Data protection law in Singapore—Privacy and sovereignty in an interconnected world*, 2nd edn. Academy Publishing.
Drake, W. J., & Wilson, E. J. (2008). *Governing global electronic networks: International perspectives on policy and power.* MIT Press.
Floridi, L. (2014). *The 4th revolution: How the infosphere is reshaping human reality.* Oxford University Press.
Gardiner, R. (2008). *Treaty interpretation.* OUP Oxford.
Gitelman, L., et al. (Eds.). *"Raw Data" is an oxymoron.* MIT Press.

Greenleaf, G. W. (2014). *Asian data privacy laws: Trade and human rights perspectives*, 1st edn. Oxford University Press.
Kuner, C. (2013). *Transborder data flows and data privacy law*. OUP Oxford.
Lessig, L. (1999). *Code and other laws of cyberspace*, 1st edn. Basic Books.
Linderfalk, U. (2007). *On the interpretation of treaties—The modern international law as expressed in the 1969 Vienna convention on the law of treaties*. Springer Science and Business Media.
Neuwirth, R. J. (2018). *Law in the time of oxymora: A synaesthesia of language logic and law*. Routledge.
Nissenbaum, H. (2010). *Privacy in context: Technology, policy, and the integrity of social life*. Stanford University Press.
Raul, A. L. (2017). *Data protection and cybersecurity law review*, 4th edn. Law Business Research Ltd.
Sieber-Gasser, C. (2016). *Developing countries and preferential services trade*. Cambridge University Press.
Wunsch-Vincent, S. (2006). *The WTO, the internet and trade in digital products: EC-US perspectives*. Hart Publishing.

Articles

Adlung, R., & Mattoo, A. (2007). 'The GATS'. In A. Mattoo, et al. (Eds.), *A handbook of international trade in services*, 1st ed. Oxford University Press.
Ancarani, F., & Costabile, M. (2010). Coopetition dynamics in convergent industries: Designing scope connections to combine heterogeneous resources. In S. Yami (Eds.), *Coopetition: Winning strategies for the 21st century*. Edward Elgar.
Antons, C., & Hilty, R. M. (2015). Introduction: IP and the Asia-Pacific "Spaghetti Bowl" of free trade agreements. In C. Antons & R. M. Hilty, et al. (Eds.), *Intellectual property and free trade agreements in the Asia-Pacific region*. Springer.
Anupam, C., & Uyen, P. L. (2015). 'Data Nationalism'. *Emory Law Journal, 64*(3), 677.
Bieron, B., & Ahmed, U. (2012). Regulating E-commerce through international policy: Understanding the international trade law issues of E-commerce. *Journal of World Trade, 46*(3), 545.
Block, R. (2014). Market access and national treatment in China-electronic payment services: An illustration of the structural and interpretive problems in GATS. *Chicago Journal of International Law, 12*(2), 652.
Branscomb, A. W. (1983). Global governance of global networks: A survey of transborder data flow in transition. *Vanderbilt Law Review, 36*, 985.
Burri, M. (2017). Symposium-future-proofing law: From RDNA to robots the governance of data and data flows in trade agreements: The pitfalls of legal adaptation. *U.C. Davis Law Review, 51*, 65.
Burri, M. (2017). The regulation of data flows through trade agreements. *Georgetown Journal of International Law, 48*, 407.
Burri, M. (2008). Trade versus culture in the digital environment: An old conflict in need of a new definition. *Journal of International Economic Law, 12*, 17.
Burri, M., et al. (2011). The protection and promotion of cultural diversity in a digital networked environment: Mapping possible advances towards coherence. In T. Cottier & P. Delimatsis (Eds.), *The prospects of international trade regulation from fragmentation to coherence*. Cambridge University Press.
Chao, T. W. (1996). GATT's cultural exemption of audiovisual trade: The United States may have lost the battle but not the war. *University of Pennsylvania Journal of International Economic Law, 17*(4), 1127.

Cowhey, P. F., & Aronson, J. D. (2008). Trade in services telecommunications. In A. Mattoo, et al. (Eds.), *A handbook of international trade in services*, 1st edn. Oxford University Press.

Dogan, I. (2007). Taking a gamble on public morals: Invoking the Article XIV exception to GATS. *Brooklyn Journal of International Law, 32*(3), 1131.

Duh, C., & 'Yahoo Inc. v. LICRA' (2002). *Berkeley Technology Law Journal, 17*, 359.

Fleuter, S. (2016). The role of digital products under the WTO: A new framework for GATT and GATS classification. *Chicago Journal of International Law, 17*(1), 153.

Gao, H. (2011). 'Google's China problem: A case study on trade, technology and human rights under the GATS. *Asian Journal of WTO & International Health Law and Policy, 6*, 347.

Gould, E. (2004). The US gambling decision: A wakeup call for WTO members. *Canadian Centre for Policy Alternatives, 5*(4), 1.

Guffin, P. J., Glover, K. J., et al. (2014). Whose governing privacy? Regulation and protection in a digital era: Foreword. *Maine Law Review, 66*, 369.

Gut, R. Q. (2002). 'Piercing the Veil of China's legal market: Will Gats make China more accessible for U.S. law firms. *Indiana International & Comparative Law Review, 13*(1), 147.

Harauz, J., et al. (2009). Data security in the world of cloud computing. *IEEE Security & Privacy, 7*(4), 61.

Horn, H., et al. (2010). Beyond the WTO: An anatomy of the EU and US preferential trade agreements. *The World Economy (TWE), 33*, 1565.

Hsieh, P. L. (2016). China-Taiwan free trade agreement. In S. Lester, B. Mercurio, & L. Bartels, (Eds.), *Bilateral and regional trade agreements*. Cambridge University Press.

Krisch, N. (2014). The decay of consent: International law in an age of global public goods. *American Journal of International Law, 108*, 1.

Lang, A. T. F. (2007). Reflecting on "Linkage": Cognitive and institutional change in the international trading system. *Modern Law Review, 70*, 523.

MacDonald, D. A., & Streatfeild, C. M. (2014). Personal data privacy and the WTO. *Houston Journal of International Law, 36*, 625.

Mavroidis, P. C. (2009). Crisis? What crisis? Is the WTO Appellate body coming of age? In T. P. Stewart (Eds.), *Opportunities and obligations: New perspectives on global and U.S. trade policy* (p. 173). Kluwer Law International.

Meltzer, J. P. (2014). The internet, cross-border data flow and international trade. *Asia and the Pacific Policy Studies, 2*(1), 90.

Mitchell, A. D., & Hepburn, J. (2017). 'Don't fence me in: Reforming trade and investment law to better facilitate cross-border data transfer. *Yale Journal of Law and Technology, 19*(1), 182.

Murray, T. M. (1997). The U.S.-French dispute over GATT treatment of audiovisual products and the limits of public choice theory: How an efficient market solution was "Rent-Seeking". *Maryland Journal of International Law, 21*, 203.

Neuwirth, R. J. (2013). Essentially oxymoronic concepts. *Global Journal of Comparative Law, 2*(2), 147.

Neuwirth, R. J. (2015). Regulatory divergence. *Journal of International Economic Law, 18*, 21.

Neuwirth, R. J. (2014). Law and magic: A(nother) paradox. *Thomas Jefferson Law Review, 37*, 139.

Neuwirth, R. J. (2014). "Novel Food For Thought" on law and policymaking in the global creative economy. *European Journal of Law and Economics, 37*(1), 13.

Neuwirth, R. J. (2013). The future of the "Culture and Trade Debate": A legal outlook. *Journal of World Trade, 47*(3), 392.

Neuwirth, R. J., & Svetlicinii, A. (2015). International trade, intellectual property and competition rules: Multiple cases for global "Regulatory Co-opetition"? *XIX Trade Development through Harmonization of Commercial Law*, 393.

Nijman, J. E., & Nollkaemper, A. (2007). Deterritorialization in international law: Moving away from the divide between national and international law. In J. E. Nijman & A. Nollkaemper (Eds.), *New perspectives on the divide between national and international law*, 1st edn. Oxford University Press.

Nissenbaum, H. (2011 Fall). A contextual approach to privacy online. *Journal of the American Academy of Arts and Sciences, 140*(4), 33.
Peng, S. Y. (2012). Renegotiate the WTO schedules of commitments: Technological development and treaty interpretation. *Cornell International Law Journal, 45*(2), 403.
Poullet, Y., & Dinant, J. M. (2006). The internet and private life in Europe: Risks and aspirations. In A. T. Kenyon & M. Richardson (Eds.), *New dimensions in privacy law—International and comparative perspectives*. Cambridge University Press.
Priess, H. J., & Pitschas, C. (2000). Protection of public health and the role of the precautionary principle under WTO law: A Trojan horse before Geneva's walls? *Fordham International Law Journal, 1*(24), 519.
Primo Braga, C. A. (2005). E-commerce regulation: New game, new rules? *Quarterly Review of Economics and Finance, 45*, 541.
Primo Braga, C. A. (2008). E-commerce regulation in a handbook of international trade. In A. Mattoo, R. M. Stern, & G. Zanini (Eds.), *Services*, 1st edn. Oxford University Press.
Roy, M. (2005). Audiovisual services in the Doha round: "Dialogue de Sourds, The Sequel". *Journal of World Investment Trade, 6*, 923.
Sarathy, R., & Robertson, C. J. (2003). Strategic and ethical considerations in managing digital privacy. *Journal of Business Ethics, 46*, 111.
Sargsyan, T. (2016). Data localization and the role of infrastructure for surveillance, privacy, and security. *International Journal of Communication, 10*, 2221.
Sedgewick, M. B. (2017). Transborder data privacy as trade. *California Law Review, 105*, 1513.
Selby, J. (2017). Data localization laws: Trade barriers or legitimate responses to cybersecurity risks, or both? *International Journal of Law and Information Technology, 25*, 213.
Shaffer, G. C., & Pollack, M. A. (2010). Hard vs. soft law: Alternatives, complements, and antagonists in international governance. *Minnesota Law Review, 94*, 706.
Shakila, B. P. (2017). Cross-border issues under EU data protection law with regards to personal data protection. *Information and Communications Technology Law, 26*(3), 213.
Singh, J. P. (2007). Culture or commerce? A comparative assessment of international interactions and developing countries at UNESCO, WTO, and beyond. *International Studies Perspectives, 8*, 36.
Teschke, et al. (2010). Public opinions about participating in health research. *Canadian Journal of Public Health, 101*, 159.
Treacy, B. (2010). Working party confirms "Controller" and "Processor" distinction. *Privacy & Data Protection, 10*(5), 3.
Whitman, J. Q. (2004). The two western cultures of privacy: Dignity versus liberty. *Yale Law Journal, 113*, 1153.
Wugmeister, M., et al. (2007). Global solution for cross-border data transfers: Making the case for corporate privacy rules. *Georgetown Journal of International Law, 38*, 449.
Wunsch-Vincent, S. (2008). Trade rules for the digital age. In M. Panizzon, N. Pohl, et al. (Eds.), *GATS and the regulation of international trade in services*. Cambridge University Press.
Wu, T. (2006). The world trade law of censorship and internet filtering. *Chicago Journal of International Law, 7*(1), 263.
Yang, A. B. (2008). International issues: China in global trade: Proposed data protection law and encryption standard dispute. *Journal of Law and Policy for the Information Society, 4*(3), 893.
Dai, Y. H. (2021). Data protection laws—One of the most important sources of competitive advantage in the context of international trade. *Journal of Data Protection & Privacy, 4*(1), 72.
Zech, H. (2017). Data as a tradeable commodity—Implications for contract law. In J. Drexl, et al. (Eds.), *Proceedings of the 18th EIPIN Congress: The New Data Economy between Data Ownership, Privacy and Safeguarding Competition*. Edward Elgar Publishing.
Zhang, G. L. (2016). China's stance on free trade-related intellectual property: A view in the context of the China-Japan-Korea FTA negotiations. *Asia Pacific Law Review, 24*(1), 47.

Reports, Webpages, Newspapers and Others

Aaronson, S. A. (2016). 3 ways to safeguard the future of digital trade. *World Trade Forum.* Retrieved April 16, 2021, from https://www.weforum.org/agenda/2016/02/3-ways-to-safeguard-the-future-of-digital-trade/

Aaronson, S. A. (2012). Can trade policy set information free? (VOX, 22 December 2012). Retrieved April 5, 2021, from https://voxeu.org/article/trade-agreements-global-internet-governance

Aaronson, S. A. (2018). CIGI Papers No. 197—Data is different: Why the world needs a new approach to governing cross-border data flows. Centre for International Governance Innovation. Retrieved March 18, 2021, from https://www.cigionline.org/publications/data-different-why-world-needs-new-approach-governing-cross-border-data-flows/

Aaronson, S. A. (2021). Data minefield? How AI is prodding governments to rethink trade in data. Centre for International Governance Innovation. Retrieved March 19, 2021, from https://ca.practicallaw.thomsonreuters.com/6-502-1481?transitionType=Default&contextData=(sc.Default)&firstPage=true

Aaronson, S. A. (2016). The digital trade imbalance and its implications for internet governance. Institute for International Economic Policy Working Paper Series IIEP-WP-2016-7. Retrieved May 27, 2021, from https://www2.gwu.edu/~iiep/assets/docs/papers/2016WP/AaronsonIIEPWP2016-7.pdf

Aaronson, S. A., & Maxim, R. (2020). Trade and the internet: The challenge of the NSA revelations policies in the US, EU, and Canada. Retrieved April 5, 2020, from https://www2.gwu.edu/~iiep/assets/docs/papers/Aaronson_Maxim_Trade_Internet.pdf

Action Plan on the Belt and Road Initiative. (2015). State Council of the PRC. Retrieved December 29, 2020, from http://english.gov.cn/archive/publications/2015/03/30/content_281475080249035.htm

Adelola, T., et al. (2017). Privacy and data protection in E-commerce the effectiveness of a government regulation approach in developing nations, using Nigeria as a case, 235. Retrieved March 24, 2021, from http://ieeexplore.ieee.org/document/7038812/?reload=true

'Adequacy decisions how the EU determines if a non-EU country has an adequate level of data protection (European Commission). Retrieved April 9, 2021, from https://ec.europa.eu/info/law/law-topic/data-protection/international-dimension-data-protection/adequacy-decisions_en

Ahmed, U., & Anupam, C. (2015). Information goes global: Protecting privacy, security, and the new economy in a world of cross-border data flows. E15Initiative. International Centre for Trade and Sustainable Development (ICTSD) and World Economic Forum, Geneva, 1. Retrieved May 24, 2021, from http://e15initiative.org/wp-content/uploads/2015/09/E15-Digital-Chander-and-Ahmed-Final.pdf

Akhtar, S., et al. (2016). Asia-Pacific trade and investment report 2016. United Nations Economic and Social Commission for Asia and the Pacific. Retrieved February 28, 2021, from www.unescap.org/sites/default/files/publications/aptir-2016-full.pdf

Albrecht, D. (2019). Measures on security assessment of cross-border transfer of personal information (2019 Draft). Your IP Insider. Retrieved March 12, 2021, from http://www.youripinsider.eu/measures-security-assessment-cross-border-transfer-personal-information-2019-draft/

Anér, E., & Rentzhog, M. (2012). Everybody is in services: The impact of servicification in manufacturing on trade and trade policy. Retrieved November 24, 2020, from https://slidetodoc.com/everybody-is-in-services-servicification-and-trade-policy/

An international "Trade in Services Agreement" (TISA)? Why this proposed free trade agreement (FTA) in services is dangerous to democracy, development, and the public interest, and must be stopped! Retrieved November 15, 2020, from https://www.handelskampanjen.no/files/documents/Memo-Proposed_TISA_June_2017_OWINFS.pdf

'APEC Cross-Border Privacy Rules System Policies, Rules and Guidelines', Art. 6.2(vi) and 16. Retrieved May 30, 2020, from https://www.apec.org/groups/committee-on-trade-and-investment/~/media/files/groups/ecsg/cbpr/cbpr-policiesrulesguidelines.ashx

References

Ariyoshi, A., et al. (2000). Capital control: Country experience with their use and liberalization. International Monetary Fund. Retrieved March 18, 2021, from http://www.imf.org/external/pubs/ft/op/op190/index.htm

Ashton, A. (2017). Recent developments in China's international trade engagement. *China Business Review*. Retrieved December 12, 2020, from https://www.chinabusinessreview.com/recent-developments-in-chinas-international-trade-engagement/

Azmeh, S., & Foster, C. (2016). 'The TPP and the digital trade agenda: Digital industrial policy and Silicon Valley's influence on new trade agreements. Retrieved March 23, 2021, from https://www.southcentre.int/wp-content/uploads/2017/09/Ev_170925_SC-Workshop-on-E-Commerce-and-Domestic-Regulation_Presentation-The-TPP-and-the-Digital-Trade-Agenda-Shamel-Azmeh_EN.pdf

Banisar, D. (2018). National comprehensive data protection/privacy laws and bills 2018. Retrieved April 5, 2021, from https://ssrn.com/abstract=1951416

Beauvais, S. D. (2014). France: Ending the cultural exception. World Policy. Retrieved March 26, 2021, from https://worldpolicy.org/2014/11/03/france-ending-the-cultural-exception/

Ben-Shahar, O. (2016). Privacy is the new money, thanks to big data'. Forbes. Retrieved October 24, 2020, from https://www.forbes.com/sites/omribenshahar/2016/04/01/privacy-is-the-new-money-thanks-to-big-data/?sh=fd2a4fa3fa2e

Berry, R., & Reisman, M. (2012). Policy challenges of cross-border cloud computing. *Journal of International Commerce & Economics, 4*, 1. Retrieved March 20, 2021, from https://usitc.gov/journals/policy_challenges_of_cross-border_cloud_computing.pdf

Big data exchange welcomes American partner. China Daily (2017). Retrieved August 23, 2020, from http://www.chinadaily.com.cn/m/guizhou/guiyang/2017-12/15/content_35308468.htm

Binding Corporate Rules (EC). Retrieved November 18, 2020, from https://ec.europa.eu/info/law/law-topic/data-protection/international-dimension-data-protection/binding-corporate-rules-bcr_en

Bischoff, P. (2021). What's the best VPN for China? We tested 59 to see which work. Comparitech. Retrieved March 15, 2021, from https://www.comparitech.com/blog/vpn-privacy/whats-the-best-vpn-for-china-5-that-still-work-in-2016/

Blaya, J. (2013). Patient privacy in a mobile world—A framework to address privacy law issues in mobile health. GHDonline. Retrieved November 9, 2020, from https://www.trust.org/contentAsset/raw-data/03172beb-0f11-438e-94be-e02978de3036/file

Bronckers, M., & Larouche, P. (2008). A review of the WTO regime for telecommunications services. In K. Alexander, et al. (Eds.), *The World Trade Organisation and trade in services*. Retrieved December 20, 2020, from https://ssrn.com/abstract=1995658

Brown, A. G., & Stern, R. M. (2011). Free trade agreements and governance of the global trading system. *World Economic Forum, 34*. Retrieved March 23, 2021, from https://pdfs.semanticscholar.org/3640/7b0d0698f580871aa8f25ab2c25355a6daf5.pdf

Bughin, J., Lund, S., & Manyika, J. (2015). Harnessing the power of shifting global flows. McKinsey Quarterly. Retrieved December 29, 2020, from https://www.mckinsey.com/business-functions/digital-mckinsey/our-insights/harnessing-the-power-of-shifting-global-flows

Building trust and confidence for a successful digital economic era. *United Nations Conference on Trade and Development*. . Retrieved March 20, 2021, from http://unctad.org/en/pages/newsdetails.aspx?OriginalVersionID=1450

Burri, M. (2013). Should there be new multilateral rules for digital trade?' International Centre for Trade and Sustainable Development (ICTSD). Retrieved March 27, 2021, from http://e15initiative.org/publications/should-there-be-new-multilateral-rules-for-digital-trade/

Burri, M. (2015). The European Union, the WTO and cultural diversity. *Cultural Governance and the European Union: Protecting and promoting cultural diversity in Europe*. Retrieved March 15, 2021, from https://papers.ssrn.com/sol3/papers.cfm?abstract_id=2389603

Business without borders: The importance of cross-border data transfers to global prosperity. United States Chamber of Commerce and Hunton and Williams LLP. Retrieved March 1,

2021, from https://www.huntonprivacyblog.com/wp-content/uploads/sites/28/2014/05/021384_BusinessWOBorders_final.pdf

Cabrera, N. (2010). How the internet affects international trade. Lilly and Associates. Retrieved April 24, 2021, from http://www.shiplilly.com/blog/how-the-internet-affects-international-trade/

Canadian Bar Association. (2000). Submission on the general agreement on trade in services and the legal profession: The accountancy disciplines as a model for the legal profession. Retrieved December 20, 2020, from http://www.cba.org/Our-Work/Submissions-(1)/Submissions/2000/em-General-Agreement-em-on-Trade-in-Services-and-t

Carlin, J. P., et al. (2017). Data privacy and transfers in cross-border investigations. Global Investigations Review. Retrieved March 26, 2021, from https://globalinvestigationsreview.com/insight/the-investigations-review-of-the-americas-2018/1145431/data-privacy-and-transfers-in-cross-border-investigations

Carson, B. (2015). 9 incredibly popular websites that are still blocked in China. Business Insider. Retrieved December 12, 2020, from https://www.businessinsider.com.au/websites-blocked-in-china-2015-7

Castro, D., & McQuinn, A. (2015). Cross-border data flows enable growth in all industries. Information Technology & Innovation Foundation. Retrieved October 24, 2020, from http://www2.itif.org/2015-cross-border-data-flows.pdf

Cate, F. H. (2008). Provincial Canadian geographic restrictions on personal data in the public sector submitted to the trilateral committee on transborder data flows. Retrieved November 9, 2020, from https://www.huntonak.com/images/content/3/3/v2/3360/cate_patriotact_white_paper.pdf

CEPA Latest News. Office of the Government Chief Information Officer of HK. Retrieved March 14, 2021, from https://www.ogcio.gov.hk/en/our_work/business/mainland/cepa/

Chapter 8: Australian privacy principle 8—Cross-border disclosure of personal information (Version 1.2). Retrieved March 21, 2021, from https://www.oaic.gov.au/__data/assets/pdf_file/0006/1230/app-guidelines-chapter-8-v1.2.pdf

Chen, J. H. (2018). China' in Robert Bond. *Getting the deal through: E-commerce 2019.* Retrieved September 10, 2020, from https://www.wildy.com/isbn/9781789150179/getting-the-deal-through-e-commerce-2018-paperback

China and the WTO (WTO). Retrieved December 13, 2020, from https://www.wto.org/english/thewto_e/countries_e/china_e.htm

China's big data exchange gains data access to Chicago Mercantile exchange. Xinhua. Retrieved August 23, 2020, from www.chinadaily.com.cn/a/201712/12/WS5a2f6beca3108bc8c6724003.html

China issues draft regulation on cross-border transfer of personal information. Hunton Andrews Kurth LLP. Retrieved March 12, 2021, from https://www.huntonprivacyblog.com/2019/06/19/china-issues-draft-regulation-on-cross-border-transfer-of-personal-information/

China Champions economic integration in East Asia despite anti-globalization headwinds. Xinhua. Retrieved December 28, 2020, from http://www.chinadaily.com.cn/business/2017-11/14/content_34525509.htm

China unveils action plan on BRI. Xin Hua. Retrieved March 3, 2021, from http://english.gov.cn/news/top_news/2015/03/28/content_281475079055789.htm

Christman, E. (2016). U.S. record industry sees album sales sink to historic lows (Again)—But people are listening more than ever. Billboard. Retrieved December 27, 2020, from https://www.billboard.com/articles/business/7430863/2016-soundscan-nielsen-music-mid-year-album-sales-sink-streaming-growth

Ciuriak, D. (2018). Digital trade—Is data treaty-ready? CIGI Papers. Retrieved March 16, 2021, from https://www.cigionline.org/sites/default/files/documents/Paper%20no.162web.pdf

Ciuriak, D., & Ptashkina, M. (2018). The digital transformation and the transformation of international trade. RTA Exchange. International Centre for Trade and Sustainable Development (ICTSD) and the Inter-American Development Bank (IDB), Geneva. Retrieved March 17, 2021, from http://e15initiative.org/wp-content/uploads/2015/09/RTA-Exchange-Digital-Trade-Ciuriak-and-Ptashkina-Final.pdf

References

Gong, S., & Shaw, N. (2015). Chinese Appellate Court provides guidance for lawful use of cookies. Hogan Lovells. Retrieved May 16, 2021, from http://www.hldataprotection.com/2015/08/articles/international-eu-privacy/chinese-appellate-court-provides-guidance-for-lawful-use-of-cookies/

Coates, M., et al. (2013). A new era for European public services cloud computing changes the game. Accenture. Retrieved May 30, 2020, from https://www.accenture.com/t20150527T211057__w__/fr-fr/_acnmedia/Accenture/Conversion-Assets/DotCom/Documents/Local/fr-fr/PDF_4/Accenture-New-Era-European-Public-Services-Cloud-Computing-Changes-Game.pdf

Commodity. Longman Dictionary of Contemporary English. Retrieved March 24, 2021, from https://www.ldoceonline.com/dictionary/commodity

Communication from the United States—Measures adopted and under development by China relating to its cybersecurity law. WTO Council for Trade in Services. Retrieved October 20, 2021, from https://docs.wto.org/dol2fe/Pages/SS/directdoc.aspx?filename=q:/S/C/W374.pdf&Open=True

Computer and related services. WTO Doc. S/C/W/45. WTO Secretariat. Retrieved December 20, 2020, from https://www.wto.org/english/tratop_e/serv_e/computer_e/computer_e.htm

Convention for the protection of individuals with regard to automatic processing of personal data. Council of Europe. Retrieved October 24, 2020, from https://www.coe.int/en/web/conventions/full-list/-/conventions/rms/0900001680078b37

Converge products, a pattern study from the center for the edge's patterns of disruption series. Deloitte University Press. Retrieved March 10, 2021, from https://www2.deloitte.com/content/dam/insights/us/articles/disruptive-strategy-convergence-of-products/DUP_1465_Converge-products_vFINAL.pdf

Coos, A. (2018). EU vs US: How do their data protection regulations square off? Endpoint Protection. Retrieved April 24, 2021, from https://www.endpointprotector.com/blog/eu-vs-us-how-do-their-data-protection-regulations-square-off/

Coos, A. (2021). Data protection legislation around the world in 2021. Endpoint Protection. Retrieved March 23, 2021, from https://www.endpointprotector.com/blog/data-protection-legislation-around-the-world/

Corr, C. F., et al. (2019). The CPTPP enters into force: What does it mean for global trade? White and Case. Retrieved March 29, 2021, from https://www.whitecase.com/publications/alert/cptpp-enters-force-what-does-it-mean-global-trade

Crawford, J. A., & Fiorentino, R. V. (2005). The changing landscape of regional trade agreements. WTO Discussion Paper. Retrieved April 16, 2021, from https://www.wto.org/english/res_e/booksp_e/discussion_papers8_e.pdf

Crosby, D. (2016). Analysis of data localization measures under WTO services trade rules and commitments. ICTSD. Retrieved December 29, 2020, from https://www.e15initiative.org/wp-content/uploads/2015/09/E15-Policy-Brief-Crosby-Final.pdf

Cross-border E-commerce contributes to China's foreign trade in 2020, with 31.1% annual growth amid pandemic. Global Times. Retrieved March 13, 2021, from https://www.globaltimes.cn/page/202101/1212876.shtml

Cybercrime Legislation Worldwide. UNCTAD. Retrieved April 4, 2021, from https://unctad.org/en/Pages/DTL/STI_and_ICTs/ICT4D-Legislation/eCom-Cybercrime-Laws.aspx

Data privacy trends in Asia Pacific's highly fragmented legislative environment. Data Protection and Security. Retrieved May 22, 2020, from https://www.mediabuzz.com.sg/asian-emarketing/data-protection-security-a-regulations-week-1/2046-data-privacy-trends-in-asia-pacifics-highly-fragmented-legislative-environment

Data protection and privacy legislation worldwide. UNCTAD. Retrieved January 4, 2021, from https://unctad.org/en/Pages/DTL/STI_and_ICTs/ICT4D-Legislation/eCom-Data-Protection-Laws.aspx

Data protection laws of the world, Russia. *Data protection laws of the world full handbook (DLA PIPER)*. Retrieved November 12, 2020, from https://www.dlapiperdataprotection.com/system/modules/za.co.heliosdesign.dla.lotw.data_protection/functions/handbook.pdf?country=all

Data protection laws of the world, South Korea. *Data protection laws of the world full handbook (DLA PIPER)*. Retrieved November 12, 2020, from https://www.dlapiperdataprotection.com/system/modules/za.co.heliosdesign.dla.lotw.data_protection/functions/handbook.pdf?country=all

Data protection laws of the world, Taiwan. *Data protection laws of the world full handbook (DLA PIPER)*. Retrieved November 12, 2020, from https://www.dlapiperdataprotection.com/system/modules/za.co.heliosdesign.dla.lotw.data_protection/functions/handbook.pdf?country=all

Data protection laws of the world-Japan (DLA PIPER). Retrieved October 12, 2020, from https://www.dlapiperdataprotection.com/system/modules/za.co.heliosdesign.dla.lotw.data_protection/functions/handbook.pdf?country=all

Data protection regulations and international data flows: Implications for trade and development. UNCTAD/WEB/DTL/STICT/2016/1/iPub. United Nations Publication. Retrieved March 29, 2021, from http://unctad.org/en/PublicationsLibrary/dtlstict2016d1_en.pdf

Davey, W. J. (2005). Implementation in WTO dispute settlement: An introduction to the problems and possible solutions. RIETI Discussion Paper Series 05-E-013. Retrieved March 22, 2021, from https://www.rieti.go.jp/jp/publications/dp/05e013.pdf

Davie, M. (2018). In brief: What is data monetization? Datafloq. Retrieved September 1, 2020, from https://datafloq.com/read/in-brief-what-is-data-monetization/3356

'Debating the future of E-commerce and digital trade in Buenos Aires. Retrieved March 31, 2021, from https://devsol.etradeforall.org/debating-future-e-commerce-digital-trade-buenos-aires/

Definition of commodity. Merriam-Webster. Retrieved March 24, 2021, from https://www.merriam-webster.com/dictionary/commodity

Definition of commodity in English. Oxford Living Dictionaries of English. Retrieved March 24, 2021, from https://en.oxforddictionaries.com/definition/commodity

Definition of data in English. English Oxford Living Dictionaries. Retrieved May 16, 2021, from https://en.oxforddictionaries.com/definition/data

Definition of information in English. English Oxford Living Dictionaries. Retrieved May 16, 2021, from https://en.oxforddictionaries.com/definition/information

DG Azevêdo meets ministers in Davos: Discussions focus on reform; progress on e-commerce. WTO. Retrieved March 31, 2021, from https://www.wto.org/english/news_e/news19_e/dgra_25jan19_e.htm

Draft annex of the trade in services agreement (TiSA). Annex on Electronic Commerce 3. Retrieved October 29, 2020, from https://wikileaks.org/tisa/document/20151001_Annex-on-Electronic-Commerce/20151001_Annex-on-Electronic-Commerce.pdf

EC. (2018). Digital single market: EU negotiators reach a political agreement on free flow of non-personal data. EC Press Release. Retrieved March 22, 2021, from https://ec.europa.eu/commission/presscorner/detail/en/IP_18_4227

EC. (2018). Free flow of non-personal data. EC Policies. Retrieved October 22, 2020, from https://ec.europa.eu/digital-single-market/en/free-flow-non-personal-data

E-commerce in developing countries—Opportunities and challenges for small and medium-sized enterprises. WTO. Retrieved May 2, 2021, from https://www.wto.org/english/res_e/booksp_e/ecom_brochure_e.pdf

Eleventh WTO Ministerial Conference. WTO. Retrieved March 17, 2021, from https://www.wto.org/english/thewto_e/minist_e/mc11_e/mc11_e.htm

Elms, D., & Lee-Makiyama, H. (2018). A roadmap for UK accession to CPTPP. Initiative for Free Trade. Retrieved March 29, 2021, from http://ifreetrade.org/pdfs/UK-CPTPP.pdf

Elizabeth, C. E. (2017). Beijing's silk road goes digital. Asia Unbound. Retrieved December 28, 2020, from https://www.cfr.org/blog/beijings-silk-road-goes-digital

Enabling trade in the era of information technologies: Breaking down barriers to the free flow of information. Google. Retrieved March 23, 2021, from https://www.google.com/googleblogs/pdfs/trade_free_flow_of_information.pdf

Erixon, F., et al. (2009). Protectionism online: Internet censorship and international trade law. ECIPE Working Paper No. 12/2009. Retrieved March 24, 2021, from https://ecipe.org/wp-content/uploads/2014/12/protectionism-online-internet-censorship-and-international-trade-law.pdf

References

E-transactions legislation worldwide. UNCTAD. Retrieved January 4, 2021, from https://unctad.org/en/Pages/DTL/STI_and_ICTs/ICT4D-Legislation/eCom-Transactions-Laws.aspx

EU strategic framework and action plan on human rights and democracy. (2012). Council of the EU. Retrieved May 19, 2021, from https://www.consilium.europa.eu/uedocs/cms_data/docs/pressdata/EN/foraff/131181.pdf

Europe vs the US—Who takes data protection more seriously? Telegraph. Retrieved April 24, 2021, from https://www.telegraph.co.uk/business/risk-insights/europe-us-who-takes-data-protection-more-seriously/

Ezell, S. J., et al. (2013). Localization barriers to trade—Threat to the global innovation economy (pp. 69–70). Information Technology and Innovation Foundation. Retrieved March 18, 2021, from https://www2.itif.org/2013-localization-barriers-to-trade.pdf

Fazlioglu, M. (2017). Transparency and the GDPR: Practical guidance and interpretive assistance from the Article 29 working party. Iapp. Retrieved March 9, 2021, from https://iapp.org/news/a/transparency-and-the-gdpr-practical-guidance-and-interpretive-assistance-from-the-article-29-working-party/

Fefer, R. F. (2017). U.S. trade in services: Trends and policy issues analyst in international trade and finance. Congressional Research Service. Retrieved December 12, 2020, from https://fas.org/sgp/crs/misc/R43291.pdf

Freedom of expression, media and digital communications framework—Key issues. (2012). EC. Retrieved October 31, 2020, from http://vtsns.edu.rs/wp-content/uploads/2020/03/Freedom-of-expression.pdf

Free flow of non-personal data: Parliament approves EU's fifth freedom. (2018). EC. Retrieved October 15, 2020, from www.europarl.europa.eu/news/en/press-room/20180926IPR14403/free-flow-of-non-personal-data-parliament-approves-eu-s-fifth-freedom

Galway project and centre for information policy leadership. Data protection accountability: The essential elements a document for discussion. Retrieved November 13, 2020, from https://www.ftc.gov/sites/default/files/documents/public_comments/privacy-roundtables-comment-project-no.p095416-544506-00059/544506-00059.pdf

Gärtner, A. (2017). Building a European data economy—Summary report on the right to data consultation. Reed Smith. Retrieved March 23, 2021, from https://www.reedsmith.com/en/perspectives/2017/08/building-a-european-data-economy-summary-report

Gehrke, J., Lui, E., & Pass, R. (2011). Towards privacy for social networks: A zero-knowledge based definition of privacy. *Proceeding TCC'11 Proceedings of the 8th conference on Theory of Cryptography.* . Retrieved March 31, 2021, from http://www.cs.cornell.edu/~luied/zkPrivacyFinal.pdf

Gehrke, N. (2017). Japan's Act on protection of personal information comes into effect on May 30. Medium. Retrieved March 21, 2021, from https://medium.com/tokyo-fintech/japans-act-on-protection-of-personal-information-comes-into-effect-on-may-30-dd7c7d476ec4

General exceptions: Article XX of the GATT 1994. WTO. Retrieved December 20, 2020, from https://www.wto.org/english/tratop_e/dispu_e/repertory_e/g3_e.htm

Godel, M., et al. (2016). Facilitating cross-border data flow in the digital single market. EU. Retrieved October 20, 2020, from http://ec.europa.eu/newsroom/document.cfm?doc_id=4118

Goh, B., & Chen, Y. (2017). China pledges $124 billion for New Silk Road as champion of globalization. Reuters. Retrieved December 28, 2020, from https://ca.reuters.com/article/topNews/idCAKBN18A02I-OCATP

Ghosh, P. (2021). China now has almost 1 billion internet users. Forbes. Retrieved March 6, 2021, from https://www.forbes.com/sites/palashghosh/2021/02/04/china-now-has-almost-1-billion-internet-users/?sh=cf1a56026d91

Goldfarb, A., & Trefler, D. (2018). How artificial intelligence impacts international trade. *World trade report 2018* (WTO) (p. 140). Retrieved January 19, 2021, from https://www.wto.org/english/res_e/publications_e/wtr18_4_e.pdf

Goode, W. (2005). Negotiating free-trade agreements: A guide. Commonwealth of Australia. Retrieved March 23, 2021, from https://www.apec.org/-/media/APEC/Publications/2005/12/

Negotiating-Free-Trade-Agreements-A-Guide-2005/2005_negotiating_free_trade_agreement_a_guide.pdf

Guo, Y. M. (2017). Digital economy cooperation to empower Belt, Road. Retrieved December 29, 2020, from http://www.china.org.cn/world/2017-12/04/content_50083923.htm

Guidelines for processing personal data across borders. Office of the Privacy Commissioner of Canada. Retrieved December 30, 2020, from https://www.priv.gc.ca/en/privacy-topics/airports-and-borders/gl_dab_090127/

Harwell, D. (2018). Facebook is now in the data privacy spotlight. Could Google be next? Washington Post. Retrieved September 23, 2020, from https://www.washingtonpost.com/news/the-switch/wp/2018/04/11/facebook-is-now-in-the-data-privacy-spotlight-could-google-be-next/?noredirect=on&utm_term=.2d318050f81d

Haupt, M. (2019). Data is the new oil—A ludicrous proposition natural resources, the question of ownership and the reality of big data (Medium). Retrieved May 16, 2021, from https://medium.com/twenty-one-hundred/data-is-the-new-oil-a-ludicrous-proposition-1d91bba4f294

Head of Department of International Trade and Economic Relations Made an Interpretation on the PRC-Switzerland FTA. (2013). Ministry of Commerce PRC. Retrieved January 2, 2021, from http://english.mofcom.gov.cn/article/newsrelease/policyreleasing/201308/20130800233165.shtml

Hellard, B. (2018). EU outlines plans to promote more data-sharing to fuel innovation. ITPRO. Retrieved March 20, 2021, from http://www.itpro.co.uk/big-data/31002/eu-outlines-plans-to-promote-more-data-sharing-to-fuel-innovation

Henke, N., et al. (2016). The age of analytics: Competing in a data-driven world. McKinsey & Company. Retrieved October 12, 2020, from https://www.mckinsey.com/business-functions/mckinsey-analytics/our-insights/the-age-of-analytics-competing-in-a-data-driven-world

Herrick, M. (2018). With GDPR in the background, digital protectionism is on the rise and it has been building for a while. Adweek. Retrieved February 12, 2021, from https://www.adweek.com/performance-marketing/with-gdpr-in-the-background-digital-protectionism-is-on-the-rise/

Hert, P. de, & Papakonstantinou, V. (2015). The data protection regime in China, in-depth analysis. Brussels Privacy Hub Working Paper. 1(4). Retrieved March 29, 2021, from http://www.europarl.europa.eu/RegData/etudes/IDAN/2015/536472/IPOL_IDA(2015)536472_EN.pdf

Hosch, W. L., & Hall, M. (2019). Google Inc. Encyclopedia Britannica. Retrieved September 23, 2020, from https://www.britannica.com/topic/Google-Inc

Hosuk, M. B., et al. (2014). The costs of data localization: Friendly fire on economic recovery. ECIPE. Retrieved March 20, 2021, from https://ecipe.org/wp-content/uploads/2014/12/OCC32014__1.pdf

How censorship works in China: A brief overview. (2006). Human Rights Watch. Retrieved April 5, 2021, from https://www.hrw.org/reports/2006/china0806/3.htm

IFPI Digital Music Report. (2015). Retrieved December 18, 2020, from www.ifpi.org/downloads/Digital-Music-Report-2015.pdf

Igor, R. (2016). Meeting the challenge of data localization laws. Linkedin. Retrieved January 4, 2021, from https://www.linkedin.com/pulse/meeting-challenge-data-localization-laws-igor-runets/

Inception impact assessment—European free flow of data initiative within the digital single market. (2016). EC. Retrieved May 22, 2020, from https://ec.europa.eu/smart-regulation/roadmaps/docs/2016_cnect_001_free_flow_data_en.pdf

Initiative on Belt and Road Digital Economy Cooperation Launched. (2017). Xinhua. Retrieved December 28, 2020, from http://www.scio.gov.cn/31773/35507/35520/Document/1612635/1612635.htm

Interpretation for the PRC-Australia free trade agreement. (2015). Ministry of Commerce PRC. Retrieved January 2, 2021, from http://english.mofcom.gov.cn/article/policyrelease/Cocoon/201510/20151001144954.shtml

Jyoti, P. (2017). Don't trust data localization exceptions in trade agreements to guarantee protection of personal data. Electronic Frontier Foundation. Retrieved November 20,

References

2020, from https://www.eff.org/deeplinks/2017/08/rising-demands-data-localization-response-weak-data-protection-mechanisms

Jyoti, P. (2017). RCEP discussions on ecommerce: Gathering steam in Hyderabad. Electronic Frontier Foundation. Retrieved April 20, 2021, from https://www.eff.org/deeplinks/2017/07/rcep-discussions-ecommerce-gathering-steam-hyderabad

Jyoti, P. (2018). The post-TPP future of digital trade in Asia. Electronic Frontier Foundation. Retrieved March 6, 2021, from https://www.eff.org/deeplinks/2018/02/rcep-negotiations-face-obstacles-member-nations-unwilling-commit

Kania, E. (2018). China's play for global 5G dominance—Standards and the "Digital Silk Road". ASPI. Retrieved March 7, 2021, from https://www.aspistrategist.org.au/chinas-play-for-global-5g-dominance-standards-and-the-digital-silk-road/

Kariyawasam, R. (2015). A new instrument for digital trade? ICTSD. Retrieved June 20, 2020, from https://e15initiative.org/blogs/a-new-instrument-for-digital-trade/

Kawai, M., & Wignaraja, G. (2009). 'Tangled up in trade? The "Noodle Bowl" of free trade agreements in East Asia'. VOX. Retrieved March 23, 2021, from http://voxeu.org/article/noodle-bowl-free-trade-agreements-east-asia

Key barrier to digital trade. (2017). Office of U.S. Trade Representative homepage. Retrieved December 27, 2020, from https://ustr.gov/about-us/policy-offices/press-office/fact-sheets/2017/march/key-barriers-digital-trade

Khan, Y. H. (2017). CPEC as Digital Silk Road. Daily Times. Retrieved December 28, 2020, from https://dailytimes.com.pk/154109/cpec-digital-silk-road/

Khaskelis, A. S., & Gallia, A. L. (2016). Russian Federation: Russia's data localization law, a violation of WTO regulations? Mondaq. Retrieved March 20, 2021, from http://www.mondaq.com/russianfederation/x/460342/data+protection/Russias+Data+Localization+Law+A+Violation+Of+WTO+Regulations

Kim, J. H., et al. (2015). Data protection in South Korea: Overview. Thomson Reuters Practical Law. Retrieved December 11, 2020, from https://content.next.westlaw.com/Document/I1d81ec834f2711e498db8b09b4f043e0/View/FullText.html?contextData=(sc.Default)&transitionType=Default&firstPage=true&bhcp=1

Kittichaisaree, K., & Kuner, C. (2015). The growing importance of data protection in public international law. *EJIL Analysis*. Retrieved May 22, 2021, from https://www.ejiltalk.org/the-growing-importance-of-data-protection-in-public-international-law/

Kommerskollegium. (2012). E-commerce-new opportunities, new barriers a survey of E-commerce barriers in countries outside the EU. National Board of Trade. Retrieved March 20, 2021, from https://www.wto.org/english/tratop_e/serv_e/wkshop_june13_e/ecom_national_board_e.pdf

Kommerskollegium. (2014). No transfer, no trade—The importance of cross-border data transfers for companies based in Sweden. 1st end, National Board of Trade. Retrieved March 30, 2021, from https://unctad.org/meetings/en/Contribution/dtl_ict4d2016c01_Kommerskollegium_en.pdf

Krajewski, M. (2011). Public services in bilateral free trade agreements of the EU. Retrieved March 15, 2021, from https://www.arbeiterkammer.at/infopool/akportal/Public_Services_in_Bilateral_Free_Trade_Agreements_of_the_EU.pdf

Kula, S. (2017). Japanese Personal Information Protection Act (PIPA)—A heads up. Mechalsons. Retrieved March 21, 2021, from https://www.michalsons.com/blog/personal-information-protection-act-pipa/24252

Kuner, C. (2011). Regulation of transborder data flows under data protection and privacy law: Past, present and future. OECD Digital Economy Papers No. 187. OECD Publishing. Retrieved January 4, 2021, from http://www.kuner.com/my-publications-and-writing/untitled/kuner-oecd-tbdf-paper.pdf

Kuriyama, C., & Sangaraju, D. (2017). Trends and developments in provisions and outcomes of RTA/FTAs implemented in 2016 by APEC economies. APEC Policy Support Unit. Retrieved March 16, 2021, from https://www.apec.org/-/media/APEC/Publications/2018/12/Trends-and-Developments-in-Provisions-and-Outcomes-of-RTA-FTAs/218_PSU_Trends-and-Developments-in-Provisions-and-Outcomes-of-RTA-FTAs.pdf

Kumar, T. (2018). 10 main differences between data and information. Loginworks. Retrieved May 16, 2021, from https://www.loginworks.com/blogs/10-main-differences-between-data-and-information/

Lanz, R., & Maurer, A. (2015). Services and global value chains—Some evidence on servicification of manufacturing and services networks. WTO. Retrieved April 1, 2021, from https://www.wto.org/english/res_e/reser_e/ersd201503_e.htm

Layton, D. W., Mintzer, S. H., & Smith, T. L. (2012). WTO panel rules against China in dispute over electronic payment services. Mayer Brown. Retrieved April 4, 2021, from https://www.mayerbrown.com/en/perspectives-events/publications/2012/07/wto-panel-rules-against-china-in-dispute-over-elec

Lee, K. F. (2020). Joins "Squawk Box" to discuss his new book, "AI Superpowers", and the U.S.-China trade tensions. CNBC. Retrieved October 17, 2020, from https://www.cnbc.com/video/2018/09/24/data-china-tech-trade-war-artificial-intelligence.html

Meltzer, J. P., et al. (2017). China's artificial intelligence revolution: Understanding Beijing's structural advantages. Eurasia Group. Retrieved September 17, 2020, from https://www.eurasiagroup.net/files/upload/China_Embraces_AI.pdf

Leblond, P. (2020). Digital trade: Is RCEP the WTO's future? CIGI 20th. Retrieved March 31, 2021, from https://www.cigionline.org/articles/digital-trade-rcep-wtos-future

Least-developed countries. WTO. Retrieved April 5, 2021, from https://www.wto.org/english/thewto_e/whatis_e/tif_e/org7_e.htm

Lillie, B. (2012). China's censorship battle between the cats and the mice: Michael Anti at Tedglobal 2012. Ted blog. Retrieved May 23, 2020, from https://blog.ted.com/chinas-censorship-battle-between-the-cats-and-the-mice-michael-anti-at-tedglobal-2012/

List of deliverables of the Belt and Road Forum for International Cooperation. (2017). China Daily. Retrieved December 29, 2020, from http://www.chinadaily.com.cn/china/2017-05/16/content_29359377.htm

Lomas, N. (2018). Europe eyes boosting data re-use and funds for AI research. Riptari. Retrieved March 20, 2021, from https://techcrunch.com/2018/04/25/europe-eyes-boosting-data-re-use-and-funds-for-ai-research/

Lund, S., Manyika, J., & Bughin, J. (2016). Globalization is becoming more about data and less about stuff. *Harvard Business Review*. Retrieved December 22, 2020, from https://hbr.org/2016/03/globalization-is-becoming-more-about-data-and-less-about-stuff

Mainland and Hong Kong Closer Economic Partnership Arrangement Agreement on Trade in Services. Trade and Industry Department of HK Homepage. Retrieved March 15, 2021, from https://www.tid.gov.hk/english/cepa/legaltext/files/sa27-11-2015_main_e.pdf

Maisog, M. E. (2015). Making the case against data localization in China. IAPP. Retrieved March 5, 2021, from https://iapp.org/news/a/making-the-case-against-data-localization-in-china/

Mandel, M. (2017). The economic impact of data: Why data is not like oil. PPI. Retrieved November 9, 2020, from https://www.progressivepolicy.org/wp-content/uploads/2017/07/PowerofData-Report_2017.pdf

Manyika, J., et al. (2016). Digital globalization: The new era of global flows. Mckinsey Global Institute. Retrieved December 19, 2020, from https://www.mckinsey.com/business-functions/digital-mckinsey/our-insights/digital-globalization-the-new-era-of-global-flows

Manyika, J., Bughin, J., et al. (2014). Global flows in a digital age: How trade, finance, people, and data connect the world economy. McKinsey Global Institute. Retrieved December 25, 2020, from https://www.mckinsey.com/~/media/McKinsey/Featured%20Insights/Globalization/Global%20flows%20in%20a%20digital%20age/Global_flows_in_a_digital_age_Full_report%20March_2015.ashx

Marr, B. (2016). Big data: 33 brilliant and free data sources anyone can use. Forbes. Retrieved September 28, 2020, from https://www.forbes.com/sites/bernardmarr/2016/02/12/big-data-35-brilliant-and-free-data-sources-for-2016/?sh=2991a6adb54d

References

Martinoa, B. D., et al. (2015). Cloud forward: From distributed to complete computing, towards a legislation-aware cloud computing framework. *Procedia Computer Science, 68*, 127. Retrieved March 20, 2021, from https://doi.org/10.1016/j.procs.2015.09.229

McAfee, A., & Brynjolfsson, E. (2012). Big data: The management revolution. *Harvard Business Review*. Retrieved October 12, 2020, from https://hbr.org/2012/10/big-data-the-management-revolution

Meaning of "Commodity" in the English Dictionary. Cambridge Dictionary. Retrieved March 24, 2021, from https://dictionary.cambridge.org/dictionary/english/commodity

Meaning of "Tradable" in the English Dictionary. Cambridge University Press. Retrieved March 24, 2021, from https://dictionary.cambridge.org/dictionary/english/tradeable

Mell, P., & Grance, T. (2011). The NIST definition of cloud computing. NIST, US Department of Commerce. Retrieved March 20, 2021, from https://csrc.nist.gov/publications/detail/sp/800-145/final

Meltzer, J. P. (2015). Supporting the internet as a platform for international trade. Brookings. Retrieved April 24, 2021, from https://www.brookings.edu/research/supporting-the-internet-as-a-platform-for-international-trade/

Meltzer, J. P., & Dreier, D. (2013). Growing the global internet economy by ensuring the free flow of data across borders. Brookings. Retrieved May 19, 2020, from https://www.brookings.edu/blog/up-front/2013/05/23/growing-the-global-internet-economy-by-ensuring-the-free-flow-of-data-across-borders/

Meltzer, J. P., & Mattoo, A. (2018). International data flows and privacy the conflict and its resolution. Policy Research Working Paper 8431. World Bank Group. Retrieved March 12, 2021, from http://documents.worldbank.org/curated/en/751621525705087132/pdf/WPS8431.pdf

Meltzer, J. P. (2013). The internet, cross-border data flows and international trade. 22 Issues in Technology Innovation. Retrieved March 4, 2021, from https://www.brookings.edu/wp-content/uploads/2016/06/internet-data-and-trade-meltzer.pdf

Meng, J., & Wei, F. (2016). China strengthens its data protection legislation. International Association of Privacy Professionals. Retrieved March 10, 2021, from https://iapp.org/news/a/china-strengthens-its-data-protection-legislation/

Michelini, M. (2017). List of blocked websites in China. Global from Asia. Retrieved December 12, 2020, from https://www.globalfromasia.com/list-blocked-sites-china/

Michitaka, N. (2014). Services negotiation and plurilateral agreement: TISA and sectoral approach. Retrieved November 15, 2020, from https://www.rieti.go.jp/jp/publications/pdp/14p023.pdf

MIIT releases 2015 telecoms catalogue. (2016). Thomson Reuters. Retrieved March 27, 2021, from https://uk.practicallaw.thomsonreuters.com/6-621-8165?transitionType=Default&contextData=(sc.Default)&firstPage=true&bhcp=1

Miles, T. (2017). U.S. asks China not to enforce cyber security law. Reuters. Retrieved December 12, 2020, from https://www.reuters.com/article/us-usa-china-cyber-trade/u-s-asks-china-not-to-enforce-cyber-security-law-idUSKCN1C11D1

Miles, T., & Palmer, D. (2012). U.S. wins WTO case over China bank card monopoly. Reuters. Retrieved April 4, 2021, from https://www.reuters.com/article/us-usa-china-wto/u-s-wins-wto-case-over-china-bank-card-monopoly-idUSBRE86F0J020120716

Mishra, N. (2017). International trade, internet governance and the shaping of the digital economy. ARTNeT Working Paper Series, No. 168, Bangkok, ESCAP. Retrieved March 1, 2021, from https://papers.ssrn.com/sol3/papers.cfm?abstract_id=2997254

Monteiro, J. A., & Teh, R. (2017). Provisions on electronic commerce in regional trade agreements. WTO Working Paper ERSD-2017-11. WTO Economic Research and Statistics Division. Retrieved March 27, 2021, from https://www.econstor.eu/bitstream/10419/163426/1/894047426.pdf

Mozur, P. (2017). China's internet censors play a tougher game of cat and mouse. New York Times. Retrieved May 23, 2021, from https://www.nytimes.com/2017/08/03/business/china-internet-censorship.html

Neuwirth, R. J. (2016). The UNESCO convention and future technologies: "A Journey to the Centre of Cultural Law and Policymaking". In L. R. Hanania & A.-T. Norodom (Eds.), *Diversity of cultural expressions in the digital era*. TESEO, Buenos Aires. Retrieved March 23, 2021, from https://ssrn.com/abstract=2884454

Neuwirth, R. J. (2014). The creative industries as a new paradigm for business and law: Of "Smart Phones" and "Smarter Regulation". In Fourth Biennial Global Conference of the Society of International Economic Law (SIEL) Working Paper No. 2014/05. Retrieved November 13, 2020, from https://papers.ssrn.com/sol3/papers.cfm?abstract_id=2450209

New China data privacy standard looks more far-reaching than GDPR. CSIS. Retrieved January 14, 2021, from https://www.csis.org/analysis/new-china-data-privacy-standard-looks-more-far-reaching-gdpr

Nielson, J., & Morris, R. (2020). E-commerce and trade: resolving dilemmas. OECD Observer. Retrieved March 7, 2020, from http://oecdobserver.org/news/archivestory.php/aid/421/E-com merce_and_trade:_resolving_dilemmas.html

Nigel, C. (2017). Cross-border data flows: Where are the barriers, and what do they cost? Information Technology and Innovation Foundation. Retrieved March 16, 2021, from https://itif.org/public ations/2017/05/01/cross-border-data-flows-where-are-barriers-and-what-do-they-cost

Online Consumer Protection Legislation Worldwide (UNCTAD). Retrieved April 4, 2021, from https://unctad.org/en/Pages/DTL/STI_and_ICTs/ICT4D-Legislation/eCom-Consumer-Pro tection-Laws.aspx

Onofrio, D. D. (2017). The future is now: Data as an asset in the corporate world. SnapLogic. Retrieved November 15, 2020, from https://www.snaplogic.com/blog/the-future-is-now-when-data-becomes-a-tangible-corporate-asset

Overview: The TRIPS agreement. WTO website. Retrieved January 6, 2021, from https://www.wto.org/english/tratop_e/trips_e/intel2_e.htm

Mainland and Macao closer economic partnership arrangement agreement on trade in services (PRC FTA Network). Retrieved April 18, 2021, from https://www.wipo.int/edocs/lexdocs/treaties/en/cn-mo/trt_cn_mc.pdf

Packel, E. A., & Haggerty, P. H. (2014). Cross-border data transfers: Cutting through the complexity. Lexology. Retrieved November 9, 2020, from https://www.lexology.com/library/detail.aspx?g=4ae7c510-e6cd-42ac-8bb0-b266794b6170

Pamlin, D. (2017). Belt and Road initiative's "New Vision". China Daily. Retrieved December 22, 2020, from http://www.chinadaily.com.cn/world/2017-11/26/content_35017323.htm

Panezi, M. (2016). The WTO and the Spaghetti bowl of free trade agreements four proposals for moving forward. CIGI. Retrieved March 23, 2021, from https://www.cigionline.org/sites/default/files/pb_no.87.pdf

Philippe, X. (1999). The dispute resolution mechanism of the WTO five years after its implementation. *Law. Democracy and Development, 69*. Retrieved March 22, 2021, from www.saflii.org/za/journals/LDD/1999/5.pdf

Podesta, J., et al. (2014). Big data: Seizing opportunities, preserving values interim. Executive Office of the President. Retrieved March 24, 2021, from file://studhome/studhome$/yb57213/My%20D ocuments/752636.pdf

Poirier, A. (2013). Why France is gearing up for a culture war with the United States. Agnes CPoirier. Retrieved March 15, 2021, from https://www.theguardian.com/commentisfree/2013/jun/07/france-culture-war-united-states

Pon, B., et al. (2015). One ring to unite them all: Convergence, the smartphone, and the cloud. *Journal of Industry Competition and Trade, 15*, 21. Retrieved March 15, 2021, from https://link.springer.com/content/pdf/10.1007/s10842-014-0189-x.pdf

Porter, M. E., & Heppelmann, J. E. (2014). How smart, connected products are transforming competition. *Harvard Business Review*. Retrieved October 24, 2020, from https://hbr.org/2014/11/how-smart-connected-products-are-transforming-competition#comment-section

References

PRC FTA Network Homepage. Retrieved June 1, 2020, from http://fta.mofcom.gov.cn/enarticle/chinamauritiusen/enmauritius/201910/41658_1.html, http://fta.mofcom.gov.cn/english/fta_qianshu.shtml

Preface of vision and actions on jointly building Silk Road economic Belt and 21st-century Maritime Silk Road. (2015). National Development and Reform Commission of the PRC. Retrieved December 29, 2020, from http://2017.beltandroadforum.org/english/n100/2017/0410/c22-45.html

Principles of the trading system (WTO). Retrieved December 18, 2020, from https://www.wto.org/english/thewto_e/whatis_e/tif_e/fact2_e.htm

Pringle, R. (2017). "Data Is the New Oil": Your personal information is now the world's most valuable commodity. CBC News. Retrieved March 23, 2021, from http://www.cbc.ca/news/technology/data-is-the-new-oil-1.4259677?cmp=rs

Process philosophy. (2012). Stanford Encyclopedia of Philosophy. Retrieved November 13, 2020, from https://plato.stanford.edu/entries/process-philosophy/

Public services international brief on the trade in services agreement (TiSA). (2013). Retrieved March 15, 2021, from https://www.world-psi.org/sites/default/files/documents/research/en_psi_tisa_policy_brief_july_2013_final.pdf

Rauhala, E. (2019). America wants to believe China can't innovate. Tech tells a different story. Washington Post. Retrieved September 17, 2020, from https://www.washingtonpost.com/world/asia_pacific/america-wants-to-believe-china-cant-innovate-tech-tells-a-different-story/2016/07/19/c17cbea9-6ee6-479c-81fa-54051df598c5_story.html?noredirect=on&utm_term=.e008b42cc8ee

RCEP outcomes documents. Australian Government Department of Foreign Affairs and Trade. Retrieved December 16, 2020, from https://www.eff.org/deeplinks/2017/07/rcep-discussions-ecommerce-gathering-steam-hyderabad

RCEP: outcomes: electronic commerce. Australian Government Department of Foreign Affairs and Trade. Retrieved December 16, 2020, from https://www.dfat.gov.au/sites/default/files/rcep-outcomes-ecommerce.pdf

Regional Comprehensive Economic Partnership (RCEP). Retrieved December 6, 2020, from https://www.dfat.gov.au/trade/agreements/not-yet-in-force/rcep

Regional trade agreements and preferential trade arrangements. WTO. Retrieved April 16, 2021, from https://www.wto.org/english/tratop_e/region_e/rta_pta_e.htm

Regional Trade Agreements. WTO. Retrieved April 16, 2021, from https://www.wto.org/english/tratop_e/region_e/region_e.htm

Reinsch, W. A. (2018). A data localization free-for-all? Center for Strategy and International Studies. Retrieved May 22, 2021, from https://www.csis.org/blogs/future-digital-trade-policy-and-role-us-and-uk/data-localization-free-all

Report on what's the big deal with data? (2016). Software Alliance. Retrieved October 24, 2020, from https://data.bsa.org/wp-content/uploads/2015/12/bsadatastudy_en.pdf

Robinson, J. (2014). The snowden disconnect: When the ends justify the means. Retrieved December 13, 2020, from https://doi.org/10.2139/ssrn.2427412

Rodrik, D. (2018). What do trade agreements really do? Revised. *Journal of Economic Perspectives, 32*(2). Retrieved April 21, 2021, from https://drodrik.scholar.harvard.edu/files/dani-rodrik/files/what_do_trade_agreements_really_do.pdf

Rossignol, D. (2015). Making one album a year is no longer enough (unless You're Adele). Drake. Retrieved December 27, 2020, from https://www.theguardian.com/music/2015/nov/30/one-album-a-year-not-enough-unless-youre-adele-drake-hotline-bling

Roy, M., et al. (2006). Services liberalization in the new generation of preferential trade agreements (PTAs): How much further than the GATS? WTO Economic Research and Statistics Division. Retrieved March 15, 2021, from https://www.wto.org/english/res_e/reser_e/ersd200607_e.pdf

Russia's personal data localization law goes into effect. (2015). Duane Morris. Retrieved November 9, 2020, from https://www.duanemorris.com/alerts/russia_personal_data_localization_law_goes_into_effect_1015.html

Saarinen, M. (2018). Data commercialization moves to insights commercialization. Fourkind. Retrieved September 1, 2020, from https://medium.com/value-stream-design/data-commercialization-moves-to-insights-commercialization-part-1-542fd625b00b

Saarinen, M., et al. (2017). Data protection in France: Overview. Thomson Reuters. Retrieved February 9, 2021, from https://ca.practicallaw.thomsonreuters.com/6-502-1481?transitionType=Default&contextData=(sc.Default)&firstPage=true

Santani, S. (2020). Why data is the new oil. InfoSpace. Retrieved August 24, 2020, from https://ischool.syr.edu/infospace/2018/02/26/why-data-is-the-new-oil/

Schedules of commitments and lists of Article II Exemptions. WTO. Retrieved December 20, 2020, from https://www.wto.org/english/tratop_e/serv_e/serv_commitments_e.htm

Schmitt, T. (2018). United States flags China's VPN ban as possible WTO violation. *Georgetown Law Technology Review*. Retrieved March 29, 2021 from https://georgetownlawtechreview.org/united-states-flags-chinas-vpn-ban-as-possible-wto-violation/GLTR-03-2018/

Schöllmann, W. (2017). Comprehensive economic and trade agreement (CETA) with Canada. European Parliamentary Research Service. http://www.europarl.europa.eu/EPRS/EPRS-Briefing-595895-Comprehensive-Economic-Trade-Agreement-Canada-rev-FINAL.pdf

Schonander, C. E. (2017). Chinese proposed cross-border data flow rules contradict an emerging international default norm for cross-border data flows. Linkedin. Retrieved March 3, 2021, from https://www.linkedin.com/pulse/chinese-proposed-cross-border-data-flow-rules-default-carl-schonander

Services and investment in EU trade deals using "Positive" and "Negative" Lists. EU. Retrieved April 3, 2016, from http://trade.ec.europa.eu/doclib/docs/2016/april/tradoc_154427.pdf

Shaping the digital single market' (EC). Retrieved March 21, 2020, from https://ec.europa.eu/digital-single-market/en/policies/shaping-digital-single-market

Shaping the future of international trade and investment. *World Economic Forum*. Retrieved December 29, 2020, from https://www.weforum.org/system-initiatives/shaping-the-future-of-international-trade-and-investment

Shoesmith, T. M., Zou, J., & Tao, L. (2017). China's new rules on cross-border data transfer. Pillsbury. from https://www.jdsupra.com/legalnews/china-s-new-rules-on-cross-border-data-50685/

Sohn, A., & Kalderon, A. (2017) Managing data as a corporate asset: Data virtualization. *Dataversity*. Retrieved October 12, 2020, from http://www.dataversity.net/managing-data-corporate-asset-data-virtualization/

Stelly, R. (2018). KORUS talks provide another opportunity for strengthening digital trade rules Disco. Retrieved January 28, 2021, from http://www.project-disco.org/21st-century-trade/011018korus-talks-provide-another-opportunity-strengthening-digital-trade-rules/#.WpYXQWddCUk

Steve Ranger. (2018). What is cloud computing? Everything you need to know about the cloud explained. ADENT. Retrieved November 1, 2020, from https://www.zdnet.com/article/what-is-cloud-computing-everything-you-need-to-know-about-the-cloud/

Stupp, C. (2015). China to Europe: We can build a silk road in cyberspace. EURACTIV. Retrieved December 28, 2020, from https://www.euractiv.com/section/digital/news/china-to-europe-we-can-build-a-silk-road-in-cyberspace/

Sullivan, J., & Jones, C. (2020). How much is your playlist worth? WIRED NEWS. Retrieved October 12, 2020, from https://www.wired.com/1999/11/how-much-is-your-playlist-worth/

Sunne, S. (2016). How data journalism is different from what we've always done. American Press Institute. Retrieved March 15, 2021, from https://www.americanpressinstitute.org/publications/reports/strategy-studies/how-data-journalism-is-different/

Sunne, S. (2016). Difference between data and information. Key differences. Retrieved May 16, 2021, from https://keydifferences.com/difference-between-data-and-information.html

Swartling, M. (2021). Data flows—Allowing free trade agreements to strengthen the GDPR. Retrieved March 18, 2021, from https://www.mannheimerswartling.se/globalassets/publikationer/data-flows.pdf

Taxamo. (2018). Digital tax trends: International plans to tax the digital economy. Taxamo. Retrieved March 10, 2021, from https://www.taxamo.com/insights/international-digital-tax-trends/

References

Thomala, L. L. (2021). Number of mobile internet users in China 2010–2020. Statista. Retrieved April 6, 2021, from https://www.statista.com/statistics/273973/number-of-mobile-internet-users-in-china/

The Amendment to the Act on the protection of personal information—Impact on foreign financial institutions. Deloitte. Retrieved March 21, 2021, from https://www2.deloitte.com/jp/en/pages/legal/articles/dt-legal-japan-regulatory-update-17may2017.html

The Belt and Road initiative. HKTDC Research. Retrieved December 28, 2020, from http://china-trade-research.hktdc.com/business-news/article/The-Belt-and-Road-Initiative/The-Belt-and-Road-Initiative/obor/en/1/1X000000/1X0A36B7.htm

The Geneva ministerial declaration on global electronic commerce. WTO. WT/MIN (98)/DEC/2. Retrieved March 10, 2021, from https://www.wto.org/english/tratop_e/ecom_e/mindec1_e.htm

The promotion, protection and enjoyment of human rights on the internet. UN Human Rights Council. Retrieved March 19, 2021, from https://www.article19.org/data/files/English_22.pdf

The WTO. WTO website. Retrieved January 6, 2021, from https://www.wto.org/english/thewto_e/thewto_e.htm

The WTO in brief. WTO website. Retrieved January 6, 2021, from https://www.wto.org/english/thewto_e/whatis_e/inbrief_e/inbr00_e.htm

TiSA factsheet. EC. Retrieved September 26, 2016, from http://trade.ec.europa.eu/doclib/html/154971.htm

Towards the WTO's Mc11: How to move forward on E-commerce discussions? South Centre Analytical Note SC/AN/TDP/2017/6. Retrieved April 25, 2021, from https://www.southcentre.int/wp-content/uploads/2017/09/AN_TDP_2017_6_Towards-the-WTO%E2%80%99s-MC11-How-to-Move-Forward-on-E-Commerce-Discussions_EN.pdf

TPP outcomes: Trade in the digital age. Australia Department of Foreign Affairs and Trade. Retrieved March 29, 2021, from https://dfat.gov.au/trade/agreements/not-yet-in-force/tpp/Pages/outcomes-trade-in-the-digital-age.aspx

Trade in the digital economy—A primer on global data flows for policymakers. International Chamber of Commerce. Retrieved March 19, 2021, from https://iccwbo.org/publication/trade-in-the-digital-economy

Trade in service agreement: Annex on electronic commerce. Netzpolitik. Retrieved October 29, 2020, from https://netzpolitik.org/wp-upload/TISA-Annex-on-Electronic-Commerce.pdf

Trade in services agreement: Publication. WIKILEAKS. Retrieved October 29, 2020, from https://wikileaks.org/tisa/

Trading into the future, the World Trade Organization, 2nd edn. Retrieved December 27, 2020, from https://www.wto.org/english/res_e/doload_e/tif.pdf

Transatlantic trade and investment partnership: Proposal for trade in services, investment and E-commerce. (2015). Retrieved October 29, 2020, from http://trade.ec.europa.eu/doclib/docs/2015/july/tradoc_153669.pdf

Turn your big data into a valued corporate asset. Forbes. Retrieved November 15, 2020, from https://www.forbes.com/sites/gartnergroup/2017/11/13/turn-your-big-data-into-a-valued-corporate-asset/?sh=d3ba0296ae30

UNESCO. (2000). Culture, trade and globalization: Questions and answers. UNESCO. Retrieved March 10, 2021, from https://en.unesco.org/creativity/sites/creativity/files/culture_trade_and_globalisation.pdf

UNCTAD. UN list of least developed countries. Retrieved April 4, 2021, from http://unctad.org/en/Pages/ALDC/Least%20Developed%20Countries/UN-list-of-Least-Developed-Countries.aspx

United Nations Conference on Trade and Development. Summary of adoption of E-commerce legislation worldwide. Retrieved April 23, 2021, from http://unctad.org/en/Pages/DTL/STI_and_ICTs/ICT4D-Legislation/eCom-Global-Legislation.aspx

United Nations Department of Economic and Social Affairs and Statistics Division. (2015). Central Product Classification (CPC) Ver.2.1. ST/ESA/STAT/SER.M/77/Ver.2.1. United Nations Publication. Retrieved December 23, 2020, from https://unstats.un.org/unsd/classifications/unsdclassifications/cpcv21.pdf

United Nations Statistics Division. Central Product Classification (CPC) Ver. 2. Retrieved December 20, 2020, from https://unstats.un.org/unsd/classifications/Family/Detail/1073

United States Trade Representative (USTR). (2016). The 2016 National Trade Estimate report. USTR. Retrieved March 17, 2021, from https://ustr.gov/sites/default/files/2016-NTE-Report-FINAL.pdf

USTR request for public comments to compile the National Trade Estimate report (NTE) on foreign trade barriers. Retrieved November 9, 2020, from www.itic.org/public-policy/ITI2017NTEPublicComments.pdf

VanDuzer, J. A., et al. (2012). Integrating sustainable development into international investment agreements—A guide for developing countries, Commonwealth Secretariat. Commonwealth Secretariat. Retrieved April 2, 2021, from https://www.iisd.org/system/files/meterial/6th_annual_forum_commonwealth_guide.pdf

Viney, S., Pan, N., & Fang, J. (2017). One belt, one road: China Heralds "Digital Silk Road"; foresees internet-era power shift soon. ABC News. Retrieved March 3, 2021, from http://www.abc.net.au/news/2017-12-05/china-presents-foundations-of-digital-silk-road-at-internet-meet/9223710

Volz, D., et al. (2018). Insight-tech firms let Russia probe software widely used by U.S. Government. Reuters. Retrieved March 19, 2021, from https://www.reuters.com/article/usa-cyber-russia/insight-tech-firms-let-russia-probe-software-widely-used-by-u-s-government-idUSL1N1OD2GV

Vrontamitis, M. (2015). Trade is going digital, finally. Standard Chartered. Retrieved December 29, 2020, from https://www.sc.com/BeyondBorders/trade-going-digital-finally/

Weber, R. H. (2015). The expansion of E-commerce in Asia-Pacific trade agreements. ICTSD. Retrieved January 10, 2021, from https://e15initiative.org/blogs/the-expansion-of-e-commerce-in-asia-pacific-trade-agreements/

What are tradable commodities? Investopedia. Retrieved August 24, 2021, from https://www.investopedia.com/ask/answers/022315/what-are-tradable-commodities.asp

What is data journalism? *Data journalism handbook*. Retrieved March 15, 2021, from http://datajournalismhandbook.org/1.0/en/introduction_0.html

Whitaker, D. (2017). The challenge of complying with China's new cybersecurity law. *Cybersecurity Law & Strategy*. Retrieved January 4, 2021, from https://uk.consilio.com/resource/challenge-complying-chinas-new-cybersecurity-law/

Winton, A., et al. (2012). Data protection and privacy in China. White & Case. Retrieved May 29, 2021, from https://www.jdsupra.com/legalnews/data-protection-and-privacy-in-china-09725/

World Economic Forum. (2011). Personal data: The emergence of a new asset class—An initiative of the World Economic Forum January 2011. Retrieved August 24, 2020, from http://www3.weforum.org/docs/WEF_ITTC_PersonalDataNewAsset_Report_2011.pdf

Work Programme on Electronic Commerce. (1998). WTO Doc. WT/L/274. WTO General Council. Retrieved March 27, 2021, from https://view.officeapps.live.com/op/view.aspx?src=https%3A%2F%2Fdocsonline.wto.org%2Fdol2fe%2FPages%2FFormerScriptedSearch%2Fdirectdoc.aspx%3FDDFDocuments%2Ft%2FWT%2FL%2F274.DOC

WTO Panel Report. (1997). Canada—Certain measures concerning periodicals. WTO Doc. WT/DS31/R. Retrieved December 27, 2020, from https://docs.wto.org/dol2fe/Pages/SS/directdoc.aspx?filename=Q:/WT/DS/31R.pdf&Open=True

WTO Panel Report. (2009). China—Measures affecting trading rights and distribution services for certain publications and audiovisual entertainment products. WTO Doc. WT/DS363/R. Retrieved April 4, 2021, from https://docs.wto.org/dol2fe/Pages/SS/directdoc.aspx?filename=Q:/WT/DS/363ABR.pdf&Open=True

WTO Panel Report. (2004). United States—Measures affecting the cross-border supply of gambling and betting services. WTO Doc. WT/DS285/R. Retrieved April 4, 2021, from https://www.wto.org/english/tratop_e/dispu_e/332abr_e.pdf

WTO Panel Report. (1991). United States—Restrictions on imports of Tuna. WTO Doc. DS21/R–39S/155. Retrieved April 4, 2021, from https://docs.wto.org/dol2fe/Pages/FE_Search/FE_S_S009-DP.aspx?language=E&CatalogueIdList=14573&CurrentCatalogueIdIndex=0&FullTextHash=

References 169

WTO regional trade agreements information system. Retrieved April 1, 2021, from https://rtais.wto.org/UI/PublicMaintainRTAHome.aspx

WTO Report of the Appellate Body. (2009). China——Measures affecting trading rights and distribution services for certain publications and audiovisual entertainment products. WTO Doc. WT/DS/363/AB/R. Retrieved April 4, 2021, from https://docs.wto.org/dol2fe/Pages/SS/directdoc.aspx?filename=Q:/WT/DS/363ABR.pdf&Open=True

WTO Report of the Appellate Body. (2007). Brazil—Measures affecting imports of retreaded types. WTO Doc. WT/DS332/AB/R. Retrieved April 4, 2021, from https://www.wto.org/english/tratop_e/dispu_e/332abr_e.pdf

WTO Report of the Appellate Body. (2000). Korea—Measures affecting imports of fresh, chilled and frozen beef. WTO Doc. WT/DS169/AB/R. Retrieved April 4, 2021, from https://www.wto.org/english/tratop_e/dispu_e/161-169abr_e.pdf

WTO Report of the Appellate Body. (1998). United States—Import prohibition of certain shrimp and shrimp products. WTO Doc. WT/DS58/AB/R, para. 120. Retrieved April 4, 2021, from https://www.wto.org/english/tratop_e/dispu_e/58abr.pdf

WTO Report of the Appellate Body. (1996). United States—Standards for reformulated and conventional gasoline. WTO Doc. WT/DS2/AB/R. Retrieved April 4, 2021, from https://docs.wto.org/dol2fe/Pages/FE_Search/FE_S_S009-DP.aspx?language=E&CatalogueIdList=14573&CurrentCatalogueIdIndex=0&FullTextHash=

WTO RTA Database Homepage. Retrieved April 2, 2021, from http://rtais.wto.org/UI/PublicAllRTAList.aspx

WTO Trade Report. (2018). The future of world trade: How digital technologies are transforming global commerce. WTO Secretariat. from https://www.wto.org/english/res_e/publications_e/world_trade_report18_e_under_embargo.pdf

Wu, M. (2021). Digital trade—Related Provisions in regional trade agreements: Existing models and lessons for the multilateral trade system. (2017). ICTSD. Retrieved October 22, 2021, from https://e15initiative.org/wp-content/uploads/2015/09/RTA-Exchange-Digital-Trade-Mark-Wu-Final-2.pdf

Zhang, R. (2015). Covered or not covered: That is the question—Services classification and its implications for specific commitments under the GATS. WTO Working Paper ERSD-2015-11. Retrieved October 22, 2021, from https://www.econstor.eu/bitstream/10419/125800/1/845007270.pdf

Zhang, X. Y. (2017). Cracking China's cybersecurity law. China Law and Practice. Retrieved October 24, 2020, from http://www.chinalawandpractice.com/sites/clp/2017/01/19/cracking-chinas-cybersecurity-law/?slreturn=20171008234213

Zhao, K. (2017). China's core socialist values. The song-and-dance version. *New York Times*. Retrieved October 22, 2021, from https://www.nytimes.com/2016/09/02/world/asia/china-dance-socialist-values.html

Zhima Credit. Alipay. Retrieved March 9, 2021, from www.xin.xin/#/home